FIGHTING THROUGH TO KOHIMA

FIGHTING THROUGH TO KOHIMA

A Memoir of War in India and Burma

by
Michael Lowry

with a Foreword by
Richard Holmes

Pen & Sword
MILITARY

First published in Great Britain in 2003 by Leo Cooper
Reprinted in this format in 2008 by
PEN & SWORD MILITARY
an imprint of
Pen & Sword Books Ltd
47 Church Street
Barnsley
South Yorkshire
S70 2AS

ISBN 978 1 84415 802 7

A CIP catalogue record for this book is
available from the British Library

Printed and bound in Great Britain
By CPI UK

Pen & Sword Books Ltd incorporates the Imprints of
Pen & Sword Aviation, Pen & Sword Family History, Pen & Sword Maritime,
Pen & Sword Military, Wharncliffe Local History, Pen & Sword Select,
Pen & Sword Military Classics, Leo Cooper, Remember When,
Seaforth Publishing and Frontline Publishing

For a complete list of Pen & Sword titles please contact
PEN & SWORD BOOKS LIMITED
47 Church Street, Barnsley, South Yorkshire, S70 2AS, England
E-mail: enquiries@pen-and-sword.co.uk
Website: www.pen-and-sword.co.uk

Contents

FOREWORD
by
RICHARD HOLMES

Mike Lowry belongs to a special generation. His father joined the army in the summer of 1914, won a well-deserved Military Cross for gallantry on the Somme two years later and was invalided out in 1919, shortly after the author of this book was born. He grew up in the knowledge that many of his contemporaries had lost their fathers in the war, and Remembrance Sunday retains a particular significance for him. Lowry entered the Royal Military College at Sandhurst in January 1938, was commissioned into the Queen's Royal Regiment in June 1939, was aboard a troopship when war broke out, and soon found himself with his regiment's 1st Battalion in Allahabad, at the junction of the Rivers Jumna and Ganges. His baptism of fire came on the North-West Frontier, where he was wounded by a rifle bullet and soon found himself commanding a company.

Frontier warfare came to an end for Mike Lowry and his battalion in December 1942 when 7th Indian Division was formed for the fighting in Burma. There was some useful training in central India before the division deployed to the Arakan under the inimitable Major General Frank Messervy. Once there, men learnt lessons in the school of hard knocks. Hungry leeches had to be removed from particularly sensitive areas by touching them with salt or, more riskily, a burning cigarette. Lowry lost his first soldier, drowned while crossing a river, and wrote to the man's parents 'with heavy heart and nagging conscience'. And then his company was involved in sharp fighting with the Japanese; it is a reflection of the harsh character of the infantry battle in Burma that it lost men to sword and bayonet in its first action.

Mike Lowry's battalion was heavily engaged in what has gone down in history as 'the Battle of the Admin Box', where the division, surrounded by the Japanese, stood fast and was supplied by air. As was so often the case in Burma, the climate, disease and parasites imposed their own strains; men were 'eaten alive with bugs, hoppers and the usual dug-out crawlers'. Ticks became so deeply embedded that they had to be prised out with a pen-knife. After the fierce fighting for the Admin Box, the battlion was flown up to Assam, where it was engaged in very bitter fighting at Kohima, losing many of its fine officers and NCOs in the process; Lowry's company was at one point reduced to two officers and 28 men. After the battle he was evacuated with malaria, bidding farewell to his company with evident emotion.

One of the reasons why I so admire this book is because of the tribute it pays to the junior leaders who helped make 1st Queens the fine battalion it was. Lowry writes with real feeling of 'these stalwart soldiers, the corporals, the lance corporals and so very often the private soldiers, who have to take on a great burden of responsibility and must make these split second judgements when operating invariably under tense conditions.' And he celebrates the fact that 'The unwavering acceptance of their dangerous reponsibilities was carried out without hesitation and with great courage'.

In an era when we have grown accustomed to sustaining heavy casualties it is worth remembering just what serious fighting against a determined adversary means. 'I buried Private West and Corporal Taylor in the area of 12 Platoon's position at 12.50 pm,' writes Lowry. And when a trusted and experienced officer was killed at Kohima, there was the shock of close-quarter death: 'I saw the contents of that clever head spread out on the ground; no grey and white matter could have been portrayed with such awful clarity.' And yet he is able to take a wider view, giving credit where it is due outside his battalion. The Admin Box could not have been held without 'a tremendous combined effort that involved pilots and crews from Britain, the United States, Australia, Canada, India, New Zealand and South Africa'. There were lighter moments, one of them coming when the commanding officer, coming under fire during a visit to forward troops, inadvertently took cover in an old latrine. And there were moment when the fighting itself had its own attractions: Lowry honestly admits that shooting the Japanese as they fell back was 'tremendous fun' and he was 'getting a kick out of this'.

This is a moving account of the part played by an excellent battalion in some of the roughest fighting in a very hard war. It is entirely characteristic of its author's generation that he modestly makes no mention of his own decorations, but the reader can see just what an inspiration he was to his company, doing its brave bit at war's sharpest end. It is an achievement well worth remembering.

Richard Holmes

Acknowledgments

I am fortunate that I have not had to rely on my memory too much when writing this book. It has been a habit of mine to make a note of events that I thought were noteworthy.

The factual elements have for the most part been taken from diaries I kept on the North West Frontier of India and in the war against the Japanese in Arakan and through to Kohima in 1943 and 1944. The latter diary was published as a book in 1950 with the blessing and a Foreword by the Colonel of The Queen's Royal Regiment, General Sir George Giffard GCB DSO; but that book has been out of print for about thirty years.

However, I have to say that the diary I kept in some detail whilst in Arakan and Kohima, was not my initiative: I shrank from keeping one as I thought I was too busy! But it was the second-in-command of my B Company, Captain Tiny Taylor (no one knew his first name, he was of course a tall man) who prevailed on me and said I really ought to keep a record of the interesting events that were happening even before we met the Japanese. To influence his request, Taylor presented me with an A4 size exercise book; and my soldier-servant (batman), Private Kingshott, then bound it in khaki cloth so efficiently that it weathered a monsoon and kept me busy in dull moments. And now today, sixty years older, the Diary which now deserves a capital 'D', sits in my desk and looks as young as many old people feel but can't gallop about.

Fortunately I discovered that my mother could never throw any papers away. Among them were my father's letters to her, his fiancée, from England and France during the First World War. Before my parents died in the late 1970s, they handed back to me all the letters that I had written to them during the Second World War.

My parents could never have met but for that First World War, and so I have begun my story with Sarajevo 1914, five years before I was born. Twenty years later my generation became involved in the Second World War.

This story covers some operations on the North West Frontier of India. Undoubtedly those hard, fit-making, disciplined months in very cold and very hot conditions gave 1 Queen's, and my B Company in particular, the ability to prove itself superior to the Japanese soldier from the earliest days of contact.

Over many years a number of ex-soldiers who were with me, and indeed some from outside the Regiment, have asked me for a copy of the original diary, but it no longer exists. Their requests, and those of the younger generation have encouraged me to write, making use of material and facts that have come my way, which I hope I have united with some accurate hindsight.

Some other memories have also played a part and have reinforced mine. I am very grateful for the views and comments of those who have helped me in recent times: Tony Lynch-Staunton, who had been my Company Commander on the North West Frontier, and kept us fairly sane with his anecdotes. And those in Burma: the late Dick Kensington who was our gallant Adjutant; Jack Sumner MC, our Medical Officer, who took our first prisoner of war in Arakan by knocking him out; Harry Haines, our 3 inch Mortar Platoon Commander, who supported all our actions with devastating accuracy; and Graham Polkinhorne, the Battalion Signals Officer, who always kept us in touch in spite of difficult conditions. And the Reverend Joe Mullins MC, an officer with me, who in due course took over my B Company and gave me details of the Company's progress and the very last battle it fought a week or so before the Japanese surrender.

I am particularly grateful to Colonel Michael Osborn DSO OBE for his painstaking work and detailed observations of the manuscript, and also to Michael Baddeley for his work and pertinent suggestions. It was very kind of Colonel Donald Eastman MC, who Commanded D Company of the 4th Battalion The Queen's Own Royal West Kent Regiment to give me permission to paraphrase and quote from the citation he wrote which earned Lance Corporal Harman his posthumous Victoria Cross, whose bravery he witnessed.

At a 7th Indian Division lunch party in 2001, I found myself sitting next to the son of the late Colonel John Shipster CBE DSO, whom I knew; as a young officer he had earned his Distinguished Service Order for bravery in Arakan. His son, Michael, was interested to read my original Diary, and very kindly said that I had a story to tell. I wish to thank Michael Stancomb for coming to my rescue on a number of occasions when I have had a computer problem; as also did my son Rob guide me over the telephone from time to time.

I shall always be grateful to Professor Richard Holmes CBE TD, the Colonel of the Princess of Wales's Royal Regiment, the successor Regiment to mine, for the Foreword he has very kindly written for this book.

I acknowledge the books referred to in the Bibliography, as I have been able to draw on them for atmosphere and for some facts. I am also very grateful to Tom Hartman, the editor of this book. He has a wealth of experience and has diplomatically put me on the correct path where necessary.

My thanks to the Imperial War Museum for permission to reproduce some of their photographs in this book. Also to Brigadier Bruce Jackman, OBE, MC, the Honorary Secretary of the Sirmoor Club, for the photograph of Brigadier Loftus-Tottenham, DSO.

For all the help and advice I have received I am most grateful, but I am the one that is responsible for what has been written.

Within the pages of the book, I refer to the remarkable British soldier, without whose loyalty and dedication I would not have a story. My children, Susie, Trish and Rob have been saying over many years: "Dad, you must write it down or we shall lose it." This book is dedicated to them.

Prologue

Twice in the twentieth century, in the space of twenty years, the industrialized nation states of Europe fought each other in the most devastating wars in history. To win the wars, or, more accurately, to prevent the aggressors from winning, meant that those countries had had to nationalize their war efforts almost regardless of the costs. For the first time in war Britain conscripted into the services, into industry, for work in the mines, farms and so forth, everyone according to their age and fitness. In reality those wars proved that there were no winners; all countries suffered for decades afterwards.

As with countless thousands of other families in Britain, I found myself as the second generation of my family to be caught up in the Second World War, which we all said would be over by Christmas; but as the first few years rolled by nobody could guess which Christmas!

To clarify the only reason for myself being caught up in the Second World War, I must go back to Sarajevo and the First World War. Fearing that the continuing crisis in the Balkans would spread further into the Habsburg hegemony, Austria, which had been administrating Bosnia-Herzegovina since the Congress of Berlin of 1878, annexed it in 1908. This outraged Serbia which feared that their Slav brothers would become absorbed into the Habsburg empire. It was the continuing friction that led to the assassination of the Austrian heir apparent,

Archduke Franz-Ferdinand, and his wife by a Serb nationalist in Sarajevo on 28 June 1914. There were also six other would-be assassins on the streets that day.

This proved to be the spark that lit the First World War which was to involve five empires. Knowing it would be supported by Germany, Austria declared war on Serbia on 28 July; Russia mobilized to help the Serbs; both, I should add, are descended from eastern slavs whose Christian Orthodox Church and Slavonic language they have inherited; Germany mobilized and declared war on Russia on 1 August and on France on 3 August. Britain had guaranteed Belgium neutrality by the Treaty of London (1839), and sent an ultimatum to Germany to halt its invasion of Belgium; the ultimatum was ignored, Britain could not ignore this nor that its ally, France, might be destroyed. The British Government declared war on Germany on 4 August 1914.

The British Expeditionary Force began to land in France on 12 August and in ten days 120,000 troops had been landed without loss. This all-regular force of professional volunteer soldiers were the trained flower of the British regular Army, which moved by train and marched eastwards and joined in the first of its bloody battles. By 23 August it had suffered 1,600 killed and wounded in the Mons area. As part of that Army that had hit the Germans at that time, I feel I must mention the 1st Battalion The Queen's Royal Regiment, as this was the Battalion that I joined soon after the outbreak of the Second World War in September 1939.

My father (to be), Graham, was 21 years old and up at Worcester College, Oxford, in 1914. He had been brought up at Cromwell Lodge in Stevenage. His father and two of his three uncles were members of the London Stock Exchange. As with thousands of others, Graham became caught up in the patriotism that swept Britain; he joined The Inns of Court Officers Training Corps. Within a few days he visited the War Office and received an interview with Herbert Creedy (later Sir), the Secretary at the War Office. He was there to ask his cousin, by marriage, for a

Commission. The Commission document, which I have, was signed by King George V on 12 September 1914; this was a quick transmogrification, barely six weeks since the outbreak of war!

Graham was posted to the 8th Territorial Battalion of the North Staffordshire Regiment and began his training on Salisbury Plain. But the atrocious weather during that 1914–1915 winter forced the authorities to move the troops to Weston-Super-Mare and train in the Blagdon and Mendip Hill areas. Within a few months my father met the Chard family who had lived in Somerset for over 300 years. Graham and Gladys Chard became engaged on 9 March 1915 and wisely decided not to marry until the end of the war.

In the meantime, in July 1915, my father's Battalion disembarked at Le Havre and spent 23 hours in trains travelling eastwards to the front. It received its first battle casualties on 21 August. Graham found himself in a flooded trench system that received daily bombardments by artillery and mortars at first light and invariably at nightfall. Those first two to three weeks of trench warfare resulted in this Battalion receiving eighty-four killed and wounded.

In a very passionate letter to his fiancée written on 25 October Graham tried to put at rest her concern about his wound: he mentioned that a shell splinter had whipped across his left hand and removed the top of his little finger.

Graham's letters to Gladys invariably began, "My very own sweet darling Gladys" and were neatly written in pencil on paper from an army notebook. In one he wrote that his Platoon was simply "topping", and went on to say: "They say they will go with me anywhere, . . . they would go to hell with me rather than go to heaven with anybody else". These words were very much out of character with my father's self-effacing nature; doubtless he was on a euphoric high as he wrote.

On the first day of the battle of the Somme on 1 July 100,000 men went over the top and over 1,000 officers and 20,000 other ranks were killed and 25,000 were wounded. The 8th North

Staffords were a follow-up battalion and put in their attack on the village of La Boiselle at 3.15 am on 3 July. This village was considered to be one of the strongest positions on the Somme, it was situated on a spur so that the approach was uphill.

The records show that it was the bombers, carrying grenades and including my father, who led the attack. The enemy trench system was complicated, as many had been partially or wholly destroyed by successive bombardments and previous fighting. Little remained of the houses and the ground was so torn up that trenches and shell craters were almost indistinguishable and the remains of barbed wire lay everywhere. Added to these difficulties of crossing this tortured ground, our soldiers had to tread over the dead bodies of British and German soldiers.

In his book *With the British on The Somme*, Beach Thomas wrote: "Boiselle, which I did not detect as a village till I was at its edge, and then recognised not by houses but by a fringe of trees . . .". Quoting the North Stafford's History: "The entire action, in fact, resolved itself into a series of individual efforts of junior officers and men. . . . The Battalion had been split up into small parties from the start of the attack." This Battalion suffered the loss in killed and wounded of 12 officers and 272 other ranks; their Commanding Officer was one of those killed, as were the COs of two neighbouring battalions.

My father never talked about this battle, although he was awarded an immediate Military Cross for his part in it. It was only after his death in 1977 that I found the *London Gazette* of 25 August 1916, which included the citation:

> Award of the Military Cross:
> Lieut. Graham Leonard Bayley Lowry, North Staffordshire Regiment.
> For conspicuous gallantry during operations. When exploring an enemy strong point with a few bombers, he found himself in the centre of a heavy bombing fight. He instantly joined in, led parties to the attack, and only came back when the strong point had been captured and made good.

I also found among his papers a letter from his one-time Platoon Sergeant from Strensall Camp, York:

Dear Sir

It does me great pleasure to hear the way that you speak about our old Platoon for it is as you say they were men every one of them and I cannot tell you how I felt when I read your name in the *Sketch* after hearing you were killed and I also heard that you had been awarded the MC which gave me great pleasure. I also had a grand report about the way you went into action in your shirt sleeves you must excuse me mentioning this but I felt I must. . . .

I have met . . . Ptes Mason, Eaton and Sherratt and Bull and they have all gone out to France again and young Eaton has been killed since . . . and I have been out again but only lasted 6 weeks before I broke down for you see I am a rib and a lung short now and that makes a lot of difference to a man what say you.

Dear Sir if you were only here and could see the cripples that come to us. . . .

Yours Sincerely
wishing you all the best of luck
196509 Sgt Heath

Those few lines echo the thousands of unsaid, uncomplaining words of loyalty and courage of the heroic British soldier, many of whom had already nearly given their life, only to have their weakened physical, mental stamina and courage tested again.

When I was about ten years old I was watching an international rugby football match at Twickenham with my mother and father. During the half-time interval my father recognized and pointed out to me Adrian Carton de Wiart VC[1]* who was wearing a black patch over his left eye and he had lost his left hand. My father told us that Colonel Carton de Wiart and some six or seven others, including himself, who had earned immediate awards for gallantry during the La Boiselle battle, were decorated with the medal ribbons on the battlefield by General (later Lord) Plumer, Commanding the 19th Division. I learnt later that Carton de Wiart's Victoria Cross was for "dauntless courage . . . and conspicuous bravery".

During most of that war my mother worked at the War Office in the Casualty Department; she was one of those who had the unenviable task of informing the next of kin that their relative had been wounded, killed or taken prisoner. There were occasions when my father got leave to England. On his first leave home from the front, one can imagine the thrill he must have felt when he climbed into a bath and then into civilian clothes. But he learnt a sharp lesson during this visit to London: men of soldiering age and not in uniform were often given a white feather by women. My father received three of them on his first thrilling, carefree day in London's West End. The significance was that the women were handing out these feathers to those they considered to be cowards, as in their opinion they should be at the front serving their country, or anyhow in uniform.[2]

In 1917 my father became very ill and was posted back to England as an instructor at Pirbright. In a letter to Gladys on 2 August 1917, he wrote, "My illness has left me with a groggy heart and my nerves are rotten. . . . Will you meet me one evening next week?" He had lost her address but sent it to "Miss Gladys Chard, C/O War Office, London"; the letter was directed on to "MS 3 Cas", probably the Military Secretary's (Casualty) Branch. I see that the envelope of this little note was Post Office date-stamped 8.15 pm 2 Aug 17B. However, Graham recovered his strength and married Gladys on 2 May 1918.

As Germany's allies began suing for peace, its Kaiser fled to Holland and the German armistice negotiators met those of the Allies on 9 November. A statement by the British Prime Minister, Mr Lloyd George, at 10.20am on 11 November said that hostilities would cease at 11 a.m that day.

By that day some nine million soldiers and five million civilians had been killed, of which Britain had suffered over 743,000

* See notes p. 263

dead and its Empire a further 140,000. This included Ireland at that time, but it became the Irish Free State in December 1921. Our family suffered, but lightly compared to some: One of my grandfather's brothers lost a son, my father's cousin, whose name is listed on the Charterhouse School memorial, and one of my father's sisters, Ida, had two brothers-in-law killed: Ronald Pyman in 1917 and his brother Colin who had been awarded the DSO and Bar, and who had died from machine gun wounds in August 1918.

In addition to the war casualties, an extreme form of influenza known as Spanish flu spread from Asia to Europe in June 1918: in Berlin on 15 October that year 1,500 died and in London during that month 2,225 people died within a week; by the end of 1918 my father became desperately ill as he in his weak state of health succumbed to Spanish 'flu.

Among my father's papers I found his medical discharge certificate, which looked rather like some citation:

Captain G.L.B. Lowry MC
The Prince of Wales's (North Staffordshire Regiment)
Served with honour and was disabled in the Great War.
Invalided from the service 1st March 1919
Signed George RI.

The Peace Conference was held in Paris, where the French Prime Minister, George Clemenceau, the British Prime Minister, Lloyd George, and President Wilson of the United States were the three very able men who carried the burden and influenced the outcome of the Treaties.

And here I wish to outline a few of the terms of the Treaty of Versailles, that was signed on 28 June 1919, as they set the scene for the following twenty years and were largely responsible for the outbreak of the Second World War in 1939: Germany was deprived of all her colonial possessions; she was to pay reparations, largely to France and Belgium; she was forbidden to have any military, naval or air forces, was forbidden to import any weapons or war materials and had to hand over the industrial area of Silesia to Poland and give back Alsace-Lorraine to France.

The Treaties of St Germain and then Trianon followed in June 1920; by these Treaties Austria ceded territory to Italy; the provinces of Slovenia, Croatia, and Bosnia-Herzegovina became part of the new Yugoslavia; other Austrian provinces went to Poland; Moravia was given to the Czechs as was the German-speaking Sudetenland; Hungary was heavily punished, her regions of Slovakia and Ruthenia were also handed over to Czechoslovakia, a new country, and Transylvania was ceded to Romania, and a small region of Vodjvodina went to Serbia.

Those transfers of territories and their peoples created new minorities that became subservient to other nationals; consequently they became running sores for decades to come and were to fuel future crises. Add these problems to the harsh financial reparations meted out to Germany and her allies, none of which could meet the financial burden, meant, certainly with hindsight, that Europe was storing up trouble for the future. The Treaty of Versailles also established the League of Nations in January 1920. But in the twenty years that followed, leading to the outbreak of the Second World War, there was never the political will to put the League of Nations to the test to resist aggression.

I was born on 30 January 1919, arriving three weeks early, at the time that my mother was concerned about my father who was still desperately ill with Spanish 'flu. After recovery, he joined the family firm of Lowry Brothers on the London Stock Exchange. My mother told me at a very young age that I must not make loud noises when Dad was in the house; I began to learn that he suffered from the intense and unremitting noises of the battlefield. In fact he never complained of the noises that my growing pains would cast off as I grew into my teens.

By the time I was four years old my father would have been just 30 and I can only remember his black hair being shot through with streaky grey-white. As the years passed I realized that he would never, if he had a choice, sleep in a small room, as he suffered from claustrophobia.

Our family, my sister Marny being born in 1921, spent almost every summer on holiday in France from 1923 until 1939; with the majority being spent on holidays at Le Touquet. Nanny would go too, which allowed my parents to play golf and tennis at which they were good. Marjory and George Edwards, who was my mother's cousin, joined us each year. Marjory and my Ma won the Le Touquet women's doubles most years and were able to spend their cash prizes at Harrods. We usually had a Citroen car that accompanied us on the cross-channel steamers, and would be holding our breath as the car was swung up on a pallet that was attached to a gantry, and was then gently lowered through a hole in the deck and secured to the ship's hold.

In 1927 I went off to my Preparatory school, St Cyprian's in Eastbourne. Before the war my grandfather, George Lowry, would take a house for the summer season, when my father would have been playing cricket for Eastbourne and the Sussex Martlets. And so it was through cricket that my father met many young men who became masters at the school after the War; in fact all his family knew the Headmaster and his wife, Mr and Mrs Vaughan Wilkes.

It is appropriate to mention here that I had already touched base in Eastbourne. During the Easter holidays, when I was about five years old, I was sitting in the passenger seat as my father drove down the promenade road towards the Wish Tower, and as we went round a roundabout the passenger door swung open and I shot out of the car and landed on my backside. My father completed the roundabout circuit, stopped for me, I jumped in again as if nothing had happened and we drove on. It was almost as if we were part of a circus act, the timing was impeccable. In those days there were no seat belts and neither was there any traffic!

Throughout her life my Ma was not by nature a person who would be late for anything, but she did have a supreme knack of just being there on time. On the day that we left our house in

Kensington by taxi on our journey to Victoria station at the start of my third term, even I, at the age of eight, realised that we were pushing it to be there in ten minutes. As we hastened to the platform we could see my steam train gently pulling away as it chuffed along at one mile an hour. My mother and the porter picked me up and put me through the first open carriage window of the moving train; I landed safely in a heap on the floor of a compartment full of old girls, probably about thirteen years old! In those days special school trains were firmly divided and locked. The girls managed to put up with me as I was apparently the only one with a bag of boiled sweets. I learnt that the girls were of Moira House School, one of whose girls I was to marry about thirty years later. But in the meantime I had no luggage and no clothes for the following day.

St Cyprian's was a member of the Boys Scouts Association, and our scouting days were taken seriously, possibly as a legacy of the War in which most members of the staff had been involved. Our Scout Troop took a prominent part in the Armistice Day parade on 11 November each year, when our small cannon was fired at the eleventh hour and our professional bugler, who was also the School's carpenter, sounded the Last Post and two minutes later the cannon fired again, and he sounded Reveille. After the parade we filed into Chapel for the Armistice Day Service. The only difference between the service of those days and today was that in those days the service was always on 11 November.

By the time I had attended my second Remembrance Service I was well aware that a number of boys whom I knew well had no fathers – they had been killed in the War. I was profoundly upset by this knowledge. And so, right through to today on what is now Remembrance Sunday, I have to say I am deeply affected by the knowledge of war as it affected my father's generation and mine. But then it was the seemingly massive loss of life in the First World War of millions of young people who fought for only a few yards of country that changed hands many times over a period of four and a half years. There were many thousands who survived who suffered physically and mentally. It was this First World War that I still find the more moving and painful.

The significance of 11 November had already impressed itself on me before I went off to boarding school. Over several years I had witnessed, while walking with my parents or my nanny, what appeared to be the whole of London suddenly going quiet as the buses, the horses, the cars and indeed absolutely everybody and everything suddenly stood still for those two minutes at 11 o'clock.

While staying at our cottage in Lyme Regis in the early 1930s, I first became aware of sinister war clouds looming over Europe. This was largely through the newspapers (we took *The Daily Mirror*, *The Daily Mail* and *The Times*), which were reporting the rise to power of Adolf Hitler in Germany and the warnings of Winston Churchill, who, both in Parliament and in his writings to the press, was urging the Government not to disarm but to rearm. By using his considerable powers of oratory at mass rallies, Hitler was able to exploit the rising German un-employment, the economic crisis and the general humiliation of the German people by their defeat in the war and the terms of the Treaty of Versailles. Hitler wanted to reverse the Treaty and reclaim Germany's lost territory and its people. He got control of the Nationalist Socialist Workers Party back in 1921, but by the time of the German General Election in July 1932 this Nazi Party had grown to over 13 million and was the largest party.

It was my mother who alerted me to the serious possibility of war. Our next door neighbours at Lyme Regis were the Jeffries: Stanton Jeffries played the piano and in many ways he was a comic little man; his wife, Vivienne Chatterton, was a very large woman with a large voice, but it was beautiful enough for her to work as a professional singer. Both worked for the BBC. They would arrive on the footpath below our terrace with Vivienne in front sailing along like a battleship coming into port. One afternoon they arrived as I was standing with Ma and Pa and they began to discuss the news headlines. With considerable emotion Ma said that she couldn't bear thinking about the possibility of another war; with Graham just managing to survive one, and now Mike, she said, probably to be caught up in another one. I was then about thirteen. My father said, "Don't worry. There can't be another war." My mother was invariably practical, although usually optimistic; my father was usually optimistic but inclined to sweep difficulties under the carpet. Their views on this occasion reflected this, although Pa could not have said much else for fear of upsetting us.

I shall always remember the day that my father rescued a man from drowning one hot summer's day in Lyme Regis. He said nothing about it to my sister or me, but Ma told us what he had done, as he had apparently raced stark naked through a crowd of people and bathers. Later the rescued man came up to us to thank Pa; it was typical of him to say nothing about it.

In 1932 my parents sold the cottage at Lyme Regis and the lease on their Kensington house. Our move to a lovely fifteenth century house in the centre of the village of Bray-on-Thames proved to be a brilliant decision. London had nothing to offer thirteen-year-olds; but there we were in the country, able to get cricket, tennis and dancing with our new friends in all the nearby villages, such as Holyport and White Waltham[3], and we had a punt on the River Thames, from which our house was barely 300 yards. The Vicar of Bray was Canon Jones, a large-girthed kindly man whose church was about 200 yards away. We had an acre of garden, an excellent tennis court, and we inherited a marvellous countryman, Mr Woods, who looked after it all.

Once again it had been cricket that influenced my father to send me to Uppingham School, where the Housemaster at Meadhurst was Frank Gilligan with whom he had played cricket at Worcester College, Oxford, before the war. After the First World War Gilligan captained the Oxford University cricket side and played for Essex. He also took out MCC teams on foreign tours. He was one of three famous cricketing brothers, the other two playing for Sussex. Of these I only met Arthur who had captained both Sussex and England.

I grew up as a wicket keeper but only received second eleven colours for cricket; apart from any declining skills, the thrill of that position, where one was always very much part of the game, never left me until the age of 65. I managed to get into the rugby football team and play hockey for the XI and only lost one boxing fight in four years. Any reader will soon perceive that sport took preference to an academic life, although musical values gleaned at the school have always been a large part of my life.

I recall the arrival of a new headmaster, John Wolfenden, who, at the age of 27, was considered at the time to be the youngest public school headmaster. He had played hockey for England, was an Oxford 'blue' and had been a Fellow of Magdalen College, Oxford. He was a breath of fresh air. He understood humanity and, being a philosopher, he would give reasons behind his decisions, which made work that much easier. His engaging smile and outstanding charisma were inspirational and encouraged me to aim high. The various governments and institutions of the day acknowledged his acumen and prodigious output, as over the years he was appointed CBE, knighted and later made a peer.

It was clear to me in my last two years at school that I was working my way towards the Army. I did become the senior under officer, which was really of no consequence but encouraged me.

Chapter 1

Training for War

I entered the Royal Military College, Sandhurst at the end of January 1938 and was posted to Number 4 Company in the Old Buildings.

It was marvellous that Sandhurst was barely eighteen miles from our house at Bray, and only four or five miles from Uncle George and Marjory Edwards at Finchampstead House, Wokingham. Lilian Bullock, one of my father's sisters, lived at Compton, near Guildford, where we had spent most of our Christmases.

It happened that Captain George Grimston of the Queen's Royal Regiment was on the staff and was in charge of cricket; he had played for the Army and for Sussex. It was he who gave me my initial interview for acceptance into the Queen's. We were to meet again when he joined 1 Queen's in the jungles of Arakan in Burma in 1943 as its Second-in-Command.

Most of my real Sandhurst friends were destined to go into Scottish Regiments: Bill Wylie and John Jeffreys to the King's Own Scottish Borderers, Alan McCall to the Cameron Highlanders and Alastair MacGeorge to the Royal Scots. Alan was in the cricket XI with me and Bill played rugby for Sandhurst. When we were not playing games, many of the week-ends were spent with us at Bray; as we poured ourselves out of someone's car, my mother would invariably greet us wondering how many would fall out of how many cars for lunch. Bill Wylie had an MG Midget and I had a square-nosed Morris Cowley of about the 1930 vintage which I had bought for £12 10s 0d. This was a very sound car and looked clean on the outside, but for some reason the starter never worked. I could only start it by crossing two wires on the dashboard, and had to stop the engine by stalling it in gear. MOTs were fortunately not introduced until sometime after the War. Our off duty menu at Bray was usually tennis and punting or rowing on the Thames, and invariably dances at Henley.

During the summer of 1938 Marny had reached the age of seventeen and a half, became a Debutante and was Presented at Court by Ma. She was lucky, because George VI was King and he took an interest in those few hundred girls being presented to him. We knew a girl a year or two older who had been Presented to Edward VIII who, as the elder son of George V, had succeeded him in 1936. But Edward had little interest in carrying out kingly duties and it was reported that he smoked throughout that presentation ceremony. He was in love with an American divorcee, Wallis Simpson, and had every intention of marrying her. The Prime Minister, Stanley Baldwin, reflected the public's opinions and masterminded Edward's abdication; his younger brother, George VI, succeeded him. Our family attended the Coronation in the previous summer of 1937, my mother, never one to miss an occasion, got some excellent seats to view the procession from a turn on the Embankment route and so we had a long view of the procession, and, as it turned the corner, we were fairly close as it passed us. After the procession, Ma made one of her typical remarks: "How funny the admirals looked on horseback."

My sister went off to France during the summer of 1938 to be 'finished off', as also had my mother who had been sent to Monte Carlo in 1913. In Marny's case our parents had made arrangements with a French family, the Beguin-Billecoqs, who had a flat in Paris XVI and a château at Chinon on the Loire. They had agreed to take Marny for a year or so. My parents agreed to have their second son, Vincent, over to us for three or four weeks of the Sandhurst spring holiday.

But before Marny went away Ma and Pa gave her a mini coming out Ball in our house with a thousand and one fairy lights in the garden. One of the guests, Cecily Barnett, was a recent school friend of Marny's and stayed with us for a few days. I fell in love with her; she was beautiful and had a bewitching voice[1].

Vincent and I spent much of our time on the river, playing tennis and riding in Windsor Park which was about four miles from home.

In the 1930s my family and my contemporaries were all too aware of Hitler's ambitions and the mounting threat that Germany was imposing, beginning with the sending of German troops into the Rhineland in 1936, in violation of the Versailles and Locarno Treaties. But now, during my first term at Sandhurst in the spring of 1938, Hitler marched into Vienna and, in so doing, had brought Austria within the German Empire. And we at Sandhurst heard with fearful understanding the fate that might overcome Czechoslovakia, with Hitler's intention of rescuing some three million Sudeten Germans from that country. Then we gathered that the Prime Minister, Neville Chamberlain, would not guarantee to help Czechoslovakia from being overrun by the Germans. It was Chamberlain's view that there was nothing the French or the British could do to prevent Germany from marching in and taking Czechoslovakia. We were not strong enough.

For some years Winston Churchill, who was not then in the Government, had been urging the Government to build up and rearm the services, particularly the Royal Navy and the Royal Air Force. In March 1938 Churchill promoted a serious plan that an Anglo-French alliance should persuade the European smaller powers, including the Balkans, to unite to resist German pressure.

However, although cool to Churchill's plans, the Government

covertly went ahead to strengthen the armed forces, with particular attention to increasing the size of the Royal Air Force. I use the word 'covertly' because it was barely 20 years since the end of the Great War and its resultant carnage was still a terrifying memory to the majority of the country: there could have been considerable opposition to overt rearmament.

These gathering storm clouds over Europe were being increasingly felt by us. Winston Churchill carried out his warnings from the back benches in the House of Commons, and these were frequently repeated in the daily press, mostly in the *Evening Standard* and *The News of the World*, which were read by millions.

One of my friends at Sandhurst was Alastair MacGeorge. He and I, his brother and a friend went off to Germany for a two-week holiday in August 1938. We stayed in a pension-style hotel at Konigswinter, a picturesque town on the banks of the Rhine with the Siebengeberge hills only a very few miles behind our hotel. We were all very aware of the shadow of war while on this holiday and conscious of the generous friendship shown to us by the German people, but we avoided any discussion on world affairs. However, I made a mental note of the alertness and fitness of the local youths (the Hitler Youth?) of about our age of 18-20 years, and I very seriously wondered whether I would meet any of them in battle in years to come.

We moved around the Rhine country, exploring the Siebengeberge and the Drachenfels, and made a memorable visit to the magnificent Cologne Cathedral, seeing for the first time its very lovely windows. We had as our tour guide a very beautiful, tall blond girl of our age who was completely bi-lingual in English and German, having been brought up in England with her English father and German mother. Alastair and I both fell in love with her, or so we thought as she was undoubtedly the most elegant girl we had ever seen in our teenage lives; her figure, style and dress were a dream. We could not let this wonderful Anglo-Saxon creature disappear out of our lives. We agreed to share her for the remaining ten days; and because we shared her there was an unspoken code that neither of us would let the side down and she knew she was perfectly safe. Alastair and I made a plan to get her over to England and invite her to our Sandhurst end of term ball in December.

I was a little slow to put the dance plan to her and so Alastair won her for much of the dancing, but it was I who made the plan to put her up in Uncle George's house at Finchampstead; in addition to some dances I took her to the ball and back to the house afterwards. She said that she had never before seen such a grand staircase; indeed it was grand. Well, she was his girl for the ball, but it was I who said "good night" at the end! It was a memorable night, but sadly it was a very brief encounter; neither of us ever saw her again.

Before that memorable ball and the Sandhurst winter term had got into its stride, the Prime Minister, Neville Chamberlain, had been to Godesberg for his second meeting with Hitler on 23 September. By coincidence, the town of Godesberg lies almost exactly opposite Konigswinter which is on the east side of the Rhine. On 28 September Hitler invited Chamberlain, Daladier (France), and Mussolini (Italy) to attend a four-power conference at Munich: they met on 29th and took twelve hours working on details of transferring the Sudetenland to Germany, with the British Government urging Czechoslovakia to accept the plan. The settlement was nothing less than a recognition of Hitler's territorial claims to the Sudetenland which was then given to Nazi Germany without a fight; hence Chamberlain's claim on his return to Britain of "peace in our Time".

The consequence of the Conservative Government policy was considerable opposition from its own Party. The Secretary of State for War, Duff Cooper, resigned almost immediately after the Agreement. In the Parliamentary debate on 'Munich' that followed in early October, thirty Conservatives abstained from voting and of these, thirteen, including Churchill, remained seated. Among those who abstained were Anthony Eden, Harold Macmillan and Duff Cooper. Both the Labour and Liberal Parties criticised the Government's handling of the crisis.

Paradoxically, the general public and almost every newspaper praised the Prime Minister's efforts to preserve peace.

But this peace which allowed German troops to occupy Czechoslovakia in March 1939 also led to an all-out effort by the British Government to overtly rearm as fast as possible.

In the meantime we at Sandhurst were reacting to events: we began to dig slit trenches and in early 1939 some regular soldiers of the permanent staff manned Lewis machine guns on the highest points of the Old and New Building complexes. There were occasions when an RAF aeroplane, as part of an exercise, would fly over the roofs and so give the gunners a little aiming-off practice.

Apart from these practical efforts of civil defence, it was our very deep concern to try and understand where Europe was going and so we did do our best to get ourselves briefed. One of our cadets, Earley, was in my Company and was a fluent German speaker. He would listen in to the German radio and then translate Hitler's speeches to us, which to us invariably sounded like a bad-tempered tirade. Whatever assurances Hitler made, one had only to look at his record and the way he had built up his dictatorship, whose aim was to create a German empire. This, I suspect, was understood even by those who had agreed with the apparent Government line of appeasement, which we could call diplomacy taken to the ultimate and which Hitler and his ilk would label as weakness.

If Britain, France and Russia had resisted Hitler in the autumn of 1938, there would have been war then. France and Britain had suffered for years from a disarmament mentality; it was doubtful that we could have effectively stood up to Nazi Germany at that time. My own view has always been that this "peace in our time" gave Britain a breathing space to rearm and build up its forces. But, as we shall see later, by mid-July 1939 the army was still very short of equipment.

My last term at Sandhurst began in January 1939 and I found myself promoted to Junior Under Officer. It was a great joy to find that some of my closest friends at Sandhurst were also

Under Officers: Alan McCall, Ronnie Bridges, Bill Wylie, Nicky Osborne. Others given a rank were Alastair MacGeorge and John Jeffreys, five of these had Sandhurst 'Blues' of one sort or another. Three of them were killed in the war, during which four of us exchanged letters.

As an Under Officer I was in charge of a platoon of cadets; giving orders to one's peers was a good addition to my learning curve. One of the resulting crosses I had to bear was to sit well up to the front in the Sandhurst Chapel. On one Sunday, very near the end of my time as a cadet, I was sitting on the middle seat of a string of five and at the end of the sermon, as was customary, we all stood up when the Padre declared, "And to God the Father . . .". When I rose I found that all five seats had risen with me; during the sermon a Cadet Under Officer sitting behind me had carefully unhitched the strap of my Sam Browne belt and threaded it through the slats of my chair so that as I rose to stand all five seats rose with me. This should not have been a laughing matter, but smiles and subdued sniggers by me and others became evident.

I can say that I had a very happy year and a half at the RMC: work and play, lots of fun and a number of excellent friends.

Many recommendations had tilted my selection to go for The Queen's Royal Regiment. Some years before, maybe 1935, a Colonel Buller[2] living in our village of Bray-on-Thames, recommended the Queen's which he had known in India and referred to them as the Guards of India. My parents knew Mrs Joan East and her parents, as I had from the age of six (they had all been members of the Roehampton Club). When Joan's first husband died she married Lance East, who was serving in the Queen's. Her knowledge and recommendation set the seal and I had other Surrey connections: an Aunt, my father's sister, lived at Compton, 3 miles from Guildford, my grandfather lived in Surrey and I was born in West Surrey.

One of the issues that affected Sandhurst was the edict that came out of the War Office that the two senior terms of the College's four companies should pass out at the same time. As far as the Queen's Royal Regiment was concerned, it meant that Oscar Palmer and Jock Haswell, who were a term junior to me, left at the same time, but I became one day senior.

All the Regular officers commanding companies at Sandhurst would have given talks to the cadets before they left the relatively friendly umbrella of Sandhurst to go out and take the buffetings and responsibilities in the wide world of the British Empire, which, by the Statute of Westminster of 1931, had become the Commonwealth of Nations, and in that year of 1939 geographically encompassed one quarter of the world and a quarter of the world's population of some 400 millions.

And so it was that our Company Commander at Sandhurst, Major E.N. Clarke of the Rifle Brigade, addressed the Officer Cadets of our Number 4 Company. I never knew him well, but well enough to appreciate that he was a sensitive man who allowed us to get on with our work, games and the business of converting us into responsible officers by his gentle guidance and with the minimum of interference. The day before we passed out of Sandhurst, the 111 Officer Cadets of our Number 4 Company were given a farewell address by him.

Major Clarke spoke with great emotion in his valedictory address to us; he was also leaving to rejoin his regiment. It was very clear that he recognized that the young men of that day were about to be launched into an unknown cauldron of warfare. I have a group photograph of him and I see that he has no Great War medals and so he was obviously too young to be called up, but I calculate that he was probably 14–15 years old at the end of that war, and so he would have been old enough to know something of the agonies of separations, sufferings and the catastrophe that had overtaken Europe's youth in that war; he would have known in some degree the horrors that his young company of cadets were about to face. There were tears in his eyes as he spoke.

After the Passing Out Parade at Sandhurst on that end of June day in 1939, there was the usual high-spirited atmosphere of achievement by the cadets. My commissioning date was July 1st.

When I went up to my parents, they were of course effusive in their elation and happiness for me; but as we left to go back to our home at Bray I noticed that my father had become rather low in spirits, non-smiling and deep in his own thoughts. I never thought of it at the time, it only occurred to me very much later, that in his mind he was possibly thinking that I was about to be caught up and engulfed in his experiences of a generation ago.

In this July period, while Marny was still at Chinon with the Beguin-Billecoqs, Ma, Pa and I and our Hillman car set off for France via Southampton and St Malo. We motored through the French countryside in glorious weather into Brittany and came to rest in a hotel in St Briac. One morning at breakfast Pa suddenly said that, from reading the newspapers, Britain was being put on a war footing, mobilizing and calling up the reserve forces, that I really should go back to England as soon as possible and he and Ma would follow soon after. Although I was aware of the proximity of war, it never occurred to me to return so soon, as I had already got a posting order from the War Office that said that I should be embarking in the 1939–40 'Trooping Season' to join the 2nd Battalion The Queen's Royal Regiment in Palestine. Anyhow, I took Pa's advice and they motored me to St. Malo.

The poignancy of that thirty-mile journey through the French countryside was made all the sadder as one saw French soldiers about to board some transport saying emotional goodbyes to their families, as doubtless the French soldiers were also being called up. The French had suffered very badly only 20 years ago; their memories and the country were still suffering.

Arriving back at the Old Dutch House on about 20 July, I found everything quiet and empty; Nora the cook was there and handed me the mail, which included a letter from the War Office telling me to report to the Hampshires "yesterday", which meant that I had to get my skates on, pack up and get myself to Corunna Barracks in Aldershot, and so the next day I motored off in my Morris with all my army kit. The country was now on the brink of war and was mobilizing its services. On my arrival

9

in Aldershot, this Hampshire Battalion was receiving many reserve officers and men who had been recalled to the Colours.

Initially I found myself as third in command of a Platoon, and on one shaking-down exercise I was the Platoon's anti-tank rifleman. At that time there were not enough of the real anti-tank rifles to go round, and so mine was a mock-up, consisting of a piece of wood built to the length and shape of the real thing with a lead weight built in to give the soldier a feel and the umpires a sight of what could be a tactical situation. It was the same with the machine guns, the old Lewis and Vickers medium machine guns; there were not enough to go round and so green flags and rattles indicated the siting of their positions!

As part of the British 1st Division, we took part in what we were told was the first divisional exercise to be held since the end of the Great War in 1918. This exercise included a long approach march followed by a night river crossing of the Basingstoke canal. That evening and throughout the night it poured with rain, visibility was restricted and water was everywhere, with the army vehicles compounding the elements into mud.

The Battalion of about 5–600 men had to get into assault boats, cross some 20 yards of water and overcome the enemy in defence behind the far canal bank; army lorries carried the assault boats to the boat offloading point; from here each boat team of eight men carried its boat to the opening point not far from the water's edge; then floated the boats, but we could not see the opposite bank because of the pouring rain; we then embarked and began to paddle; for a moment we could not understand why the four paddlers were not moving us forward, until it dawned on us that we had launched the boats in a gigantic puddle of about 100 yards in width and about 50 yards short of the canal.

This setback, the wind and the rain and the pyrotechnic noises of this make-believe battle were an excellent introduction to the fog of war for us; many of us were to find that real war would invariably produce its own fog and that so often the best hard-worked plans would sometimes go awry.

Having received a movement order to report to the Movement Officer at Euston station on 30 August, my attachment and training with the Hampshires ended and I motored back to the Old Dutch House, where I spent a very grim and deadly last night in that lovely house; the voices, laughter and dogs all had gone. I said goodbye to Nora and Woods the next day, took a taxi to the station, having left my car in the yard, and was at Euston by tea time and miraculously met up with Ma, Pa and Marny as we had arranged by telegramming each other.

Marny had came over from Chinon, and quite separately our parents had arrived from Brittany. They had had a ghastly job trying to get back to England with the car. They had motored to St Malo, only to find a queue that stretched into tomorrow, and so they moved on to Cherbourg where it was insuperably worse. All British holiday-makers were scuttling back to England in great haste, to any French port to board any boat that could take them.

St Malo appeared the easier bet to them and so back they motored. These queues were being 'policed' by French members of the Automobile Association and, as with many others, we were members of that organization, but there was a difference: Ma could speak fluent French and easily talked her way to the head of the queue by saying that her son was in the British Army and was about to embark overseas and that she had got all his equipment in the car and had to get back to England that day. Only Ma could have done this with a straight face, and, anyhow, whatever would I be doing with my military equipment in France?

It was by a stroke of genius and considerable good fortune that we did all four meet up in London that late afternoon. None of them had had any time to go home to Bray. My parents made some hasty arrangements: booked us all into the Euston Hotel, where we had an early supper and they had taken tickets to see a marvellous Review called *Sweeter and Lower* with Hermione Gingold and Hermione Baddeley. It was just about the funniest show I had ever seen, with one of the Hermiones wearing her

Picasso hat which she proceeded to eat as it was made up of grapes and lettuce leaves. The other Hermione performed on the 'cello with her legs apart and got her knickers and everything else in a twist!

Our family had a marvellous and memorable last evening together before the war that was to keep me away from them for five and a half years.

On the following day, 31 August, the platform farewells by soldiers, families and friends at Euston station were very emotional, with war imminent and families being split for an unknown length of time and in many cases to unknown destinations. But our soldiers' goodbyes were as nothing compared to those hundreds of parents on the next platform who were embracing their very young children as the children were about to board another train that was evacuating them out of London. Their situation was all the more painfully tearful as the children wore labels round their necks giving their names and destinations, which to some would have been completely unknown, and they carried small cases with a few possessions These wartime partings have been re-enacted down the centuries: after two and a half thousand years Homer's description in his sixth book of the Iliad of Hector's parting from his wife, Andromache, and their little son, all in tears, is probably one of the most poignant stories of a farewell to war and synonymous with the experiences of families at Euston station on the eve of another.

Chapter 2

Convoy

By 11.50 am on 2 September 1939 we were on board the Cunard White Star liner H.M.T *Britannic*, a twin-screw 27,000-ton liner, at Greenock, where a convoy of ships was forming up. This, I was sure, was about to become the very first convoy of the war. One of our first tasks was to help stock the ship with stores, which included drinks for the various bars. But it was not long before many of us, including Brigadiers, were painting the ship grey. I and others were lowered in a lifeboat to paint the ship's side. Being just out of Sandhurst meant that we three young officers (Oscar, Jock and I), together with about thirty others joining their regiments, were at the bottom of the pile when it came to the allocation of cabins: we found ourselves in a 4-berth on 'D' deck right on top of the propellers, or so it seemed. There were 1600 passengers on board, of which 1200 were presumed to be 1st class: they were made up of some 80% Indian Army and British Army officers and Warrant Officers and Sergeants most of whom were returning from leave, and the remaining 400 or so being civilians in the Colonial administration, the police and bankers or merchants. On this first night on board we ran out of all alcohol before the bars officially shut. During the next two days barrel after barrel was loaded from a smaller ship. The rumour was that the ship had reloaded with 90 tons of alcohol. (Could that really have been true?)

In between painting the ship and packing sandbags around

the ship's bridge, on 3 September we heard the Prime Minister, Neville Chamberlain, announce on the wireless at 11.15 am that, to fulfil its obligation to Poland, Britain was at war with Germany. For two days Poland had been bombed as the German forces advanced; we learnt that the wailing of the air raid sirens had already sounded their ominous alarms around London.

That evening the news was flashed around from ship to ship and over the loudspeaker system to say that "Winston is back". This meant that Winston Churchill had returned to the Admiralty as First Lord, which he had left after the disastrous Dardanelles campaign in 1915; this news appeared to be an enormous boost to everyone's morale. We were due to sail on 4th, but on the morning of that day, the SS *Athenia* was sunk by a German submarine in St George's Channel and so it was not until 5.30 pm on 5 September that we departed from Greenock and sailed down the Clyde. This became our first experience of moving around the deck of a darkened ship at night: no lights to be shown, so all hatches, doors and portholes had to be closed down and of course there could be no smoking on deck.

By 8 September our course, and those of the other ships, zig-zagged south-west, west and even north, so we were well out in the Atlantic, having moved well away from the Bay of Biscay. Our journey was to be full of zig-zags to try and conceal from enemy submarines our true course across the seas. We were part of a convoy of ten merchant ships and we had as our escort between ten and twelve destroyers and a battleship that brought up the rear of the convoy until we got to Gibraltar. It was on this day, as my letter to my parents confirmed, that our escort dealt with an enemy submarine and sunk it in broad daylight; it was discovered far too close to us and the *Duchess of Bedford*, another troopship. As we suddenly put on full steam and drew away we only saw a little of this action, when two of our destroyers got astride the enemy submarine a few hundred yards apart and dropped about ten depth charges that shot up into the air, the explosions taking place some fathoms below the surface.

At the time of this naval action I was playing deck tennis with three others and so had as good a view as anyone.

During our journey through the Mediterranean most of the junior officers had taken to sleeping out on deck: this was not because of the heat but rather to escape from the stifling air and smell, mostly of old orange peel and feet, that permeated 'D' deck from the open doors of all cabins. Security made it necessary that all portholes be shut, and, because this was a North Atlantic Cunard liner, the fans and ventilation systems proved quite inadequate.

We went to 'boat stations' every day wearing our lifejackets; when not at stations we must carry them everywhere. We kept fit playing deck tennis, walking around the ship and making use of the gymnasium, tug-o'-war and so forth.

It was a great boost to our pride and morale to see so much of the British and French Navies in the Mediterranean. At Port Said I had thought that I would get instructions for Palestine, but heard nothing, so I went ashore with most of the ship's passengers; a few of them got off here to take up their appointments in Egypt. Some of the Egyptians had a great sense of humour, or perhaps they were seriously trying to build up their family trees. One would say, "My grandfather's name is 'Mackay'. Is your name Mackay?" Sometimes there was a variation of this, as the name might be Macdonald; whatever, it was clear that the Scots had left their mark. It seemed that nearly the whole ship had descended into Simon Artz to buy silk sleeveless shirts and civilian-type Bombay bowlers (sunhelmets). None of us younger officers had any adequate hot weather clothes; but because I had been posted to the Queen's 2nd Battalion in Palestine, I had been talked into buying a very expensive Wolseley helmet from our Regimental tailors, Hawkes of No. 1 Savile Row, who advised me that the Wolseley was just the hat for officers in Palestine! It was a marvellous looking sun hat, shaped rather like the Royal Marine full dress white helmets of the 21st century; but I never saw another of the thousand or so officers on that ship ever wear one, so I presumed it was not part of the fashion in India and bought myself a civilian Bombay model. Jock, Oscar and I, along with some other ex-Sandhurst cadets, had a marvellous party ashore at Port Said; we had been on the ship for sixteen days and felt overdue for a party. The last person to swim back to the ship arrived at midnight and we set off to sail down the Suez Canal at 00.30 am!

The Canal was a memorable part of our journey to the east, there being a hot, dry heat on deck. The *Britannic* was almost too large for the canal; one gathered that it was only half-filled with water and fuel; even so we did undoubtedly do some gentle bumping along the bottom. As we passed several 'stations' going down the Canal, which is 103 miles long, there were groups of British troops wearing khaki shorts who shouted to us to "get your knees brown". Towards the southern end of the Canal there is a noticeable bend and, as one looks back to the ship behind, that ship appears to be floating along on the sand. There is no water to be seen anywhere near it. That was the only ship of the desert seen so far; it was a true optical illusion! We arrived at Port Tewfik at about 4.30 pm on 18 September, where *Britannic* filled up with water and fuel and set off into the Red Sea at 6.30 pm.

For those of us travelling on the Red Sea for the first time, we experienced a heat that was ferocious, and hit one as if a furnace door had suddenly opened in front of the face, and roasted air jumped at us from the ship's deck as the sun above delivered its fierceness.

With no large fans in the dining saloon or lounges, smoke room and bars, and the ship's ventilators and blowers not designed for really hot weather, and with what little wind we had blowing hot air from behind us, moving with the ship, there was no escaping this oven-like existence. Additionally all bulk-head doors and portholes had to be shut at night and on 'D' deck they were closed all day, as they were near the water line; the accumulation and the pungency of smells had mostly been compounded by days of dormancy. The general temperature on my deck was 120 F, in the kitchens and bakery it was

150 degrees; it so happened that I went in there to find a steward and checked on conditions. Before breakfast on the boat-deck it was 110 in the shade. This was a dripping heat of high humidity in which we changed our shirts some three times a day until we gave it up and resorted to shorts and a towel. There were twenty-three cases of heatstroke and one old steward died while we travelled through the Red Sea. There was a period when we were about 100 stewards short, and so we took it in turns to serve drinks in the bar and wait at our own tables, moving between the dining saloon, kitchens and pantry. Those poor, loyal stewards, they certainly had a dreadful time.

For some of us it was the first time that we saw flying fish and were entranced by their movements. Shoals of them usually appeared about level with the ship's bows and moved gracefully with us at about 11 mph. We kept down to this speed to enable a cargo ship, the slowest in the convoy, to keep up with us; it was quite fascinating watching those fish. They would normally swim just below the surface and only in warm water, but when disturbed by ships they would rise up into the air, propelling themselves by thrashing their tails, and then would glide forward for about ten yards by the aid of their large fins a foot or two above the water and then return into the sea and so avoid a fry up, then take a well earned drink before repeating the cycle. This flying fish sideshow was the Red Sea's only saving grace.

Bombay was sighted at 7 am on 26th. It was good to see that the *Duchess of Bedford* was also making her way towards this Indian port. This ship had always been known as the drunken *Duchess*, although I couldn't believe she was ever any more half seas over than we might have been on occasions. We had really only met at Port Said, but we had watched her progress daily, as she was our next-door neighbour, and checked that she was safely with us; some days she would be drunkenly weaving behind us and sometimes veering to the right slightly ahead of us as we changed course to confuse the enemy!

Throughout the journey the ship's clerical staff were busy typing out menus, and, very importantly, the daily newssheets which kept us in touch with Britain and the world, via the radio: this gave us a feeling of being able to share some thoughts with our families at home. The farewell dinner on board that last night was proof of our grateful thanks to Captain A.C. Greig OBE RD RNR and the ship's crew. All passengers were given a copy of H.M.T *Britannic*'s passenger list.

Chapter 3

India and The North West Frontier Province

Within half an hour of being alongside at Bombay most of us knew where we were going. The three of us Queen's officers and Captain Michael Fletcher, who had been on leave, were to move to join our 1st Battalion in Allahabad. The organization was quite first class, the only hold-up from our point of view, was me spending what seemed hours with the customs over my 12-bore shot gun, on which I had to pay £2.10s. Jock, Oscar and I took a taxi to our allotted hotel, the Taj Mahal. We thought that maybe we were more special than most, as our taxi flew a Union Flag on its radiator; we were soon to learn that there were other taxis which flew the Flag, and that the taxi drivers thought that they were all rather special driving around with Union Flags and consequently inflated their charges!

We found ourselves in the best hotel, maybe the second best, in India. The Taj Mahal Hotel had been converted into an officers' club at short notice; most of the civilians who had been there had to make way for about 1,000 officers who had landed from the *Britannic* and the *Duchess of Bedford*.

The Hotel gave us a five or six course meal that night, followed by a cabaret and dancing. We were only there two days and two nights, but we managed to explore some of the city and bazaars. Our senses were really hit as we took in our first

19

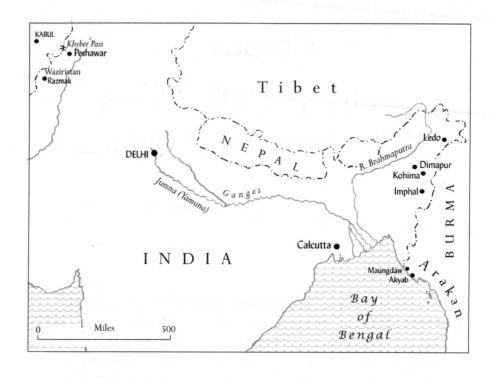

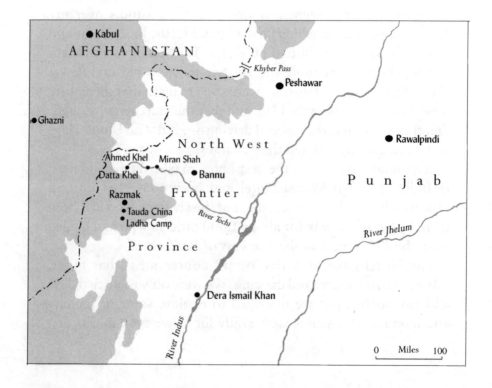

impressions of eastern living: the smells were deep, pungent and what to us seemed fetid and was almost at the same time reprieved by the fragrance of eastern incense; strong though it was, I much preferred it to the stench of feet, BO and orange peel on 'D' deck! During the afternoons and as dusk quickly descended we were staggered to see Indian bodies lying on the pavements, pedestrian islands and almost anywhere; they all looked quite dead, and the more so as their faces were covered with a shroud. We were to soon learn that this was a habit of the continent, the Indians would doss down when and where they felt inclined and cover-up their heads to keep off the flies.

At 11.30 am on 29 September we left by train for Allahabad about 1,000 miles away. Our immediate reaction on arriving in the Officers' Mess was that its furniture and silver were magnificent and a heart-warming and refreshing sight. We were very impressed with the high standards of dress and in particular our very smart, beautifully starched khaki uniforms that awaited us; getting into a pair of starched trousers seemed initially to be as delicate an operation as getting into a suit of armour might have been. Each of us had our own bearer, an Indian servant, who did everything, clothes laid out, cigarette cases filled twice a day; my shoes were taken off my feet as I read a book. These bearers would not let us do anything; they wanted their sahib to look smarter and better served than any other officer. I later learnt that they were completely honest with their own officer, but might borrow from the sahib next door! We were, as new boys, also impressed by the way people moved about to go to their work; they walked tall.

It didn't take long before one was riding; first my company commander, Major Jack Phillips, lent me his horse and then Oscar Palmer and I were all but given a good looking one after a few days.

Apart from a tradition of being a Regiment second to none and not accepting second best, this Battalion was fortunate and indeed blessed by having an outstanding Commanding Officer, Adjutant and Regimental Sergeant Major, the key personalities in any battalion: the Commanding Officer was Lieutenant Colonel J.B. Coates MC, who appeared to me to be a terrifying man with the eyes of a hawk. He missed nothing; when he was inspecting us from behind, we trembled at what he might find wrong as those eyes piercingly drifted their way down from the back of the head to the feet.

As my Company Commander was on leave and his second in command was away, I found myself, a five-month-old 2nd Lieutenant, as the Company Commander on one day in Allahabad. At about 7.30 am, in the period before breakfast, I was studying the company accounts when I heard the clatter of hooves approaching towards our office block and then there appeared the Colonel braking his horse from a gallop with all four feet skidding along the sandy track as he reined in. The CO was purple-faced, with a vein through his forehead that appeared ready to burst; and then he let fly at me: "I have just seen the untidiest platoon of my whole life ambling down the ranges, and it is yours; I will see you later." His blast and the pitch of his decibels made most of what he said unknown to me, but it didn't need translating. And then the CO shot off as his spurs invited his charger to get a move on. I was shattered, my army career finished before I had seen any war. After breakfast I received the expected summons to his office. There was a standard form for the Commanding Officer to invite his officers to attend his pleasure, which had two lines typed: "the Commanding Officer will see you immediately" and "the Commanding Officer will see you at . . . hours". In this case the second option was crossed out and had been signed by the Adjutant. I trembled along to his office and stood in front of him as he bawled me out. "Never again . . ."

That night there was the weekly Guest Night, the occasion when the Battalion's Band would be playing and when we wore our scarlet tunics. Prior to dinner we assembled in the anteroom, where the Battalion's three Colours[1] and magnificent silver were displayed. Then, a few minutes before dinner was announced, from the body of the room Colonel Coates came across to me and said in his normal quiet, dignified voice, "I want you to sit next to me this evening, now don't be afraid, I am really quite nice". And so he was. During his period of command, he taught me more about standards, discipline, tactics and the sensitive way to handle subordinates and get the best out of them than most senior officers. He temporarily commanded a brigade in Burma; after the war I got to know JB well and visited him in a retirement home in Kirby Lonsdale shortly before he died.

Again we were fortunate to have Captain John Metcalfe as the Adjutant of the Battalion. He was an excellent adjutant, always impeccably turned out, tall and a very intelligent staff officer; he had possibly an overbearing personality, which could be a little frightening. But there was no need to fear so long as one could attain his standards.[2] The third of the trio who impressed everyone and ensured that high standards were maintained in all corners of the Battalion was Regimental Sergeant Major Gus Hartridge MBE. He also saw that no one, including young officers, was going to get away with the second rate. A very tall, impressive and strongly built man, his real strength lay in the fact that he made himself known to the private soldiers and corporals in their canteens, and the Sergeants' Mess; he was a model for all and respected by all ranks. One of the reasons he was so well known and respected by even the junior ranks was that he taught the young soldiers and band boys under the age of 17, just as they came onto man service, such subjects as the art of survival, welfare, cleanliness, health and self-discipline.

For us young officers to arrive in a Battalion of this high calibre was an impressive start to regimental soldiering. The legacy of those standards was to have an inbuilt effect on the dedicated performance of the Battalion in the battles of the future, and that of course was what extracting those standards from all ranks was all about.

For three months, from November 1939 to the end of January 1940, with Captain Ian Thomson, two other subalterns and myself and about 100 men, it became our 'B' Company's turn to be stationed in the Allahabad Fort, which overlooked the

Jumma River near its junction with the Ganges and some five miles from the rest of the Battalion. This was excellent; we were self-contained for all training, sports, games, shooting and horses, barbers, canteen, indeed for everything, and a telephone call could warn us of any impending descents from on high!

An Indian Army Officer, Ramanaj Singh, who was on attachment to us, was the brother of the Maharaja of Rewa and was particularly kind to me; we would go off in his car to shoot duck on 'his' jheels, or lakes, usually from the back of an elephant which paddled in the lake and was trained to the gun! When the guns were ready, his or his brother's servants would let off a firecracker and up would go hundreds of duck. On other occasions we would walk up snipe through the marshes. We were very fortunate to receive a number of shooting invitations, mostly from local Rajas: on one occasion it was duck and snipe for junior officers, followed by muggar (an Indian crocodile) and panther for senior officers, Rajas and princes!

Swimming in rivers had always had a fascination for me; I had done this for years in the Thames at Bray, much against my parents' wishes and the horror of my sister. With the River Jumna passing just below my window in the fort, it was not long before I was in it. I can only say it was cool but it really was a dirty river; the Thames was drinking water compared with the Jumna that moved slowly during the dry season; sometimes dead bodies floated down and dead cattle would lumber past; turtles were also swimming and picking up tit-bits wherever they could, which led to those watching warning me to swim on my back!

I took my turn to be the Orderly Officer; one of our duties in the Allahabad Fort was to open and close the Treasury, which apparently held a large percentage of the Government of India's money. In this part of the Indian Treasury alone, there was so much money that it took a dozen Indians two months to count it all. In my letter to my parents on 6 December 1939, I wrote that "The Indians are counting one cell which will take them a week. I hold the keys of the Treasury, open it in the morning and lock the Indians inside the cell to count the cash. I then open it again at about 3 p.m. to let them out and close it up behind them. I have now held the keys for five days."

Every Sunday we had a church parade and one Sunday in the Fort the padre warned us that the organ had broken down and that we must use our own! As good as the padre was in leading the singing, I am afraid he had far too much opposition: the soldiers had their own idea of what the tune should be, and the woman (a senior soldier's wife) behind me had a strong voice, but she was still singing to the tune of the previous hymn.

When letters started to arrive by air they took about twelve days and came in twice a week by a Sunderland flying boat, which would land on the river about 400 yards from my window in the Fort. The throb of its engines pushing the two propellers was a stimulating experience and raised morale, as it signalled our contacts with our families in Great Britain some 8,000 miles away. Even in those war days when we were all anxious to receive letters that never came, we recognized that this twice weekly service was truly remarkable; this flying boat was skirting around the war zones.

In February 1940 the whole Battalion marched off some 35 miles to a training camp. It was the first time that I appreciated how cold were the Indian nights in winter; in reality it is the tremendous contrast, when in the middle of the day it can be 85 degrees (F) and at night it may be about 40 degrees. On some of the training exercises I found myself acting as company commander, which allowed me to command my platoons from the back of a horse. On these occasions I would be in the saddle for some six hours. At the time I thought that it was important and fun to go charging about on a horse, up, over and through scrub, but as I became more mature I realized that this was not the way to command troops who had to walk, stalk and run, although it was all right for umpires! In the training exercises there was invariably an enemy which would have been an element of another company. There was an occasion when two soldiers volunteered to dress up in native clothes and, leading a camel, moved in among the 'enemy' to find and report back their defensive positions. They were magnificent 'spies'; I think the cockney likes to dress up and act, but after time their old training got the better of them, as gradually they found themselves marching in step and the 'enemy' soon debagged them and put them away into custody.

After a fortnight's hard training and running about with packs on our backs, we marched back to Allahabad very fit. The troops invariably sang for most of every march, night and day; it was non-stop with all the words well known to them. They were always one jump ahead of the officers, as at the drop of a hat they would imperceptibly change into their own unwritten version which had an entirely different meaning. Two verses later the officers would gradually realize that their version had been overtaken! One of the disciplines the Queen's always carried out on marches, which, because of the heat would normally be done overnight, was that before we were due to come to the usual ten-minute halt in each hour, a whistle was blown on which everyone stopped singing and marched to attention. When halted, platoons would post two sentries with fixed bayonets, each one facing onto different sides of the road or track, so each company of about 100 men would have at least six sentries posted. This was an outward sign that, in spite of troops relaxing, the unit was alert and would deter any body of locals making a grab at an unwary soldier's rifle.

Before returning to barracks from a march it was customary to have breakfast at about 5.00 am, (not light until after 6.00 am at this time of year), then shave, after which we then changed into clean and beautifully starched shirts and shorts, and so marched into barracks, maybe 3–4 miles away, looking very smart after 14 days away. Most of the junior rank soldiers would not claim that this was good for their morale, but merely bullshit; in fact it was good for morale, and as one marched into barracks with the Battalion Band playing Regimental marches, there was no doubt that the soldiers stood a few inches taller.

As officer in charge of boxing, I had been selected to box for the Battalion in the District Championships in Lucknow in

February 1940. The Battalion lost to the Royal Welch Fusiliers and I lost my fight, but it was reported to be the best fight of the evening and resulted in letters to me from the CO and my Company Commander confirming this: their reporters had been the Brigadier and the General Commanding the Lucknow District.

I mention this, as on my return I needed to change trains at Delhi for Allahabad. Knowing that Indian trains in wartime rarely ran on time, I asked the Anglo-Indian assistant station-master, "What time does the 10.00 pm train for Allahabad arrive?" His reply was beautifully courteous and given in a manner that was no surprise to him, but how fortunate I was that that 10.00 pm was not four hours late but 24 hours late, when he replied, "You lucky man sahib, yesterday's 10 o'clock train will be here in fifteen minutes"! Indian railway platforms were a sleeping bedlam: steering one's way through the bodies was enlivened by the continuous chatter and shouting of Indians as they tried to find their platforms and this cacophony was orchestrated by discordant notes from engines' whistles, shunt-ings and brakes screeching; to this can be added the discontented voices from the coolies who descend on one as they try to claim the favour to carry your luggage into the compartment.

The mention of trains reminds me of a warning a travel agent gave me in Bombay, when he said that it was not unknown for porters to occupy the unreserved seats and then sell them to the highest bidder!

The North West Frontier Province —The Khyber Pass and Waziristan

At the end of March 1940 I was fortunate to be included in a party of the Battalion that was sent on a mountain warfare course, up to the top of the Khyber Pass in the Landi Kotal area on the border with Afghanistan and about 30 miles from Peshawar. The ten of us were: two officers, Arthur Lockyer and myself, RSM Gus Hartridge and seven NCOs. Our task was to learn from some Indian Army experts how to conduct this very specialized form of warfare, as we were due to start a tour of duty in Waziristan before the end of the year.

It was a thrill for all of us to be going to the famous North West Frontier. I recorded in a letter home: we left Peshawar at 10.30 am in lorries and made a steady, very steep and twisting climb through rugged hills on both sides of a good tarmac road, although there was frequently a precipice on one side; we passed a number of outposts including Jamrud Fort; the Queen's Regimental badge of the Pascal Lamb was prominently displayed on the side of another fort. We arrived at Landi Kotal at 12.15 pm, where we discovered we were at about 3,500 feet.

This part of the frontier is Afridi country and all appeared to be peaceful, indeed there was peace; however, we always had to carry arms and ammunition just in case. The cold and the biting wind carved through us like a knife. During our three weeks training, we took part in discussions, training exercises that involved advance guards, picketing, patrols and rearguard operations, and night marches going up and down 2,000 feet. It was very, very cold. The Queen's were mostly attached to the 1st Bn The Punjab Regiment. The training was exhilarating, very efficient and we became very fit.

The NWFP was divided into the 'settled' and 'tribal' territories. The Queen's were to become part of the Razmak garrison in the very unsettled area of Waziristan, some 300 miles to the south-west of the Khyber Pass. We arrived there at the end of October 1940. The tribes were mostly Wazirs and Mahsuds, they were all Pathans and fiercely independent and would always fight tenaciously for their freedom; tribal and village loyalty was strong and could induce unrest with a nationalist-type fervour. For decades they had felt restricted by the British and caused security problems when they thought they could get away with it. In the 1935–1938 period some 40,000 troops were tied down on the NWFP. A decade or so ago the Afghans had made some minor incursions across the frontier that had unsettled the tribes. The Second World War against Germany and

Italy made it all the more necessary that Indian peace was secure, as those axis countries tried to stir up trouble by circulating their propaganda and it was our knowledge at that time that their influence, the supply of aid and money to Afghan tribal leaders had emanated from the German and Italian Embassies in Kabul, and was proved to be effective. About forty battalions of British and Indian infantry were tied down and could not be used directly against Germany and its allies during the Second World War.

The strategy of the Government was to prevent any instability from seeping, and maybe cascading, down the frontier mountains into India, and so the task of the Indian and British Armies throughout the frontier was to ensure that any uprising could be contained and that peace was secure. This Razmak 'fortress' had been built and first garrisoned in the 1920s as part of this British Government's strategy which was connected to the British being able to remain in India.

Razmak was a well-found hutted camp, strongly fortified with a stonewall perimeter of about four and a half feet high and an extensive, deep barbed wire fence at about 30–40 yards from the walled perimeter; the whole camp was guarded by sentries and a number of picquets of about platoon strength round the perimeter, maybe up to about twenty-five men each, ready to rush out to take action. About half a mile out from the Razmak camp were some six permanent camp pickets built on features that dominated the area around it, each manned by about 25–30 soldiers.

The Razmak Brigade Garrison had to ensure that the lines of communication in our area were safe. Razmak was about 75 miles beyond railhead at Bannu. The Queen's were the only British battalion in this six-battalion Brigade Garrison, the others being two Gurkha and three Indian battalions; the garrison also included a mountain gunner regiment of the Indian Army, and sometimes a two-gun section of 6-inch howitzers of the Royal Artillery, elements of the Royal Corps of Signals, Royal Engineers, and their counterparts in the Indian

Army, a troop of Indian cavalry with its armoured cars, and supply services; an important part of the garrison was a strong medical element, both British and Indian, and a hospital.

There were other smaller military garrisons on all the lines of communications between us and Bannu, and a number of forts and posts, manned in this area by the Tochi Scouts. Razmak lay on a plateau at about 6,500 feet and was overlooked by mountains a half to a mile or so away on its north and south sides that were several thousand feet higher. Much of the country was dotted about with scrub; some 6 miles along the road to the north was Razmak Narai which was just over 7,000 feet. From there the one and only road gradually dropped down through the hills and many hairpin bends on its way to Bannu which was about 5,000 feet lower.

The fact that the Battalion had been selected for service on the Frontier was a tremendous honour and proved that our reputation in the Indian Command was very high. Frontier warfare required the Battalion to be ever alert and highly disciplined, and demanded a physical fitness whereby all ranks could march and run 10–15 miles, go up and down hundreds of feet on the craggy boulder-strewn hills fully armed and equipped and be able to fight at the end of the day.

The local tribesmen were all potentially our enemy and would take every opportunity to catch us off guard to capture a rifle or ammunition. Of course they were not all fighting men, but those that were not would pass on intelligence and information about our movements. They would put us under constant surveillance night and day to check that we did cover ourselves with, say, a section of men as we approached an obstacle; they would soon learn whether we used the same route each day and at the same time. We had to be ever alert even when tired. If we did not keep up a high standard, then one day we would become a target. The tribesmen knew all their country, short cuts, tracks and places suitable for ambushes; they were absolute masters at lying in wait for days on end for the right target, they had supreme patience; they had practised shooting at different ranges in distant valleys, they could not afford to waste ammunition and so were usually excellent shots.

Their ambushes were carried out at close range so that they were certain to succeed, and, if anyone remained alive amongst the desperate confusion of a sudden close-quarter battle, the tribal assault party would come in with knives to finish off the rest or at least make off at speed with the rifles and ammunition of their enemy along their rehearsed route. The Pathans' speed of action was essential to them, so that it was all over before our troops could react and bring down artillery and machine-gun fire on to the enemy; at least that was their aim.

Another method used by the tribesmen to test out the efficiency of a unit was to carry out spasmodic sniping to assess our reaction. And many times they would try out a unit's reaction during the withdrawal phase of operations, which was well recognized as the sub-unit's or battalion's weakest moments.

The road to Bannu had to be opened twice a week. Our garrison would open the road as far as Razmak Narai and other garrisons along the 75-mile route would complete the road protection down to the railhead at Bannu. On these occasions usually empty lorries would go down, although probably containing people going on leave or to be evacuated, and lorries with fresh supplies of food and ammunition and people joining their units would fill the incoming convoy of lorries. Two battalions and supporting mountain artillery were required each time we opened the road in our sector.

The method a battalion adopted to protect the route was to have an advance guard company of about 100 men moving well opened out astride the road, with following companies in turn putting up pickets on both sides of the road onto hills overlooking the route. Each picket, usually not less than twenty soldiers, would move out and climb its objective in extended line, possibly two sections of five or six men each in the leading echelon with a third section in depth. Just below the crest there would be the slightest pause and then a charge to the top and occupy the sangar (a rough stone shelter) and improve the stonewall protection. Over many decades many of these hills had been used as pickets before, which would have been another reason, if one were required, for leaving all positions scrupulously clean. On arrival the platoon signaller would signal back to its company, usually by flag in morse, that it was in position. These pickets would stay up guarding the route all day until all road movement had finished and the rearguard gave the sanction for the withdrawal of the pickets in sequence as the troops 'rolled' up towards their return to Razmak. It was during this phase of picket withdrawal that tribal ambushes could be expected when the Pathan tribesmen could be lying up within 30 yards. The tribal fieldcraft and expertise to move in close and undetected were renowned.

Immediately the withdrawal signal was given by the Commanding Officer, it was acknowledged and the picket 'flew' down the hill. The two flank men of the last section wore orange screens on their chests to indicate to gunners and all commanders that there were no troops behind them or on their flanks. Not only was covering fire from artillery and machine guns made instantly available to hit the enemy, but the picket would almost certainly have had to put out its own local covering fire across a defile or some obstacle. The picket withdrawal was done at the quickest possible speed, that is to say running and jumping down and over the rocks and boulders, right until it was well through and to get out of the way of the rearguard troops. If there was a casualty on the way down, the picket had to move back up to the best tactical position and have dead and wounded evacuated; no one could be allowed to fall into the Pathans' hands; they were renowned for mutilating bodies.

1 Queen's went out on its first road opening on 4 November 1940. During the withdrawal the Pathans fired twenty-seven rounds at us, over our heads, and we fired thirty-four rounds at them. It was our experience on this occasion and on many others that we rarely saw the tribesmen who were doing the shooting. On this, our very first operation to withdraw, someone had left

32

six magazines of machine-gun ammunition on a ridge and so back we went to put in an unopposed counter-attack to retrieve them. That was a salutary lesson for our first day: check every detail before moving! To lose an empty rifle bullet case was a serious crime: nothing must be lost that could be re-used by the tribesmen, for they had their own arsenal for making and repairing rifles, and facilities to re-fill empty used cases. We had left that morning at 7.0 am and returned at 6.30 pm. Although winter was on its way, the days had a hot sun, the air was dry and the men would get very thirsty.

There was a patrol that had to be done daily outside the perimeter: the dumping (of rubbish) patrol around HMS Razmak, so named as it had a high chimney stack, where garrison rubbish was dumped and burnt; we had to make sure it was free of any enemy and that there were no booby traps. When all was completed, the patrol would take up defensive positions while the dumping carts from all units were unloaded.

We learned of a ghastly ambush suffered by the Devonshire Regiment along the L of C about six miles beyond the Razmak responsibility. One of their piquets was withdrawing down a series of small features overlooking the road when they were surprised, two soldiers were killed and four wounded. The repercussions of this were that the Hyderabad Regiment had to go out as the road had to be opened again to bring in the casualties and the Queen's had to take over the Hyderabad's posts in Razmak at 4.00 am. The following day, 14 November, the Battalion were out again on a normal road opening. I had noted in my diary that 'B' Company were once again advanced guards and, as the commander of 11 Platoon, I varied our route past the Kooly Camp and the Khassadar Sarai (a tribal levie encampment). On one occasion our 'B' Company had to piquet the Devons' razor-topped hills where they had suffered the ambush: it really was a ghastly, steep and gullied series of thin hillocks, dotted around with six-foot-high scrub. The ambush permutations open to an enemy were almost limitless.

Khassadars were a form of armed tribal levies who were

trusted local villagers, which the army sometimes used as guides and for information regarding tribal movements, and the forming of lashkars (large, potentially hostile, gangs), but they came under the control of the Political Agents and lived in Khassadar posts; another of their tasks was to patrol and check the telephone lines. Needless to say, some were more trust-worthy than others and so we had to be careful that we did not give away too much information. Many of us had fond memories of the head Khassadar at Razmak, 'George the Khassadar', who worked very largely with our Battalion; he was a wonderful character and looked absolutely the part wearing crossed bandoliers of ammunition and proudly carrying an old Lee-Enfield .303 rifle; we believed him to be an honest rogue. Some years later I heard that he received the BEM from the Governor of the Province and was rather joyfully drunk through most of the ceremony.

By the end of November 1940 it was evident that the Wazir tribesmen were becoming a little more active: another British soldier of the Devonshire Regiment was killed on operations near their camp a dozen or so miles from Razmak. One night in early December 1940 there was a fire in the wood contractor's yard in the bazaar area of Razmak Garrison camp; this resulted in the picket party and fire fighters arriving on the scene. Within minutes a volley of some thirty shots were fired at the party and one of our men of the Drum's Platoon, Drummer Reed, was shot in the stomach; Tony Lynch-Staunton who witnessed this, told me about this tragedy; the Maharatta Light Infantry Regiment also had two casualties from the volley. Very often these fire incidents had been instigated by tribesmen through their friends working in our Razmak camp, they then knew that they will have had night targets lit up in the camp. It was a sad routine that always followed after a soldier died or, as in this case, killed on operations, that his very personal effects were sent back to his next of kin and his other personal property was auctioned off to his friends with the proceeds being sent to his home.

Intelligence reports coming in from Brigade HQ during the first days of December made it clear that there was a build-up of Mahsud tribesmen 15 miles south of Razmak in the area of Ladha and Kaniguram, where there was a large factory for making tribal rifles and ammunition. Various bridges had been damaged and road blocks had been set up. It was apparent that both the Wazirs and the Mahsuds were building up a large lashkar (a gathering of hostile forces); the numbers were reported as about 1,000 armed men. This was the first occasion that I heard the word 'Jihud' mentioned; there are a number of interpretations given to it; in its simplest form it could be a holy war declared by Muslims on the unbelievers of Islam. Each intelligence report was making it clear that the tribesmen were moving closer to Razmak.

It was evident that Razcol would be going out on operations to break up this lashkar of Hayat Khan, the tribal leader in the Ladha area. The Battalion had already been out on two training column operations and so we knew how to organize our mule loads of blankets, ammunition, food and water, cooking pots and oil burners, 3-inch mortars, Vickers medium machine guns, barbed wire and picket posts. The supporting arms of mountain gunners and their supplies were also on mules: mules allegedly could climb and descend anywhere a fully armed soldier could go. They invariably were in strings of three. Should they break loose and somehow had to be caught, there came the problem of dodging the centre forward and the pots and pans that cascaded around one. More than one mule and its load went over the khudside from the narrow tracks that threaded their ways along some of the precipitous slopes.

Our Battalion of seventeen officers and 458 men moved out of the Razmak camp at 0830 hrs on 7 December and joined the Razcol Brigade column for operations against the tribesmen. Included in the order of march were: 5/8 Punjab Regiment, 1/10 Gurkha Rifles, 4/8 Punjabs, 1 Queen's, 1/19 Hyderabads. The Brigade's (Razcol's) objective was at first to set up a brigade perimeter camp at Tauda China about seven miles away, before moving on to Ladha, if it was necessary; we expected to be out on operations for up to 12 days.

The column's advanced guard and pickets on both sides of our route went forward but not before the supporting mountain artillery and Vickers machine guns were able to give instant supporting fire. For nearly three hours we were unopposed and then, suddenly, at about 1100hrs there was a burst of fire from our left as we advanced; we moved forward about another 500 yards and then halted as other pickets went out for the column's protection. As we progressed it became increasingly apparent that the Punjabis were being strongly opposed on a mountainous feature called Pakkalita Sar, which was over 7,000 feet up, some 500 feet higher than us. That whole Battalion became committed to this battle on these high, craggy, sharp-featured mountains. At this stage none of the bullets appeared to be aimed at our battalion, but were passing over our heads; however, the cracks of fire and the tack-dum sounds appeared remarkably close. This was the first time that the majority of our soldiers had heard any noise of battle to this degree, and it was the first time that I 'spent a penny' on my knees as we sheltered in the nullah bed (dry water course). As the Punjabi pickets tried to withdraw they were ambushed and so back they would go to occupy more favourable ground and collect their casualties.

It was appreciated that the mountain gunners and the Vickers machine gunners who supported the troops could not put down effective fire because of the confused fighting, and the exact position of our own troops was not certain. This fierce battle went on for the remainder of the day and much of the night.

During the afternoon our Battalion, with the remainder of Razcol, arrived unopposed in this camp at Tauda China, put out protective forces and built sangars and perimeter defences.

B Company had to find a camp picket for the night, so our Company Commander, Captain Ian Thomson, went out with a platoon to supervise building the sangar and to see them settle in. But because of the battle he was obliged to remain with the picket and was ordered to stay there for the night, and so I found myself commanding 'B' Company. Our Battalion was called out at about 1600 hrs and moved to where the Punjabis would be withdrawing and so help them into camp. I remained out as rearguard for two hours. By then it was dusk, getting very cold at this height of about 7,000 feet and the bullets were still flying; it was very nearly impossible to tell from where and in which direction they were actually going, although it was certain that no man of my company fired a shot; as a general rule you do not fire at night at something you cannot see and give your position away, but in this case we were expecting the Punjabis to come through us and so there was certainly no firing by us. During this time many wounded Punjabi soldiers passed my Company.

On returning to camp later that night we leant some of the horrors of the battle: the Punjab Battalion had had their CO, Lieutenant Colonel Faulkner, killed, and apparently many of their officers. During the course of that evening I met their shattered Second-in-Command, apparently the only British officer not killed. That evening Corporal Simmonds of my Company was killed by a sniper's bullet while he was sentry on the camp perimeter. No one could have had much sleep that night, as the battles on the hills continued and machine guns and artillery were firing from this Tauda China camp. This only died down in the early hours of the morning. We had to be very much alert as the Punjabis tried to filter into the camp through my 'B' Company; the majority were wounded, some were without arms and equipment and some were almost naked. We later leant that a number of Punjab sub-units were ambushed, shot and knifed as they tried to make their way into camp. It was a ploy of the Pathans to follow up the wounded and dead of their enemy and strip them of all weapons, ammunition and clothing, indeed everything, and then the women would carry out the mutilation of the soldiers' genitals.

On Sunday 8 December we had a clearer idea and a confirmation of the extent of the disaster to the 5/8th Punjab Regiment: apparently the Mahsuds had overrun a number of pickets, a total of sixty-nine were killed, a large number of rifles and thousands of rounds of ammunition, many grenades, equipment and wireless sets were lost to the tribesmen and it was later said that a further ninety men were wounded. Because of the battle, the road back to Razmak had to be re-opened to evacuate the casualties on the next day. As I was the acting Company Commander of 'B' Company, the CO, Colonel Evans, briefed me to take out the company in an advanced guard role and then to occupy the features 'Razor' and then on to Sharkai Sar. Before we had moved more than 200–300 yards we came across an unforgettable sight of horror and almost disbelief, as strewn across our front as daylight was breaking were twenty or more naked corpses of Indian soldiers, whose bodies were frozen solid, and there were also two large army vehicles into which the bodies were being placed. The temperature at night had dropped to well below freezing point. Our young minds, which were new to the shattering reality of bloody war, then had to contend with our real task of having to climb the Razor piquet; the name was indicative of its knife-edge quality and it was a very difficult climb. Most of our thoughts were taken up with the possibility of being opposed by these Mahsuds whose morale by now must have been very high. I then took the other platoon onto Sharkai Sar. This was an almost perpendicular feature; we had to climb some of this hill on all fours, covering fire having been dropped off from time to time. In the forefront of my mind was, where have last night's tribesmen of several hundred melted to? Odd shots had been fired at us from the area of a village and from 'Crag', which was very much a part of yesterday's battle area, but we were not directly opposed. During the day we saw the Bombay Grenadiers, who had been sent up to reinforce Razcol, march with great pride along the track below us towards Tauda China, followed by a section of British Royal Artillery 6-inch medium guns. As I watched the Bombay Grenadiers pass us about 400 yards away, I thought that they were a very impressive Battalion and one with which the tribesmen would not wish to get too involved; of course this was only a marching discipline, but the outward signs count for a great deal.

In the course of the day the main feature of yesterday's battle, Pakkalita, was bombed by the R.A.F. Some of us had an instinct that these two aircraft were not in reality bombers; we thought that 25lbs bombs were being thrown out of a door! Perhaps not; anyhow it was an aerial gesture.

December 9th was a rest day for the Razcol Brigade. The Battalion spent much of the day digging slit trenches and bivouac holes of about two feet deep. Even the tribesmen had a rest, as there was no sniping, which usually began at about 4 pm and continued perhaps intermittently until about 11 pm. On this night one could see their fires burning in the hills and hear their watchdogs barking as the tribesmen returned to their sarais (villages) during the night.

It was very, very cold at night and, first thing in the morning, the veneer of ice in my mug had to be broken before I shaved; the wind from the east was known to us as the 'breath of death'. Later in the day the sun and wind combined to raise the temperature, but it was always cold enough to wear a leather jerkin over our sweaters and possibly a greatcoat. Sometimes at first light, while we were 'standing to', sections of our Machine Gun Platoon would open up on their fixed lines of defensive fire; this had a prophylactic effect to deter an enemy. It was often unkindly said, in jest, that the machine gunners were heating up their shaving water or maybe it was for their early morning tea. In any event, their shafts of short bursts of staccato firing were powerfully reassuring.

From time to time my 11 Platoon of B Company would take its turn to do a camp picket, which would be about half a mile from Tauda China camp, around which there would be a total of five or six other pickets of platoon strength of some 20–30 men. To prepare for this entailed a considerable amount of hard work by the platoon commander, platoon sergeant and the three section commanders. Apart from the daily cleaning of arms and ammunition, loads had to be gathered and sorted into mule loads, where a mule could carry 160lbs, 80 on each side of it: two boxes of a thousand rounds of reserve ammunition, grenades, coloured Very lights, two or more days' rations, cooking equipment and oil and the all-important water, possibly two packals of 8 gallons, one on each side of a mule. Each man had one groundsheet, a greatcoat and two blankets, each of 5lbs; our rule of thumb was that a mule carried thirty blankets. Time was always required to roll the appropriate loads into tidy, tight bundles. Then the loads had to be fitted onto the mules; would the loads balance and how steady were the mules, which one was going to object to carrying the sometimes noisy cooking pots which made a rather unnerving repetitive clang as one mule in the string of three kicked and bucked? By and large they were well-trained and behaved, but we had to ensure that we gave them no cause to complain!

When in these camp pickets it was important to patrol the dead ground within, say 30–50 yards to ensure that no enemy were lying up to make a rush attack. This would always mean that the picket 'stood to' in case the patrol got into any trouble. Sometimes platoons were up in these piquet positions for two to five days; and sometimes we would have to build the sangars and put up a protective wire fence; this would involve more mules and a further party of men to protect us as we worked. 11 Platoon had a succession of excellent cooks; L/Cpls Hole and Glover were absolute aces at converting and camouflaging bully beef into something it wasn't; on occasions we had bacon and eggs for breakfast, which always tasted better in these raw conditions.

The security of the picket by day was usually left to two sentries, while the remainder were busy washing, cleaning weapons and carrying out the thousand and one other necessary chores or resting and writing letters. At night probably two or three pairs of sentries would be necessary. Sentries were on duty for two hours, then four hours off duty, the night sentries being staggered, so that in reality a new man came on duty every hour. This helped sustain the morale of the man who had already done

one hour. In the second hour of sentry duty at night the eyes could become weary and blurred; it was very easy for men imagining that the bushes in front were moving and that they were creeping tribesmen, although sometimes they might have been!

Reading my diary for Tuesday, 17 December 1940, and for some following days, the entries were in ink, as I wrote it up from my hospital bed, after being evacuated back to Razmak two days later:

On 17 December the road was opened to Razmak and 'B' Company were doing the picketing on the right of the road: my platoon moved up the slopes of one of the route pickets accompanied by an artillery Forward Observation Officer (FOO), an Indian Havildar, our 11 Platoon objective was a feature called 'Whalebone'. Captain Ian Thomson, our Company Commander, came up and visited us at about 10.30 am., all was well. At 1200 hrs some of my men started firing as they reported seeing tribesmen; when they fired again I could see that they were firing onto the ridge above us about 500 yards away; and so I called for the gunners to shell that area. We received the orders to withdraw at 1450 hrs; on this I put out a section to our rear to cover our withdrawal. I withdrew with the last five men of the Platoon and the signaller, and as always it was at the double. As we galloped down over the boulder-strewn hill, a volley of shots came in amongst us. I shouted to keep going, and then another volley of bullets spattered around us, and one hit Private Boyne in the leg and he could not move, and a ricochet hit me in the face, which knocked me down and concussed me for 10–15 seconds; although it was probably only some five seconds as the serious significance of the situation also 'hit' me fairly quickly and I shouted "back to the crest" as soon as I could and yelled to the signaller "casualty". A minute or so later we were back on the crest returning the fire with rifles and machine gun on to the enemy which I am sure no one had yet seen as they were camouflaged amongst the craggy outcrops and the shoulder-high scrub. Private Gorman gallantly knelt to signal our plight with his flag in morse code; he was an outstanding target for the tribesmen. Within a few minutes the Company Commander with a Company HQ escort and stretcher bearers arrived. While covering the movement of the stretchered Boyne, Ian Thomson and I operated our Vickers Berthier light machine gun, and the artillery and Vickers medium machine guns fired beyond us and to our flanks as we made our otherwise uneventful withdrawal at speed, jumping from boulder to boulder.

An interesting sideline to me being wounded was that I immediately put my hand to the back of my head as I assumed that if a bullet had hit my face then it must have come out at the back of my head somewhere. But no there was no blood coming out of the back of my head, so that was almost all right! The other point was that it did not hurt on impact but just became very numb; the pain came later. As I returned to the camp, some of the soldiers were concerned that I had lost half my face, as it and the field dressing were oozing blood all over my face.

That evening Captain Davies (RAMC) of the Field Ambulance took out a piece of lead barely half an inch from just under my right eye. I took a look in a mirror – a very neat job indeed. He put in other stitches just below the right cheek. The following morning I wandered over to the Field Ambulance and stopped a rocket from the duty medical officer and the major commanding it for being out of bed; but they put it very nicely. The major commanding was really charming and went out of his way to make things pleasant and comfortable. While having the wound re-dressed I saw L/Cpl Fraser of 'C' Company having his face attended to; he had also been wounded on the same day as me but half a mile away.[3]

My morale received an excellent boost on this day, as I received a long cheery letter from Mum.

On 19 December I recorded that the last two nights have been the warmest I have spent on this Razcol operation, as the Field Ambulance lent me three blankets. I must say it was a marvellous change and a relief to be told to lie in bed in this camp and not to go leaping around in the dark trying to put on boots with frozen hands, and I need not try to take any notice of the background clatter of small arms fire, machine guns and artillery firing.

I had to report to the Field Ambulance this morning, as our own medical officer told me that I had to go into hospital in Razmak. I felt saddened to have to do this as Razcol was about to move on towards Ladha to disperse the tribes around there. But I did seriously consider myself fortunate to have had a lucky escape. However, it was as well that I was sent to hospital as I had a searing headache, half the face was black and I couldn't see out of my right eye.

And so I was backloaded with some others in an ambulance. At the Razmak hospital I was given an X-ray. The following day I was given no breakfast as I was due to be given an anaesthetic before the surgeon did some lead picking, which he did for about one and a half hours, prodding and cutting. The injections wore off about four times; apart from this it was not too painful as another piece of lead was extracted from just below the right eye. What was so incongruous about all this was the fact that I was taken in and out of the operating theatre on a stretcher, when I had been walking quite happily to the bathrooms. I heard that Fraser and Boyne were progressing quite well. Captain John Metcalfe, the Adjutant, came and visited me in the afternoon.

Snow fell on Christmas Eve, and it snowed again on 25th. It was the first time ever that I had spent Christmas Day in bed. I was still suffering from headaches and so did not touch any beer that was being given away. Three of us in the ward tried to make the most of the occasion and, not surprisingly, our morale was boosted by some Queen's soldiers in the hospital who came in to see us at half-hourly intervals to toast us with more rum, and each time they came in they were one stage worse, or maybe better, being miles away in their own world but they were very happy and entertained me.

As a concession to tradition, the surgeon allowed me out of bed to see the troops' Christmas dinners. Fraser and Boyne seemed to be recovering all right[4]. As I wrote in my diary, I felt shaky on the feet. We had a bit of a party in the ward, I had bought some crackers and pulled them standing around a table at tea-time. We really did very well, with turkey, Christmas pudding and an issue of cigarettes.

While in hospital I learnt that on December 20th the Battalion had three more casualties, one of which was fatal. Because of an increased tribal activity, during which both the Mahsuds and Razcol got some casualties, the road back to Razmak was opened to enable Tocal to join Razcol at Tauda China camp. On 30 December the Government terms to the tribesmen were due to run out, but in the last hours they were accepted. The terms included: the tribes to disperse and to hand over so many rifles. This was followed by Tocal taking over from Razcol at Tauda China and Razcol moving on to Ladha on January 1st 1941.

Colonel Crispo Evans thought that, as I was so much better, I could return to the Battalion at Ladha and surprisingly said to me that my return to the Battalion would do the men good to see me again! Unfit though I was, I agreed, although I knew it wasn't going to do me any good! I returned to B Company on 8 January and shivered with aches and pains for the remainder of the operations, I thought I was getting pneumonia or the next worse thing! On that night I attended an 'O' [orders] group in the very warm, dug-in Officers' Mess tent. They were the orders for tomorrow's operations.

As the CO was himself sick, the orders were given by the 2IC, during which there was much laughter as he invited us to take a look on the map at the 'e' in 'Bare Spur', which a Punjab Regiment was to occupy: the general mirth arose because we had all written in 'Bare Spur' on our maps in pencil and so the position of the 'e' could have differed on our maps by as much as 400 yards on the ground! Present at those orders was the Political Officer, John Dring[5], who gave us his updated intelligence on tribal movements, numbers and morale.

Further operations proved that the lashkar had dispersed, but it also proved that small elements were still in the area of our

44

operations, as sniping continued during the next two days, when casualties occurred both to Razcol and to the Mahsuds. To soften the enemy up, after a warning, some of their houses were destroyed and the tribal gatherings bombed by a couple of RAF aeroplanes. The final Government terms between the Political Agent and the tribal elders were agreed, which allowed Razcol to return to Razmak on 13 January. The return was unopposed, but the tribesmen made us realize that they were still keeping an eye on us as they fired on the column from Sharkai Sar [the perpendicular feature I had occupied on 8 December after the Punjab battle].

The two officers who joined the Regiment with me, Oscar Palmer and Jock Haswell, were also very much involved in these operations: Oscar, as a platoon commander in 'D' Company, took a large share in their operations. His Company Commander reported that on Christmas night there was an alert as explosions and Very lights went up from his camp piquet. This was almost immediately followed by their signaller's lamp flashing "Happy Christmas". This was an inspired and typical gesture from the picket commander, Oscar, who had an enlightened sense of humour for most occasions. During these operations and others, Jock Haswell was proving himself as the Brigade Intelligence Officer.

In between operations and road-opening days, there were many activities that kept us occupied within the Razmak Camp. There were a number of sports grounds and a marvellous roller-skating rink, which was tremendous fun, mostly taken up by inter-platoon competitions; this rink was an excellent fit-making institution.

Many were the times when snipers, usually from a low hill feature known as Bakhshi, which was some 800 yards from the perimeter, would open up at us very often while we played hockey on the pitch which was inside the perimeter. Sometimes we would stop play but mostly we toughed it out and played on. The sniper was known as Bakhshi Bill and was probably two or three men, as they took it in turn to zero their rifles against some mark on the perimeter wall, with a couple of rounds for luck amongst the hockey players. On an occasion when Colonel Evans went down the road on leave in a convoy of vehicles it was ambushed by tribesmen somewhere beyond Razmak Narai and beyond our responsibility. In his young days he had been an Army 100 yards champion. He told us that on that day he would have beaten all records as he sprinted back to get under cover round the last bend.

In March 1941 I was given a month's leave and I see, in a letter to my parents dated 9 March 1941, that my address was the "Peshawar Club Peshawar, North West Frontier". I mentioned that Lord Haw-Haw had made a propaganda broadcast over the radio from Germany last December (1940), concerning the fighting on our part of the Frontier and how his references to our operations had made us laugh. As I said in the letter, this was the first leave that I had had since arriving in India at the end of September 1939. In the few days I spent in the Club before moving on to Delhi I managed some dancing on the first night, then tennis, bathing, cinema and squash. After a riotous party in the Club on the Sunday when a band played at 12 noon to a vast crowd "such as I have never before seen the like in India. This drinks party and music went on until 1.30 pm", then on to lunch in the dining room until 3.15 pm. Later that afternoon I went on to play golf with a great friend of mine, Ronnie Bridges, who had been an Under Officer with me at Sandhurst. "We rashly only took four balls with us . . . and finished up with only one between us"! Ronnie was my age and had joined the Indian army. We never met again. I later learnt that he was very badly wounded in the Burma campaign, lost the sight in both eyes, but never recovered.

I arrived in Delhi by train on 11 March and found that every worthwhile hotel was absolutely full and so went on to Old Delhi where I spent the remaining three weeks of my leave in the fabulous Hotel Cecil, which was run by a ruthlessly efficient Swiss woman. It was so overcrowded that furnished marquees had been set up in the large gardens and I had been given one of

46

these. It was the custom at that time for an officer's Indian bearer to accompany his officer on leave and this meant that one was superbly looked after with crisp, clean clothes and ironed shirts, trousers, shorts etc. This was a necessary luxury in the steaming heat of Delhi which at that time of year was becoming increasingly hotter.

In my letter to Ma and Pa of 19 March 1941 I thanked them for their letter posted on 21st January which had therefore taken just on two months to find me: this was not too bad really as it had been sent down from Razmak to the Peshawar Club and then on to the Cecil Hotel. My letter said how fit I was and that I weighed about 12 stone, (my boxing weight had been 11.5 stone). I extolled the fine virtues of this Hotel, reputedly the best in India; its food, I wrote, was as good as anywhere in England. It had about 100 bedrooms and thirty large tents for the overflow; it was very clean and modern inside, superbly furnished, lovely swimming pool and tennis courts. "Everything is done on a magnificent scale and you get individual attention. The Hotel is permanently full and about twenty people get turned away each day. At the moment there are nine Indian princes and their staff here to attend the Viceroy's meeting of the princes. For all that it is not outrageously expensive. You get such nice people here and fortunately not all military. There are Dutch, French, one or two Austrians and many Americans and Canadians. I have met two Old Uppinghamians staying here, one is a knight and the other was Keith Mackenzie, captain of hockey when I was playing in the team: he was serving with a Gurkha regiment."

I will make the most of this long letter to my parents as it gives a flavour of wartime life in India, in that peaceful city of Delhi in early 1941; so I quote: "I hadn't been in the hotel gardens half an hour after breakfast my first morning when suddenly from nowhere I was pounced upon by a woman. This led to an introduction, . . . at lunch time I was passing through the verandah when the woman's mother . . . invited me to sit down and have a drink and then go and have lunch with them. Well, for two

47

days I never had a meal to myself. These two, mother and daughter, were Canadians and had been touring the world . . . Mother was obviously trying to get this uninteresting woman off to some unwary man. Mother must have been 55–60 and the daughter looked barely ten years younger!

"Well, on the third day (of my hols), I realized the game . . . I used to keep a wary eye and quickly dived into the swimming pool when I saw the depression approaching. She used to suddenly sink and whirl her tentacles around my neck. One couldn't be callous or unkind to them but I wished to appear hopelessly foolish all the time. All this was rather amusing to others in the hotel who had doubtless been through the same routine.

"I have been having a terrific time here. For three weeks I have only had three nights in before 2.0 am, usually far later. There is something on every night . . . breakfast at 9.0 am, then read the paper, write letters . . . at 11 o'clock I go and bathe and sunbathe until lunch. After lunch I repeat the bathing, play tennis, see an early flick, back to dinner or out to dinner; then dance or out to dance and when that finishes go on to another dance and 'home' by 0330 am."

But I did spend much of the leave hiring horses, as on many days before breakfast I went out riding with the young daughter of a Colonel and his wife, who were spending their leave in the hotel. I had been swimming and dancing with a lovely girl called Jean Bruce-Hay, who was a teacher at a rather upmarket school in Delhi; I had first met her in Allahabad at the end of 1939; she was a marvellously happy outgoing girl of 20, whose address in Delhi I can never forget even after 50 something years, – 8 Aurangzeeb Road.

There was dancing in the Cecil, although the Imperial Hotel, which was almost across the road, had a very traditional, possibly pre-war, or even pre-1914, atmosphere that was very British and had more character than the excellent Cecil Hotel and so Jean and I invariably elected to go there.

One certainly rubbed shoulders with the great on that holiday.

Continuing my letter home, "The other evening Jean and I inadvertently tripped up Lady Auchinleck, the Commander-in-Chief's wife while doing an old fashioned waltz." We had been dancing at the Imperial Hotel and somehow our legs got intertwined with Lady A and her partner, and the four of us finished on the floor in gales of laughter. I was told that Lady A was always tremendous fun.

The General, we were sure, was far too busy organizing India's war effort to go dancing. After the war I heard that Field Marshal (as he became) Sir Claude Auchinleck and his wife had separated and occasionally I would bump into him at our Club, The In and Out, or exchange a good morning in Hatchards, the bookshop across the road in Piccadilly. He had retired to Morocco and returned to England in the summer.

That wonderful holiday had to come to an end. I noted in a letter of 2 April, "I must finish off now, as I am leaving Delhi in three quarters of an hour for Razmak and it is now 6.30 am! Had a perfect leave. Very much love from Mike." I was back in Razmak on 6 April; my next letter of 24th said how homesick I was for that superb holiday and how it had "hit me with a h . . . of a bump coming back to this place". It will be noticed that the language and courtesies of those days did not allow me to spell the word 'hell' out in full!

I noted that the temperature in the Razmak area in April was fairly ideal – cool at night with a hot dry heat by day. I found myself officer in charge of hockey and boxing. The Battalion held its athletics meeting at which our 'B' Company won the inter-company athletics shield and I managed to win the Battalion 880 yards. It was quite incongruous that I should win this race, as I was not at all interested at school nor at Sandhurst in running anywhere, except possibly after some ball!

Having quietened the tribes in the southern parts of Waziristan in the winter and consolidated the success in early spring, considerable unrest began to erupt in the north, where, almost daily, outrages were being committed, mostly against civilian lorries that were held up and robbed. This trouble had intensified since February last year and spread up the Tochi valley; the terrorists had proclaimed the Fakir of Ipi as their leader and imposed fines on the local inhabitants for supporting the Government. The tribal artillery shelled the Boya and Datta Khel posts, held by the Tochi Scouts, which were being repeatedly attacked by the tribal ground forces and suffered casualties both in the Fort and whilst on patrols.

At that time the Tochi Scouts were mostly officered by the British, and the recruiting of the soldiers that made up the 'Scouts' was drawn from Pathan tribes, but the Wazirs were never included as they had proved fickle, unreliable and treacherous. Training and ambition was to provide some excellent Pathan officers for the Tochi Scouts and other Frontier units.

The final straw, which sparked off our summer operations, came when the Tochi Scouts' fort at Datta Khel was besieged and cut off, with all roads being blocked, and the local Khassadars and inhabitants refusing to sell food to the Government forces. This meant that the fort had to be supplied by air.

Lessons had been learnt that, once the tribal gangs had sniffed success, local recruits would be encouraged to join and in time the problem could escalate into a large-scale operation which could destabilize Afghanistan and its neutrality in our war against Germany which had an embassy in Kabul. Certainly unknown to me then, but it became known later, the Germans planned to drop paratroops in the area of Datta Khel; this in turn could encourage dissidents in India.

Over the centuries the Tochi valley had been an important trade route to and from Afghanistan and it was from Ghazni in Afghanistan that raiders came down the Tochi Valley into India.

The Government decided that a major operation involving three brigades was necessary to relieve the Datta Khel fort and disperse the tribesmen. Both Razcol and Tocol, based in Bannu, were ordered to advance up the Tochi Valley and 1 Infantry Brigade to come up from Abbottabad to protect the lines of communication. Our column from Razmak (Razcol) included:

one Section of Royal Artillery Medium guns, two Mountain Batteries of Indian Artillery, Royal Signals and Indian Signals, 1/ Queens, 5/8th Punjabs, and 1/10th Gurkha Rifles[6]. Also in the column were the 4/12th Frontier Force (an infantry battalion), Field Ambulance, two Mule Companies, a Supply Issue Section (with motor transport) and one Troop of Scinde Horse (armoured cars).

The forward troops crossed the start line at 6.40am on 16 June 1941, 1 Queen's was in the main body and crossed at 0815 hrs. The Rearguard arrived in Gardai camp at 1645hrs, some 15 miles from Razmak. I mention the details as an indication of the length of this column, which had literally thousands of mules, much motor transport, some cavalry armoured cars and at least ten artillery guns. From Razmak Narai the route twisted and turned as it gradually descended from 7,000 feet to about 2,000 at Miran Shah, where the heat became progressively severe.

Much of the route had been picketed for us and so our progress had been fast. Apart from an attack by a gang on one of the camp piquets, when a bomb was exploded close to it and some of the gang climbed onto the sangar wall but were beaten off, there was no opposition until we were in the Ahmed Khel camp, which was at 3,203 feet and 19 miles from Datta Khel.

The Battalion spent two weeks in Ahmed Khel camp on the north side of the Tochi River. The ground to the south was flat for nearly a mile. It was saturatingly hot in this camp and indeed anywhere. The air was solid in its immobility. I recollect someone saying that the temperature rose to 118 degrees F in the shade, but there really was no shade; quoting from a letter home in June 1941, I wrote that the temperature was usually about 110–112F (in the shade). While on these operations I made a rather successful ice box, on the same principle as the hay box, in which we kept some of the troops' beer and the Company's butter.

Whenever we were in camps the kite hawks would appear from nowhere during daylight; they were scavenging after any food they could lay their claws on. If we were too slow eating our sandwiches, these shite-hawks, as the soldiers had quickly renamed them, would swoop down and take a sandwich out of one's hand before it reached the mouth. We had to learn to be quick eaters. On one occasion some soldiers thought they would give the kites a lesson by sewing a sandwich to an army blanket: the effect was that the kite dived and picked up the sandwich with its talons and came away with the blanket which the kite dropped almost immediately. I think the lesson to the kites was that a 'bird in the hand was . . .'!

Water on operations on the NWFP was invariably a problem; as a yardstick we were restricted to one water bottle (2 pints) a day. I can remember shaving in the dregs of my tea-leaves, which had given me such nectar five minutes before. There had to be strict discipline on water consumption, as it was rarely known when the next refill would be possible. At this time we were near the river in which the troops would wash, try to launder their clothes and bathe. In reality it was only a little stream and the water was not very good, having been doubtless soured by innumerable villages upstream.

We learnt one day that some tribal ration lorries had been held up and looted. Sniping did occur spasmodically during our two weeks at Ahmed Khel and intelligence reports said that there were gangs that totalled over 500 in the Tochi Valley. Our Vickers guns were often in action and were credited with some kills; an Indian officer and Indian soldiers were killed one day. Enemy bodies were brought in on occasions. The Battalion carried out some sweeps and searches through the villages; on 28 June B and C Companies carried out a search and found some live rounds, knives and swords but no rifles nor pistols. On 29 and 30 June there was heavy sniping of the camp after the evening stand to from a village south of the river; shells were fired into the village and then the firing ceased. The next day permission was given to the tribesmen to come out and bury their dead.

Because Razcol had decided to engage all suspicious persons

moving near our troops both in and outside the camp the tribesmen largely left us alone and consequently we suffered from only a few sniping incidents. On 25 June a bulldozer, known as the Yellow Monster, arrived to help us improve the track systems as we advanced; it probably did the work in a day that 100 men with picks and shovels might do in a week. At all events, it saved us a great deal of hard work.

1 Infantry Brigade joined us on 3 July to take over Razcol's Ahmed Khel camp, and so released us to move on to Datta Khel. The intelligence information was that the enemy was surprised to hear that the column was advancing along the Tochi Valley to Datta Khel from Razmak, as it had assumed that the most likely line of advance would be the shortest, i.e. north-west from Gardai and down the Mami Rogha Algad. Reports stated that large gangs were in the hills on either side of the valley and that they would oppose the advance. This route had very thick scrub and the hills would have been difficult to picket; the condition of the road was not known and so, as the columns had animal transport, carts and MT, the longer way round along the main road via Miran Shah and Ahmed Khel was chosen to relieve Datta Khel.

The Razcol Brigade moved on to Degan early next day. Many miles ahead of us there had been some heavy rain in the mountains and suddenly the Tochi River gave us plenty of muddy water. By 6 July the river was in spate and caused delay to units trying to cross to secure the route and on this day it was estimated that the hostile tribes numbered 400–500 opposing our advance, and they inflicted five killed and ten wounded to the troops of our Column.

As we advanced towards Datta Khel Battalion HQ and B Company were heavily fired on as we moved round Drewasta Corner, thereafter known as Windy Corner! From here onwards the ground flattened out towards the Datta Khel Post. On 7 July tribesmen shot up our administrative troops and killed two mules and wounded five others, which had to be put down. The loss of mules was an administrative headache, as the loads had to be redistributed; a further task was to bury the dead mules as quickly as possible, otherwise they would blow up into almost untouchable, disintegrating, smelly carcasses. In the meantime the troops returned the fire which appeared to have the desired effect. A number of road blocks also slowed up our progress as they prevented the movement of wheeled transport; in addition we found that nearly all the culverts were either damaged or destroyed. Once the Indian Army Sappers and Miners had cleared the obstacles and, with the help of that outstanding worker, our bright yellow bulldozer, the Column continued its advance. The Battalion arrived in camp at Datta Khel at 1700 hours.

Razcol stayed in this camp for twenty-eight days. Having relieved Datta Khel Post, Razcol had to turn its attention to the punishment of the offenders, and so a list of houses and villages was drawn up for demolition: in this process two villages were completely destroyed, as were certain houses and towers in Khanirogha and in Datta Khel villages. Most villages and houses in these tribal areas were strongly built with walls some two feet thick made of wattle and daub; invariably a village would have a watch tower. All this punishment could be done from the camp which was about 250 yards from the Tochi Scouts' Fort. We learnt that Razcol had killed thirty-nine and wounded twenty-eight on 6 and 7 July; this was possibly a conservative figure because the names of those casualties were actually known to us.

The weather had been blisteringly hot throughout, but it was cooler than the Ahmed Khel area, as since then we had climbed to 4,600 feet. Our time in Datta Khel, apart from local security and helping the Sappers destroy houses, was spent in road opening for troop movements and resupply. Another major task was to improve the tracks; the Battalion made an excellent 400 yards of road with picks and shovels on one day, although it was not strong enough for wheeled transport.

15 July was noted as a turning point in the tribal attitude when a Jirga, a meeting between tribal leaders, of the Madder Khel

tribesmen and a Political Agent, was held outside the Fort; also present was the District Commander and the Political Agent of North Waziristan. The tribesmen's demands had now turned into humble requests. They constantly emphasized their loyalty to the Government, and on behalf of all tribesmen in the Tochi Valley they asked that no more demolitions be carried out. They were told very firmly that the demolitions were only just beginning! I should make it clear that the tribes were always warned which and when their houses were going to be demolished and so give time for the inhabitants to move away.

As the days moved on, it was good to see that one of the villages destroyed was Drewasta of 'Windy Corner' fame. Sporadic sniping occurred on most days and Razcol did receive some casualties, but the enemy certainly took many more than we did, as we were able to drench them with artillery shells and occasionally aircraft were made available to dive-bomb their positions.

Captain Jack Wyatt, who had been commanding A Company, was evacuated sick in July, and so I was transferred from commanding 11 Platoon of B Company to command A Company for the remainder of these operations. During my time in B Company on this particular operation Captain Tony Lynch-Staunton had been my Company Commander.

The Commander-in-Chief, General Sir Archibald Wavell, who had only been out in India for ten days, visited Column HQ on 20 July and was introduced to all COs and chatted with some men of A Company in their protective positions, and, as their Commander, I was one of those introduced to the great man, who stayed on for lunch and left at about 3.00pm.

Razcol left Datta Khel on 5 August for Boya, 14.5 miles towards Miran Shah. More demolitions were carried out at a number of villages on this part of our march back to Razmak, notably Boya, Isha Algad and Banda, where the Battalion had been formed into working parties and demolished all the houses they had been allotted, with the Sappers dynamiting the thickest walls. Much of the marching was done in the Tochi nullah bed, which was very tiring as the surface was rocky and stony and the shallow, winding river had to be crossed and recrossed many times. As we advanced towards Miran Shah we lost height and the weather became hotter; we arrived at one camp, which for some inexplicable reason was being built in the nullah (the water course) bed. While getting the positions and the administration together, a violent dust storm arrived at 4.45pm, followed by heavy rain, the growth and speed of the rivulet increasing to a degree that a water bore shortly took its place and rushed through the camp. It is possible that the Battalion held the record that day for striking a camp; for as the tents were being struck and moved, and cooking pots and all the paraphernalia of administrative necessities (personal weapons and ammunition were always carried on the man) had been moved safely to the bank, a wall of water roared down the nullah, which included mud, sand, stones and tree stumps, making it a fair percentage of solids. The heat of the next morning dried out most things.

The lower, flatter country near Miran Shah, Isha Algad and Ahmed Khel was very malarial because of the abundance of mosquito-breeding areas. This was in the 1940s before any prophylactic anti-malarial pills, such as mepacrine and paludrine, existed. The only defence against the disease at that time was quinine, which in reality only kept the temperature down. The Battalion suffered from the ravages of this disease which resulted in a large number being evacuated and some were to suffer relapses over future years. Malaria takes the form of causing the sufferer to have a very high temperature, 105 not being uncommon, accompanied by intermittent uncontrollable shivers as the body see-saws between very cold and very hot. Evacuation and bed had to be the answer; but Colonel Evans and four or five other officers, including myself, never suffered from it on these operations as we were whisky drinkers, though in this I was not in their league, but probably in the fourth eleven. They always swore that that was their preventative medicine. I was to catch the disease a week or two after our return to Razmak and it was to return to me a number of times over the next few years.

As Razcol turned the corner at Miran Shah, Tocol left the Column to return to Bannu. It was noticeable that in the later stages of this operational column, and more certainly as we turned the corner from Miran Shah on our way back to Razmak, we had negligible opposition. This was probably due to the fact that the tribesmen had taken a hard knock and did not want any more punishment.

Two British regiments which were not part of Razcol or Tocol were very helpful to us, namely the Suffolks of 1 Infantry Brigade, who began to build the protective walls of our perimeter camp before we arrived at Idak and saved us much hard work, and the Warwickshires who gave our troops baths when we halted for the night at Gardai on our return journey, which was 15 miles from Razmak. Somewhere on that route back, about 15–20 miles from Razmak Narai, a Battalion signaller, using his heliograph, signalled the fort on the Narai, asking them to tell the troops' canteen in Razmak to make sure the beer was cold and that there was plenty of it for the return tomorrow!

Shortly before we reached Razmak Narai as the column wound its way up towards 7,000 feet again, we were overtaken by two lorry loads of sailors. Our cockney soldiers made many instant sallies. One I remember was, "Now get out your oars and row". They were a party from the destroyer HMS *Kelvin*, which had been badly damaged in the battle off Crete and had come on to Bombay for repairs. Regardless of their Lordships' views in England, the ship's Captain turned his blind eye and got his sailors out of Bombay to see something of India. And so we were fortunate to be able to go to town and play the 'HMS *Excellent*[7] card and our naval connections that gave us an excuse to have some very memorable parties with *Kelvin* in Razmak. We had an open-air Garrison concert party, to which Bakshi Bill was not invited, but even so he entertained us with some wild west sniping, forcing us to continue the parties indoors in the messes and canteens.

An almost unbelievable statistic became available after our return, but it was true according to the Battalion diary:

	Officers	Other Ranks
Marching out strength	17	524
Number evacuated sick	7	420
Number of reinforcements	4	133
Number who never missed a day throughout operations	4	54
Marching in strength	15	287

I was lucky that malaria kept away from me until after we had returned, but I did have a day off operations as I was overtaken by a plague of boils on my left arm and hand. Before lancing a boil between the thumb and the left forefinger the doctor said, "Just wait a moment. I'll spray it and it won't hurt". He sprayed it and it did hurt because, as he later said, he had sprayed it with water! The boils hung around for about 18 days, during which a second lance was necessary, when not even water was used! This was the only sickness I had in all the 75 days of these operations, although the CO told me to take one of those days off.

The Tochi operations began on 16 June and ended on Friday, 29 August 1941. We covered 348 miles as measured on the map, but we must have covered considerably more on our feet, as we walked, although more often than not we ran, sideways off the tracks and climbed up and down several miles of hills and mountains.

In my letter to my parents written on 4 September, I began it by saying, "Now over two years since leaving you. It is a terrible long time and it has felt a long time but on the other hand it has passed quickly as so much has happened ... What a pleasure it was to arrive in this place (Razmak Camp), even though it is called a cemetery with lights, after eleven weeks of very extensive frontier operations ... in country that has immense geographical difficulties, . . . the terrible heat . . . in contrast to our winter campaign. The conditions were very exacting for British troops; it was considered that both tactically and in health we did well."

In that letter I contrasted the types of sickness we had in the winter and the summer operations: in the rather severe winter the pattern of sickness was 'flu, sore throat, pneumonia of all types, and Spanish 'flu amongst the Indians; in the summer heat and the humidity of the lower heights, the ailments were mostly malaria, sand-fly fever, dysentery and other stomach illnesses; any cuts and mosquito bites turned into terrible sores that flared up and went septic in a matter of hours; some men had bandages over their exposed limbs, including their faces. It was said that the air and soil were very rich, and doubtless we did not eat sufficient fresh fruit and vegetables.

I also wrote in that September letter that, as my bivouac hole was dug down 2–3 feet (for protection against sniper fire), water from the flooded river had made a lovely tide mark on my mosquito net; during the seventy-five days I had five cold baths and two hot baths. This was not quite as bad as it sounds as there were three camps where we could bathe in a stream, which were being used by "all the troops on the column, the mules and the dhobis who were the laundrymen washing our clothes." Doubtless we were using second-hand water much of the time; whenever we refilled our water bottles we would drop in a couple of water purifying tablets. Whatever the quality, the tablets apparently did the trick and allowed us to drink as we were usually fairly desperate for another little drop and the taste was always absolute nectar!

Before I had time to finish that last letter I had to stop as I was suddenly hit by malaria and went into hospital. I restarted that letter on 20 September, about two weeks later, saying that I was still in bed but out of hospital: "Alternatively streaming with perspiration and shaking and shivering all over; . . . with about seven blankets and a hot water bottle, with a sledge hammer going through the head".

It was about this time in 1941, two years after I left home, that I heard that my parents had sold our lovely house at Bray. This was a very great shock, although it made sense for them. Nora the cook had been called up for something, the gardener had gone off to do his bit and my sister had become a VAD and served in time in Portsmouth, Paisley and the Isle of Man. Those growing-up days in Bray were idyllic and left a memorable imprint that has stayed with me all my life. Such is the destruction and unplanned movements caused by war. Ma had said in her letter that on the day they left Bray she wept buckets. At that time we also owned a house in Windsor and a cottage in Henley that was alleged to be part of a stable block that had been owned by Henry VIII. Henley remained with us until the 1950s. But in 1941 Ma and Pa moved down to St. Ives in Cornwall, where they remained for the rest of the war; my father joining the Home Guard and then, as the possibility of German troops landing in Britain receded, he joined the Observer Corps and my mother helped to run a troops canteen. In one of her later letters in the war she reckoned that she was doing her bit for the war effort working in a troops canteen, as on occasions she had to dance with the American troops.

From 1942 little artistic St. Ives apparently came very much alive as it became a training ground on sea and land for the Royal Marines and later a Marine Commando unit was based there.[8]

In this same letter home I thanked them for the cigarettes they had organized to be sent to me. The saga of these cigarettes began way back in Allahabad in the early days of 1940, resulting from a throwaway remark I made in a letter home to the effect that there was a shortage of the recognized brands of cigarettes. In due course a reply from my mother said that she had got in touch with Uncle George who was a Director of the Imperial Tobacco Company, then in Bristol. I never thought any more about this; but more than a year later the Indian manager of the troops' canteen sent me a note to say he had some cigarettes for me. I thought I was about to collect a carton of several tins of

Players. The manager told me that I was lucky because his boss in Delhi had told him to give me a tin of 50 cigarettes, and "Here it is," he said as he pulled a tin (which was rationed) from off the shelf!

The kindness and trouble taken by my parents for my welfare surfaced again after I told them how bitterly cold it was on the North West Frontier in winter. Some six or so months later I received a parcel from them that contained knitted green-matching mittens, scarf and a balaclava helmet, which arrived in the heat of a Frontier August: this, as I said in my 'thank yous', did not matter as they would serve me well "throughout this war". And as indeed they did and, some 60 years on, after travelling some 20,000 miles, my son Rob is now the proud owner of the balaclava.

I made the point at the beginning of this description of our frontier activities about the decision to send this Battalion to the North West Frontier for operations. The Queen's endorsed the confidence the generals had of our abilities. It was clear that our reputation during the twelve months or so was one of excellence. As did all units, we suffered some casualties, but generally speaking the tribesmen left us alone. Any time the Mahsuds, Wazirs or some lesser tribes had tried to make inroads against us they got a bloody nose; they never tried to ambush us and we never lost any ammunition or weapons to them. The tribesmen were probably the best umpires in their frontier warfare games.

During November 1941 my Company Commander, Tony Lynch-Staunton, became ill and returned to England. I was then transferred back to 'B' Company to take over command. We missed Tony's laidback approach to life and on occasions his seemingly bottomless pit of almost unrepeatable stories.[9]

We left the North West Frontier in November and moved to Ambala in the Punjab for six months. For much of this time I went back to the School of Physical Training as the Officer in charge of the Officer's Wing which was similar to our PT School in Aldershot. I was not keen to go there and leave my 'B' Company and miss some training for the real war somewhere.

The CO made a compromise with the staff that I should go to the PT School but remain to run only two British Officers' courses.

I returned to the Battalion in time to move back up to the other end of the frontier in March 1942, when the Battalion found itself prepared to keep the peace in that famous frontier cosmopolitan city of Peshawar, which was near the 'mouth' of the Khyber Pass. Here the Queen's were the only British regiment and our most important role was internal security, as it was in this frontier city that various tribal elders would swap their experiences from the hills and schemers in the bazaars could foment trouble that had influences further afield; and indeed within this city was a troublesome sect of people known as the 'Red Shirts' who looked for trouble. The Governor of the Province (NWFP), the Government Political Agents and the senior military commanders and their staff would also confer in Peshawar and assess the frontier situation.

The Peshawar Cantonment was well founded for the entertainment of all ranks. It was not surprising that many officers from the battalions on the frontier outposts, including those from the Tochi Scouts, came down to Peshawar for long weekends to let off steam. It was in the Peshawar Club that the revolving ceiling fans in the dining room became a target on occasions for someone to try and prevent a fan rotating by first stopping it with a hand and then with one finger. One evening a member of the club put a bullet through a fan blade from his revolver; not anyone of the Regiment I would add. It was a lively city, catering for many tastes. I attended most Saturday night dances in the officers' club. Of the few women I knew in India I was delighted to meet Jean Bruce-Hay again, this time in the Peshawar Club. Needless to say she was, as always, a breath of fresh air and boosted my morale considerably; she was still a delightful bundle of fun. She gave me many happy memories of wartime days in India. After the Battalion left Peshawar we never met again.

The Battalion went up the Khyber Pass to Landi Kotal on the border with Afghanistan to reinforce the Indian defences. The presumed enemy had been the Russians, who had suffered three centuries of Mongol occupation, since when it had sent armies across central Asia, with its eyes and heart on the riches of India. But the Germans were also possible invaders with the connivance of Kabul. To meet the threat from wherever, and I certainly had no idea, this meant digging, or trying to dig, in the all but solid rock. On many occasions we would be drilling and blasting the holes with gelignite; my company carried out more than thirty explosions on a number of days. Down in the Pass itself, Royal Engineers and the Indian Sappers and Miners were also blasting and setting up dragons' teeth (large concrete triangular blocks) to prevent vehicles, in particular tanks, from getting into India through this Pass.[10]

However, this diversion for us on the Afghan border at Landi Kotal was rather short-lived. Suddenly, we were all told to pack up and go back to Peshawar. The strategists were beginning to realize that the Germans and the Soviet Union had much more on their minds than to strike across Central Asia, as the German invasion into the Soviet Union had penetrated as far as the outskirts of Leningrad by the late summer of 1941 and had moved towards Stalingrad during 1942. There had been devastating casualties on both sides; in a period of over two years nearly a million people of the Soviet Union perished in their successful effort to prevent the Germans getting a foothold in Leningrad. In a referendum in 1991 the citizens decided that the city's name be changed back to its original Sankt Petersburg.

The 7th Indian Division

Moving down from Landi Kotal in November 1942, the Battalion remained in the Peshawar District, but had to pitch its bivouac camp near Nowshera, a very much smaller town than Peshawar, some 25 miles or so to the east, where the frontier hills gave way to a flatter, greener countryside; it was still very hot by day but at this time of year it became very cold at night.

During the few months here we were re-equipped with some motor transport, although we kept the mules, but our Victorian-type pith helmets, or topees, made way for the practical bush hat, whose wide brim kept the sun and the rain to some degree off our faces.

On weekends we were allowed to send parties of an officer and twenty men from each company to Nowshera Junior Ranks Club, officers' clubs and a cinema. This was a little unexciting, but, whatever its shortcomings, the town had more to offer than a freezing cold bivouac and a canteen. This opportunity to have a meaningful break encouraged good training and behaviour to qualify for some fun. My company had been boosted during this period by the addition of a tall, gangly officer, Captain Tiny Taylor. In the one and a half years he was to serve as my second in command in 'B' Company no one ever learnt his Christian name; he was always known as Tiny. He was an intelligent man from the Channel Islands and was about two years older than me. Soldiering didn't come naturally to him, lacking the spit and polish, and very often something like a bootlace but his heart was always in the right place. By trade he was an architect. He had a great sense of humour; he was reliable and, later, was to prove both gallant and fearless in Burma.

The first time Tiny took a party of soldiers on the bus into Nowshera he had clear instructions to catch the 10.00 pm bus back into camp. By about 10.45 all the Battalion soldiers had returned to camp, all that is, except Tiny's party. I was very worried, as it appeared I had lost an officer and twenty men.

At about 11.00 pm that night the Peshawar-Nowshera-Lahore train stopped opposite our B Company camp which was barely 200 yards away. This stop was not in any timetable, but then we heard the whooping cat-calls from some cockney soldiers and Tiny Taylor's voice shouting to me in the cold moonlight, "Teek hi sahib, we are all here. I pulled the communication cord, it stopped the train and I thanked the driver, so all is well." I do not believe that anyone outside my Company ever heard about this incident. I never asked Tiny if he had paid the driver and the Battalion never had any complaints from the railway!

In December 1942 the Battalion joined the 7 Indian Division, which mobilized in the Hazara District of the NWFP in the Kashmir foothills; together with the 4/1st Gurkhas and 4/15th Punjab Regiment, 1 Queen's formed the 33 Indian Infantry Brigade. All of the Divisions' nine Infantry battalions had been on active service on the North West Frontier, hence the Division's Golden arrow emblem pointing to the north-west. By the time we began our training for Burma, the Battalion's excellent musicians of some thirty Bandsmen had had to put their instruments into store and take on further training to become full-time first aid experts and stretcher-bearers and integrated into the rifle companies. They formed, together with the Battalion's Medical Officer, our Regimental Aid Post, through which our casualties would be channelled. It was very sad to realize that this magnificent Band would probably not be heard again until we had won the war, and for us at that time the prospect appeared to be years ahead. The Band had been a tremendous morale-booster, playing on the march, in the troops' canteen, the Officers' clubs, the Officers' Mess, the Warrant Officers' and Sergeants' Mess, and loaned to many units without a band.

An addition to the Battalion were the tracked Bren-gun carriers; to begin with this new Carrier Platoon rather thought that it was a troop of tanks. There was an element of elation to think that we had got tracked vehicles and some additional motor transport. Within a week of the carriers' arrival, one was very sadly involved in an accident, when a carrier ran over the legs of a private soldier on a night exercise.

This Division was the first to receive any proper jungle training, which we did at Chindwara in the jungles of the Indian Central Province and in the Seoni Forest of Kipling's *Jungle Book* fame. The training was very tough, initially to give individuals and the section-size units confidence in fending for themselves in the jungle. One can recollect the many times when there was an acute shortage of water and we felt almost completely exhausted; most of us could have drawn parallels with the operations on the NWF. The training taught us to go miles out on compass bearings through fairly thick country behind our objective, and so to establish an ambush position behind the enemy and not get lost; we learnt a great deal about the Japanese, their movements and habits, one of which was that they did not to take prisoners. We were beginning to hear from some of those who had been driven back in previous battles of 1942–1943 that the Japanese was a fearless soldier and was good in the jungle.

We were to learn many important jungle training lessons. One was that, as we moved forward on a compass bearing supposedly in a straight line, there were of course a hundred and one bushes and trees on the direct compass line; it was often proved that some soldiers would nearly always move instinctively to the right around an obstacle in their path, others always go round to the left of it. If one continued moving like this for, say, 1,000 yards, the objective could be missed by a large margin. The soldier had to bear this in mind and make compensating corrections as he moved. At the time, but certainly reinforced in the operational year or so to come, the most important jungle 'trick' that I learnt was that the answer to noise was silence; this was particularly important when moving at night – to freeze for as long as it takes and let the enemy make the mistake and make a noise – although it could have been a monkey following us in the trees!

I was fortunate to be sent on the advance party to Arakan in Burma in June–July 1943. I and my batman, Private Kingshott, joined Lieutenant Colonel Mattingly, the CO of the King's Own Scottish Borderers, and did attachments to the Royal Norfolk Regiment in Arakan. We found ourselves marching in the continuous drenching rain, the monsoon being at that time at its height as we joined one of their companies in positions by the Naf River. We journeyed down this tidal river in a sampan with an outboard motor; because of the addition of the monsoon rain water, this was a hairy, choppy thirty minutes with the river not quite lapping over the gunwale of this small craft, that carried its pilot and some mail and rations to the company outpost where we were to spend a few days patrolling on the Teknaf peninsula.

We returned to our Battalions in time to pass on our new-found knowledge and to take part in the Divisional final exercise *Panther* that lasted 15 days. This exercise proved to be the most exhausting and toughest of them all. Then it was on to Ranchi, about 200 miles west of Calcutta, the rear base of XV Corps, at the time when the wrath of the monsoon weather was belting out its annual emotions, and from where the whole Battalion began its move to Arakan in Burma in August 1943.

Chapter 4

The Arakan

Our move into the Arakan included a five-day train journey to Madras. As the orderly officer on one of those nights and having to be awake all the time, I asked the engine driver if I could stay on the foot plate with him and the fireman; he was happy for me to do so. Except for refuelling with water, coal and wood, there were no stops, although it was necessary to pause from time to time to fit in with the movement of other rolling stock; whenever we stopped the orderly officer had to check on the train security and the sentries. After an hour or so, having studied the driver's movements, I asked if I could drive the train: the engine driver agreed that I could and so I paid attention to his instructions of "slow downs" and "more steam"; it was almost uncanny that the driver, now turned passenger, never had to say "turn left" or "right here"! I enjoyed controlling the big lever and the wheel, as I drove the engine for some three hours. The driver only allowed me once to move the train off from a start; this I learnt was the most difficult part of driving a steam train. I discovered that trying to coordinate more steam and a little less brake and keep the speed under control at the same time so as to avoid a judder and break the couplings linking the carriages and to keep the whisky in the Colonel's glass was an art that could not be learnt in a night. I failed that one test, but the Colonel told me he slept well!

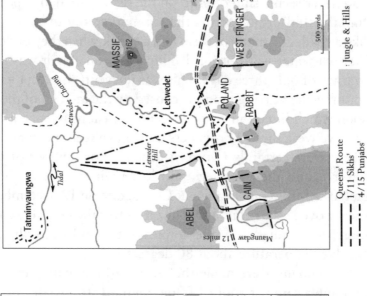

33 Brigade - Area of operations 7-25 March 1944

MASSIF
162
Letwedet Chaung
Tidal
Tatminyaungwa
Letwedet
Letwedet Hill
POLAND
WEST FINGER
Buthidaung 1 mile
RABBIT
ABEL
CAIN
Maungdaw 12 miles
500 yards

Queens' Route
1/11 Sikhs'
4/15 Punjabs'

Jungle & Hills

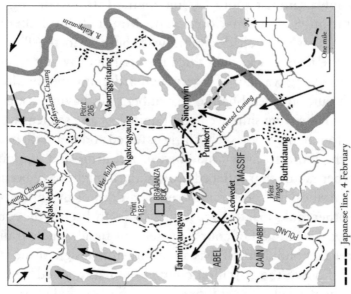

Japanese Encirclement Threats 4-5 February 1944

R. Kalapanzin
Maunggyitaung
Ngakyedauk Chaung
Point 206
Ngakragyaung
(Wet Valley)
Laung Chaung
Ngakyedauk
Point 182
BRAGANZA BOX
Sinomyin
Punkori
Letwetet Chaung
Tatminyaungwa
Ledwedet
MASSIF
West Finger
Buthidaung
ABEL
CAIN
RABBIT
POLAND

N
One mile

Japanese 'line, 4 February
Encirclement thrusts

At Madras the Battalion and the 4th/1st Gurkhas embarked on HT *Santhia* to sail across the Bay of Bengal to Chittagong in September 1943. The Gurkhas, who, with a very few exceptions, had never seen a ship or been on the sea before had expected to find the ship's route across the sea marked out in straight lines like a road, and many of them had a shock when they discovered that sea water was not for drinking. Fortunately it was a short journey of only three days. This was uneventful, except we were to suffer the heaving motions caused by the tail end of the monsoon which lifted our troop ship on occasions to such a degree that we were sure its propellers must have seen the light of day. There were certainly two days when a fair number of troops never found their sea legs and lost their stomachs! We disembarked from our steamer at Chittagong on 12 September and then moved on by train to Dohazari. Over the next five days we marched 85 miles in a rather unpleasant humid atmosphere with the day temperature about 80 degrees F.

B Company were made the rearguard company, arriving in Pondiywa camp at about 1.00pm on the 18th. According to the Battalion Second-in-Command, Major John Pakenham, B Company's march discipline was the best in the Battalion, with the fewest sick; only three men fell out. By any standard, our marching was not of a very high order; no one should have fallen out, but then I had to remember that, having just got off a heavily heaving ship, we hadn't quite lost any sea legs we may have found, our bodies felt a little battered and were still heaving and the more so as we marched in full arms and equipment. Another factor that reduced the standard might have been that the Battalion had been reinforced by a draft of five officers and 125 other ranks in late August; they had only been in the country five weeks and had of course missed our tough jungle training! John Pakenham himself was an unforgettable sight as he strode up and down the Battalion column: he had hooked up everything he needed, or so it looked, on to his belt and cross straps, items such as water bottles, compass, a bush knife and his revolver and he wore his bush hat at an angle that was entirely his own. The troops called him 'Hop along Cassidy'. He was certainly not carrying anything other officers were not, but somehow he looked incongruously different as he lolloped past the ranks. John P had one of those open, happy, beaming faces that was always smiling; while his quick progress up and down the Battalion checking its marching and security was always an accurate assessment. John P was not a regular soldier, but had been an enthusiastic member of one of our Territorial Battalions between the wars.

While at Pondiywa we learned that the Battalion was the Brigade reserve and that, on that day, 18 September, our 7 Indian Division took over from 26 Indian Division and became responsible for all operations in Arakan. We were still some twenty miles from any Japanese positions, but of course in this sort of jungle country there could be no front line. The Naf River and a maze of rivulets and chaungs (usually large tributaries of rivers), some of which were tidal, and the monsoon rains had made many of the rivulets unseen patrolling hazards in some flooded erstwhile paddy-fields; at this time of year the valleys were impossible for wheeled or even tracked vehicles and were hazardous for mules. In the valleys there are a large number of isolated pimples and long ridges from 50 to 200 feet high covered in thick primary jungle with tall clumps of bamboo. Many of these small hills were ideal positions from which to ambush and control the valleys by day.

There was still about a month of monsoon rain to come. In these parts of Burma an average of about 170 inches of rain can be expected in a year (the UK averages about 28–30 inches). Of this, some 142 inches fall between June and September and, as the rain tails off, the temperature of about 80 degrees is all but equalled by a stickily uncomfortable humidity. It was during the monsoon periods when we were in and out of water-filled paddy-fields and chaungs that we suffered the explorations of leeches around our bodies; new British blood was apparently nectar to them. The leeches would usually get their sustenance by entering our boots through the lace-holes. They got so

71

bloated by this apparent bottomless pit of blood that they would never have seen daylight again had it not been for the pain the men felt as the swollen leeches tried to share a boot which only just fitted a swollen foot. Some leeches were doubtless old soldiers at the game and raced up the inside of a man's clothing and took more juicy blood from around the crutch. They were the devil to extract as their strong suckers at the mouth and the rear appeared to be glued to the human skin; just trying to pull them off was usually unsuccessful, whereas touching them with salt or a burning cigarette end usually did the trick, but doing it in some sensitive places was an art. You can't always light a cigarette and salt isn't always to hand.

It was here that we built our first operational bashas out of bamboo, usually for two or three men. The sentries would be doubled at nightfall, when, just before dusk, the whole company, and indeed the Battalion, would stand to. As part of our fitness training we continued to wear our packs between 12.30 pm and 13.30 pm each day, as the enemy were unlikely to attack us in daylight. In our turn we sent out patrols on a Battalion roster. The month that we were here and at Tumbru, a few miles further south, emphasized the problems the Brigade had regarding its supplies. Because of the heavy rains the roadways were closed for six days out of seven; our alternative route for all supplies of food, ammunition and baggage was by sampans negotiating the twisting chaungs that were tributaries of the Naf River. This performance could take up to six hours in a day, one reason being that the river was tidal and there were two high tides a day.

For two weeks in September and October the Company carried out persistent patrolling, mostly by my two officers, Pen Ingham and Tiny Taylor, with three or four men each. Much of this concerned chaung and river reconnaissances and escorting the supply sampans on the river; another of their tasks was to locate crossings for the 33 Brigade mules.

On 30 September Corporal Morris and two men of the company went absent at about 5.30 am and left me a note to say that they were fed up with the hanging around and wanted to get at the Japs, so had left with that intention, but were sorry I couldn't come with them! Corporal Morris was a very effective and efficient NCO and an articulate cockney, as also were the two men. I believed them to have got itchy feet and genuinely wanted 'to get at them'. But this was an inexcusable, irresponsible action to have taken. I suspected that they would see a spell of detention before they saw the enemy, unless someone's bullet got them first. All very sad and such a waste; we never saw them again.

Up to October we had had considerable rain and then the monsoon stopped suddenly on 3 October as if the Almighty had controlled the taps, knowing that we had all had enough; then the sun became scorchingly hot. Shortly after the end of the rains my B Company was joined by Joe Mullins, who became the commander of my quite excellent old 11 Platoon. This period was largely devoted to swimming training, working up to swimming in full kit which included a steel helmet, a rifle and equipment but not the pack. Considerable time was spent with sampan boat drill and practising assault landings from a tug and barges on the Naf River.

It was not long before we lost Pen Ingham to Brigade as their Intelligence Officer. I was very sad to lose him as he was a fine commander of men and stood head and shoulders above some others. From Tumbru we moved down-river to Nhilla, which was a rambling mixture of largely bamboo and wooden huts around the chaungs that feed the tidal Naf River. From this point it was assumed that the Japanese were dug in on the Burmese mainland a mile or two across the Naf River in the area of Maungdaw and Buthidaung; we did not think the enemy were dug in on our side of the river, but they undoubtedly patrolled it.

The Battalion's task was to defend the Teknaf Peninsula. Only the 4/1 Gurkhas of our brigade had so far had a brush with a Japanese patrol. The mosquitoes were very much in evidence and spent much of their time sampling the new, young English blood; mosquito nets and anti-mosquito cream were a must every night both by law and for comfort, except that the sentries could not drape themselves in the netting. At night the jackals came into their own when their screeching howls cut through the silence as they moved amongst the litter in the villages and then were joined by the village pye-dogs whose barking added to a discordant cacophony as they chased off the jackals.

During October we had put out day and night standing patrols to give us early warning of enemy activity, and continued with our intensive patrolling, reconnaissance and fighting patrols, and training with sampans by day and night. By mid-October my company of about one hundred men could all swim fully equipped, although not with the fairly heavy pack.

As a result of this tougher training we suffered our first fatal casualty in Burma. I was putting a fully armed platoon through its swimming training in the Naf River when Private R. Smith drowned on 14 October 1943. We immediately stopped our training and a number of us dived in search for him, having first taken our equipment off. We were of course well out of our depth. He would have been pulled down and out with the movement of this tidal river; we failed to find him. We were very saddened at this loss and it did affect my conscience as to whether I had taken sufficient safety precautions, the more so, as I was swimming a few yards from him and had seen it all happen. His steel helmet had slipped down to the back of his neck and the swirling water got caught in it and pulled him down. He was a very good lad, one of the younger soldiers who had come to us towards the end of our training on the North West Frontier. With a very heavy heart and a nagging conscience at this our first loss, I wrote to his parents.

The days ahead for me and the company proved to be overflowing with activity and preparations for our first major operation.

I soon overcame my grief at losing a man whilst training, as we became more heavily involved. Then, three months later, by which time my company had lost other men in battles against the Japanese, I received a very moving letter from Private Smith's parents. In the year 2,000, as I went through my original diary and correspondence, I re-read their letter and considered it worth including in this account as it illustrates the awful days, weeks, months and years that loved ones were going through in time of war, and in our case being separated by many thousands of miles. One can sense the unselfishness, the caring and stoical attitude of this grieving mother and father:

161 Lower Addiscombe Rd
East Croydon, Surrey
Jan: 27-1-44

Dear Sir,

I wish to thank you for kind letter of my dear Son's death, Pte. R. Smith. We are very proud to know that he died doing his duty, and it is a comfort to know that you and fellow officers made such efforts to save him. Please convey our heartfelt thanks for all they have done, and may I just add, that the last letter I received from my son, was telling me about you, and if need be he would give his life for you. God bless him.

Thanking you for your sympathy and condolences.

Yours Truly

His (Mother)

Mrs. Hetty Smith

May God bring you all safely through this terrible war.

On that sad night of 14 October I received an urgent message from the CO to report to him at once. He gave orders for B Company to carry out a raid on a village, Letha, close to Maungdaw across the Naf River. This operation was ordered at very short notice by 7 Indian Division; I learnt that my company was to create a diversion while another brigade carried out an operation a few miles to the north of Maungdaw. The plan and all administrative arrangements were to be done by me. A 'V' Force Agent, Captain Ginsberg, came with us as a guide with local knowledge of terrain and the people.

I had under command two detachments of 3" mortars which were to be fired as part of the diversion, to be escorted and portered by one of my platoons and my other two platoons to operate as a fighting patrol. Before this party left by steamer for Teknaf, about twelve miles down the river, I rescued two crates of beer off the jetty for consumption on our return. The aim of this raid was to do nothing more than create a diversion; we had not been given any specific target other than to bombard that village with mortar shells; no information was really known of the enemy, other than that the Japanese were in the area.

To transport my B Company across nearly two miles of tidal water, consisting of over ninety fully armed men, carrying rations, two 3" mortars and seventy-two 10lb bombs (which had a range of 1,500 yards), we needed twenty-seven sampans. In the event, we needed only eighteen sampans to transport two platoons and company headquarters. The remaining nine sampans were quite inadequate to carry the mortar detachments, its bombs and the combined escort and porter platoon, so a khisti was commandeered. This ungainly, unwarlike vessel with its high stern looked very like a Chinese junk and was propelled by sail, and so some sort of wind as well as the tide were important factors! At least by this time, mid-October, we had got rid of the monsoon. The crew for all these little boats were of course Burmese with whom my officers and junior commanders could only communicate in sign language. I had to presume that they were going to be loyal to us and would not give us away. I found the thought of this operation and the unknown factors a little daunting.

The operation had of course to be carried out under cover of darkness regardless of whether the two to three-mile-an-hour tide was coming in or going out. There were many considerations that affected my plans to cross the river: how long would the night crossing take and whether I should take a compass bearing with all the bows of our flotilla of eighteen sampans pointing slightly down or upstream. No one had any ideas how this top-heavy-looking khisti would perform with its precious cargo. Would the wind, which was light, be sufficient to sail against the incoming tide, in fact would it get across at all?

I calculated that it would take two to three hours for the sampans to cross. This was a generous margin that allowed for some possibly uncontrolled drifting; and, to ensure our boats would not be beached on a falling tide, it meant that we needed about three hours before the ebb began. By that time we should have landed on the far bank. Before setting off at 2115hrs we had muffled and greased the rowlocks to cut down the creaking noises of this armada, and the boatmen had to stop talking and put out their cigarettes!

I had assumed that our landing on the far beach would be resisted by the enemy and so our disembarking needed to be done quickly and on a fairly broad front, but initially my overriding concern, prayers and preparations were to ensure that we would all cross safely to the far unknown banks with an armada that depended partly on paddles and oars and a great deal on God! I feared us being swept out to sea, so we had to beat the tide which would turn at about midnight.

We began our crossing with Tiny Taylor's 12 Platoon on my left and Svenson's 10 Platoon on the right; this gave us a nine-sampan front with about five–six yards between each boat, or visibility distance, with the platoon commanders on the inside so that I (with the HQ in the middle) could immediately contact them. Once at 'sea' we were soon pleasantly gliding at two miles an hour slightly 'up hill' to our objective, which was to be about 1,500 yards north of Maungdaw. I say 'uphill', by which I mean the incoming tide was taking us further north than I intended.

We paused from time to time to allow the mortar group in the khisti to keep with us, but it was very slow and continued to drift northwards on the incoming tide. By 11.30pm there was no sign of the khisti and the all-important mortars, by which time we had arrived on the east bank of the Naf about 800 yards north of where I had planned to make a bridgehead. Here we halted in a mangrove swamp. I was confronted with an option either to wait for the khisti to come down on the morning tide, which would turn in forty minutes, or to go on and establish a bridgehead. I decided on the latter as there was no knowing whether we would see the missing boat in time; anyhow, I thought that if the khisti was seen on its own sailing in daylight up the Kanyin Chaung it should not cause too much excitement.

So we paddled downstream as the tide had slackened and turned in to the Kanyin Chaung, disembarked and formed a bridgehead and firm base, where I left one platoon which had also to ensure the security of the sampans and their rowers. Having done a reconnaissance before first light, I sent out two standing patrols to give early warning of enemy activity and sent a platoon well forward within a thousand yards of Maungdaw.

While on a further recce at 3.00am, by which time we were about 2,000 yards forward of our landing point, I met an officer and some men of the King's Own Scottish Borderers also on patrol. Neither of us had any idea of the existence of the other! Heavens, that could have been catastrophic for both of us. We swapped intentions and went on our ways. In the meantime, by about 6.30am it was daylight and a radio message from our bridgehead Platoon told us that, after a sampan reconnaissance, the khisti with the two mortars, all their bombs and some twelve soldiers, could still not be seen. So I decided that we must carry out our task of a noisy diversion by using the three company 2 inch mortars and small arms fire. At 8.30am I went on another recce with Captain Ginsberg as far as the Tat Chaung, a small river to the north of Maungdaw. From here he pointed out some suitable targets in the town.

A further message was received from the bridgehead Platoon at 10.30am to say that the khisti had come down on the ebb tide and was sailing into the Kanyin Chaung, having earlier been grounded on a mud bank. I had been really worried about losing those men and their equipment; the khisti could have been grounded, sunk or captured. So many ghastly thoughts.

Some local villagers helped speed up their move south by becoming porters and carrying the mortar detachment's bombs to us over 2,000 yards to the south and 500 yards or so from the targets. This was a gruelling task for the soldiers and the porters who had moved very quickly with their heavy loads. The mortars were ready for firing at 11.30am! It was certainly not thick jungle through which they had to move, but down a track where visibility was about ten yards. Fortunately for us there were no enemy. If the enemy had seen us they would have been overcome and dumfounded by our speed and brazenness!

I considered the loss of security as a result of using local people, however, and also considered that we had already compromised ourselves by so much daylight movement. So the best thing was to move everything quickly and proceed with our diversion task as a matter of urgency. The targets chosen were the British Oxygen sheds and a plantation; we purposely avoided any buildings and possible living areas to avoid civilian casualties. As soon as we had unleashed all the 3-inch mortar bombs we covered ourselves back to the sampans and the khisti; with the help of the outgoing tide we raced down the Kanyin Chaung for nearly 1,000 yards until we reached the Naf River. The sampan element of the raid reached Teknaf on the other side of the river at about 4.10pm. Alas, once again the khisti had its tidal difficulties, coming in with the tide at about 0115hrs on 17 October!

Apart from suffering from some leeches and mosquito bites, the Company, its armada and Burmese sailors were all safely back at base. The raid was saved by the fact that there was no enemy; there was absolutely no trace of any and I do believe that Maungdaw had been empty of people. I cannot believe that we would have been sent on this mission if the Japs had been there; our arrival would probably not have been discovered during the night but our withdrawal in daylight could have been disastrously expensive in casualties.

The behaviour of the local inhabitants we met was very encouraging. They were obviously pleased to see us and their enthusiasm to help us became a little embarrassing, but we needed their help at that time and it probably saved some forty minutes.

We re-embarked in the twenty-seven sampans and departed from Teknaf at 8.30am, arriving at Nhila at 1.30pm. It was a great honour for B Company to have carried out the Battalion's first operation actually in Burma.

The rest of October was spent in field-firing exercises with every conceivable weapon and long operational patrols from coast to coast. All this period was in reality a very prolonged training, but under operational conditions as nothing was known of any Japanese positions on the Teknaf peninsula, although they were known to have patrolled on the peninsula. Consequently there was an edge and an air of expectancy in this tough training.

On 29 October we drew up green battledress; previously we had been wearing khaki drill which we ourselves had had to dye green. As we drew out this battledress from the stores we changed immediately and we looked very odd. I should have had size eleven but had to take size fifteen. Unknown to us at the time there was a shrinkage factor which reduced my fifteen to about size twelve in a month or so.

Then came a very strong report from 'V' Force that the Japanese were about to put in an invasion of the peninsula, as there were a number of sampans visible in the Maungdaw area. On 7 November the Battalion was visited by General Slim. Along with some other officers and men, I was introduced to him; he wished us good luck for the future. A story went around that one of the soldiers said to him, "We are right behind you, sir." "Don't believe it my boy, I am about two hundred miles behind you," replied Slim. If true, this reply was typical of his ability to put others at ease and win their respect. He was a very

80

large man with a lovely expansive, sensitive expression, usually with a large smile, and by his firm unequivocal speech anyone meeting him instinctively recognized the presence of a strong, inspiring leader[1].

By 9 November 1943 we became aware that we were on the move, as we had to pack up our kit and personal belongings into what was known as 1st call and 2nd call kits, which we could not carry and would catch up with us at the end of a march or an operation; on this occasion we loaded them onto the steamer jetty.

This packing up was followed by the company carrying out the mammoth task of stacking about 900 maund (each maund is equivalent to 83lbs), so about 3 tons of non-essential baggage, between midnight and 2.00am. This was about two-thirds of the Battalion baggage. The company carried out this work quite magnificently, the sense of humour of these, mostly cockney, soldiers was as good as any show. The next morning the Battalion embarked on a Creek Steamer and on some barges and sailed at 5.00am back up the river to Bawli to the north, arriving there at about 8.00am. From here we marched to the Goppe Pass at the foot of the western side of the Mayu Range some five miles away.

We were still not near the Japanese who were a good deal south of and on the other side of the Mayu Range, but there was no knowing where we might bump into them. We found ourselves in this "grand jungle position", still training but under operational conditions; we crawled into our positions and sleeping areas. I made the comment in my diary that our track discipline, camouflage and the wiring-in of the position was terrific. Joe Mullins had by now been transferred to command C company. Some of the orders for this position included – no smoking between 10.00pm and 6.30am, no talking on Mondays and Thursdays between 6.30pm and 6.30am, and a complete 'brown out' was imposed for those who possessed hurricane lamps!

Divisional HQ was only a few hundred yards away up the

road towards the Goppe Pass. We contributed to their security by finding two section posts and an air raid post.

On 12 November I took the Company out on a toughening-up training march for over ten miles. This was no ordinary march as we were wearing full equipment and I made it more interesting by making it tactical, not keeping to any tracks but cutting our way through the thick virgin jungle foothills of the Mayu Range. Before turning back, I put the officers and NCOs through some map-reading.

Our Brigadier, Loftus-Tottenham, visited the Battalion at 8.30am on 13 November and spoke to me about the fitness of the men and how were we off for clothing and equipment. In fact we were well equipped. We carried out a tactical advance up the Goppe Pass during the morning. At one of our halts our Divisional Commander, General Frank Messervy, joined us and spoke to a number of men, one of his questions being what did we think of our new Mark IV rifles and another was about the behaviour of our mules, (which carried our ammunition, water and, if the situation required, our rations, blankets and cooking pots!). We liked our new rifles as they were marginally lighter and the bayonet was shorter, being about nine inches long, and they were first class tin openers for the bully beef and cheese!

On turning south down the ridge for about 1,500 yards, we halted and made a safe harbour, did some map-reading and made some tea. While up here we studied the most glorious views: there was the Pruma Chaung flowing into the Naf River and beyond the river there was the Teknaf peninsula and beyond that again we could see the Bay of Bengal, possibly only twenty miles away.

Returning that day to our position on the Goppe, we had in fact only covered 9 miles but it was stinking hot, with encrusted salt sweat showing through the men's equipment. That evening the Brigadier visited the Company and congratulated us on our camouflage.

Further training on a toughening-up march on 14 November. Again it was not the distance we moved but the heat and the difficult country we traversed. The CO had given us the task to reconnoitre a route from the main Wabyn track into the Mayu hills. As we went down the Wabyn road at about midday it was very hot and my batman, Kingshott, who was walking behind me, suddenly passed out and keeled over into the ditch. I was very shaken as I hadn't realised that perhaps others might be feeling the heat and I hadn't allowed them a drink of water. The company stretcher bearers attended him; we moved a few hundred yards up the road into the shade and by chance had halted near 5th Indian Division's rear HQ signal office and a medical inspection room (a tent). Kingshott was backloaded down the road to the Battalion. By the time of our return at 3.50pm he had recovered. In the meantime we left the road and then went through miles, so it seemed, of streams and across paddy fields. At 1.00pm we brewed up more tea. For this welcome morale booster all men carried in their kit a solid fuel burner, and precious water was tipped into one half of their mess tins. Within five minutes the water boiled, we drank and became new men again!

During the afternoon we did more map-reading; then, after some fifteen miles, we returned to our company position. I had intended this to be a tough exercise and it became clear that a number of the chaps were fairly exhausted. This was part of the training, for which we had carried full-scale Field Service equipment, ammunition and two days' rations in the heavy pack.

15 November was a day of rest, when we had a voluntary church service in our camouflaged area at 11.00am. It was a good short service attended by almost 100% of the Company. The next day was taken up with interior economy, that is to say the mending of clothes, cleaning and washing almost everything, the priority being our bodies. Later that day I carried out a detailed inspection of all arms and ammunition.

The 17th and 18th were spent on further training: tactics, fighting patrols, recce patrols, ambushes, First Aid, map-reading and navigation. The Divisional mobile cinema visited the

Battalion on the 17th, a magnificent effort thoroughly appreciated by all. Further entertainment on the 18th was given by a very funny live show, provided by E.N.S.A.

On this day Private Kingshott, Sergeant Robinson and I went out to reconnoitre the ground for another company exercise as we moved over the Goppe Pass, on the top of which we called in at B Company the 4/1 Gurkhas, who held a defensive position there. On returning towards our own position on the home side of the Goppe Pass I saw a most extraordinary sight. There was a man sitting astride a horse, wearing a bush hat, a short but rather unkempt beard, no shirt, green slacks, no shoes, his feet dangling out of the stirrups. I am sure he carried no military weapon except a dagger/bush knife in his belt. One fine man, possibly an orderly, walked behind the horse.

This incongruous pair was coming down from the enemy side of the Pass. Then I realized that the horseman was Tony Irwin who had been a cadet in my company at Sandhurst and who I had known well four years ago. His unconventional dress was no surprise; when at Sandhurst he was invariably dressed to a level which was just inside the acceptable! He was the greatest fun, loved a party and had an intelligence that he preferred not to exploit. He never rose above the rank of Gentleman Cadet, as an unpromoted cadet was known in those days; he was possibly the only GC I knew really well. I became his friend and was invited for lunch with his parents, his father at that time, in 1939, being the General Officer Commanding Aldershot District. I remember handling his father's 1914–1918 army pistol, with which he was armed on the Western Front on the occasion when he led a successful fighting patrol and was awarded the DSO.

Within a year of the start of the 1939 war Tony Irwin had himself been awarded the MC during the withdrawal to Dunkirk. We had a brief chat on the Goppe Pass and when I learnt that he was one of those brave but unconventional British officers serving with 'V' Force. This small force spent much of its time between the opposing forces and often behind their lines.[2]

Some soldiers in the Battalion had been abroad for six or seven years, so on 22 November seventy men had to be repatriated to the UK and we in 'B' Company were to lose six men, including a sergeant and some NCOs. It was sad to see them go, as these older soldiers were a source of knowledge and an important part of the company team, men to whom the younger men instinctively looked for guidance. I, in my optimism, had hoped I had got the same team for ever.

The XV Corps Commander, General Christison, visited us and chatted to many men of the three platoons while they were training. He remarked how fit they were. I was invariably amazed, although I shouldn't have been, how much the men appreciated visits from senior officers who they would probably never see again. These marvellous, humorous men with their smiling faces gave back so much in their enthusiasms. Conversely, if they were not happy or busy, they were a clever bunch and could run a few rings around some, if the commanders held too loose a rein. But I was happy and proud to know that this B Company behaved brilliantly and did not take advantage of their officers' shortcomings. We were to discover that we needed each other for survival. Some of them I had known now for three years or so and I was blessed and very fortunate that we all had a fair understanding and confidence in each other. As each soldier does not wish to let his mates down, and as a company is made up of a number of interlocking mates, I can say that we had a first rate team.

On the evening of 22 November the CO and all the Company Commanders went to have dinner at 7 Indian Division Headquarters. After all the visiting generals and General Frank Messervy's excellent hospitality, it came as no surprise to learn on 24 November that the Battalion was to pack up everything for a move forward over the Goppe Pass, through the Mayu Range. This evening a number of war correspondents visited the Battalion and all Company Commanders met them.

I took an Australian, Mr. Gardner of the *Sidney Herald Tribune* around B Company. He met quite a number of men and had a plate of hot stew with us. The men got a load of thoughts off their chests and talked about the forgotten army among other topics. Gardner spent about two and a half hours with us and as he left he said, "It is impossible to lose a war with men such as these". I said, "It is beyond one's imagination to think otherwise, their humour won't allow it"! In my letter home at this time I mentioned that I was writing at night by the aid of a piece of string soaked in rifle oil, coiled out of a tin; it gave out a ghastly light which meant that I had to be so close to it that as I puffed a cigarette I frequently blew out the light. It was also in this letter that I recounted the number of things that we had made out of bamboo which added to our comfort, such as the basha floor. The roof was made of bamboo interlaced with leaves and there was the bed, a plate and the bamboo mugs. Bamboo was everywhere We also used it for our security; if barbed wire was not available for defence, by sharpening one end of a six-to-eight-foot pole and embedding the blunt end in the ground, then angling the exposed sharp points of the poles to about 30 degrees towards an expected enemy route into our position we had a reasonable alternative.

The following day was one of rest and packing up. That night I closed the Company up and slept in a fairly tight laager as it was to be a very short night. At 11.50pm we loaded up the mules, then at 0.40am the whole Battalion moved out with B Company leading. Between 8.00am and 11.00am fifty-three Liberator bombers (US) went over and pasted the area just a few miles ahead of us.

It was a terrible march in pitch blackness through the jungle, bumping into each other and sometimes stepping on air. Three mules went down the side of the Pass carrying with them their loads of cooking pots and blankets, which were eventually retrieved. We arrived in Goppe at 6.45am and here we rested until 11.30am, when we moved on again and halted at 4.00pm. We dug in immediately and harboured fairly close in the jungle as we were due to move forward on the morning of the 27th. It had been a stinking hot and muggy march of barely 30 miles over two days, made the worse as we carried full marching order, which included the pack, an entrenching tool (for digging a foxhole), two days' rations, full-scale ammunition, and, for most, two grenades.

Soon after our arrival at our next temporary stop at Limbabi at about 12.30pm, having gone through the usual security drill of posting sentries in each platoon's three-section area and then pushing out some standing patrols to give us early warning of enemy movement, the troops would be making a cup of tea. Tea, always known by the troops as 'char', a corruption of the Urdu word 'chae', is a life-saver and always a great morale-booster. Provided the operational conditions, security and time allow, the char restores the energy and does a little something towards quenching the thirst. All else being equal, I encouraged the men to make a mug whenever possible, but so often it wasn't and the water situation had to be considered.

For the first time in years I felt, as I wrote in my diary, "not so hot – went at the knees, presence of malaria". This was a poor choice of words, as in fact I was boiling over, alternating with shiveringly cold shakes! My first bout of malaria I had contracted after the Tochi Column in the summer of 1941, since when it had returned a few times. As on other occasions, one can work through it, and this was one of those occasions. One jolly well had to work through it, although again, the word 'jolly' is a little inappropriate.

Having loaded up 200 Battalion mules, we moved off again at 1.45pm to a position about a mile ahead, but to get there we had to make a detour of over 3 miles to ensure not being seen by the enemy, which was by now only 2,000 yards away. It took us about two hours to get to our objective, which we had to make into a strongly defended area and so we dug in hard during what daylight we had left. That night we heard a Japanese patrol open up on our left, probably in the Somersets' position (of 114 Brigade), and there was mortar fire on both our flanks for about an hour and a half. The next day, 29 November, was largely a

87

rest day that included washing clothes in a nearby chaung and we were given a talk by an Australian Brigadier who had had jungle fighting experience.

The following day I gave my officers and NCOs a series of talks on the impending operations.

Chapter 5

Bayonet, Sword and Grenade

No man who was serving in the Battalion on 1 December 1943 can ever forget it. It was known as D-Day for the 7th Indian Division. So far the brigades had been infiltrating over the Goppe Pass but now the real advance began. The Battalion moved out at 1.00am, B Company leading, moving first west, then south, and arrived at our first long halt at 4.30am. Here we harboured in thick scrub jungle and made some breakfast. The thunder of mortars and 3.7 inch artillery shells and the cracking of small arms fire broke the comparative quiet of the last few days as the Gurkhas drove a wedge into an enemy position at first light.

At 1.00pm we moved south again to a position a thousand yards away from the Japs. The day was very hot, causing dryness on the roof of the mouth; the stifling heat, added to the humidity, gave us a feel of dehydration. So it was not surprising that many of us felt a little tired after marching for the last five and a half days, each carrying three days' rations. At about 4.00pm my Company, less one platoon, were warned for a fighting patrol and then, a few minutes later, I met Brigadier Loftus Tottenham, the Commander of our 33 Infantry Brigade, who gave the four patrols (two Queen's and two Gurkhas) a briefing; we were to move off after dusk and "bring back some heads of these yellow bastards". We left at 8.00pm, as did C Company, on our different easterly bearings. Their objective was Point 206, about half a mile away to the north of us, ours being the jungle-covered hill and spur to the north of Ngakragyaung village; this feature dominated the village and an east-to-west track running through it. We were given no information about the enemy. B and C Companies' aims were the same: first, to see and probe the feature for enemy occupation; secondly, if there were no enemy there, we must take possession of the hill and the Battalion would follow up and hold it in strength from 5.45pm on 2 December.

It was dark, with a clear sky, but with a disappearing moon as we set off in single file towards the enemy from our company defensive position, moving along a single-file track that became known at once as 'wet valley' because of the atrocious swamps through which tracks ran. Before leaving the jungle-clad hillocks at the eastern end of Wet Valley, I dropped off 11 Platoon which took up a strong defensive position in an ambush-type role, overlooking open paddy fields. On reaching the open paddy, I halted the Company and re-formed it with platoons in line ahead and each with two sections up, 12 Platoon leading. Tiny Taylor, the platoon commander, and myself were between the two leading sections, which were in single file. Company Tactical HQ with my wireless set tuned to Battalion HQ, but switched off (there had to be wireless silence) were immediately behind me. Then followed Sergeant Hole's 10 Platoon. We had about a thousand yards of paddy fields to cross; most of it was waist high and some up to the neck. To avoid rustling noises as we moved was impossible, so a slow rate of advance, with halts for listening every twenty odd yards, was the order. An alternative route was by way of a track to Ngakragyaung, but that was asking for trouble; we should keep away from tracks when possible!

At about 9.30 we reached the outskirts of Ngakragyaung just north of the junction. We heard talking near one of the houses, then voices began shouting at us. Now, by the light of the setting moon we could just see the owners, some fifteen yards away. They were frightened and cautious, it appeared, as they moved towards us. We watched them and froze into the long paddy. Meanwhile I moved Corporal Charman's section of 12 Platoon around to their right. We saw five, all told. They knew we were there, although at first they did not realize who we were, nor we them, as they could have been villagers. Suddenly the forms fled, shouting and scrambling in panic through a house and up on to the hill behind. It soon became obvious that they were Japs, but I did not want to open fire at this stage, for fear that the Japs who were undoubtedly occupying the hill discovering our real location before we drew closer to them. I ordered 12 Platoon to advance a little quicker and take to the track and through the end house, a bamboo-type basha. There was more scrambling in this one-floored building, as other Japs there were hurried out, shouting warnings to the posts on the hill in front of us, but not before one Jap had been bayoneted by Corporal Williams' section. Halting the rest of the patrol, I moved with 12 Platoon just off the track. We had not got more than twenty yards when a continuous stream of stabbing flames spouted at us from about forty yards away on our left. Someone in the right-hand section of the Platoon was hit; we heard the groans. The Platoon was temporarily pinned down, the firing being continuous in long bursts from a machine gun. Sergeant Philpot dropped off here with the 2-inch mortar and, with the rest of the Platoon, I ordered Tiny to infiltrate farther south and encircle this post with a right hook.

Some minutes later I had word from Tiny that they could get on no farther. They were now within grenade-throwing range and had worked round the enemy's left and rear. But all hell was now let loose; he had established the location of a further light machine gun on the enemy's extreme left. Apart from the volume of metal flung at him by machine guns and rifles and grenades, Tiny said the jungle here was trackless. I told him to contain the Japs while I moved the rest of the patrol up a spur on the left. I added that it would be a good thing if we captured that light machine gun! 10 Platoon moved forward slowly, crawling. The enemy obviously could not see us. It was inky black and we had not fired. However, they began a furious blitz on our flank. Another machine gun from our left was firing back diagonally across our front and a light machine gun, recognized as a 'Tashio' 96, from the centre. Company Headquarters remained in the area of the track and the foot of the spur to ensure our line of communication for a withdrawal, but all the efforts of the signallers failed to contact Battalion HQ. Kingshott and I moved up with 10 Platoon; but this was slow because of the small arms fire immediately above our heads. Eventually we reached the high ground, where the Japanese and ourselves exchanged grenades, but the enemy were still on slightly higher ground and could roll them down on us; an enemy grenade discharger was also lobbing grenades at us and one of our own 2-inch mortar bombs, firing from behind us, dropped a bit short and very close to us.

Throughout this time the Japs themselves were kicking up a terrible row in their positions, shouting orders and chattering. They gave me the impression that they were panicky. They were firing wildly and madly at this stage. I considered that we had got as complete information as possible without committing the Company to unnecessary casualties. The Japs certainly had one machine gun and two light machine guns, but I was sure they had a third, unless they had changed the position of the one on our right. I was not certain how many men of 12 Platoon were missing, although I learnt there were ten, and one killed and one wounded. 10 Platoon, I was sure, had not suffered any, mostly through luck, but also because the enemy machine guns appeared to be firing on fixed lines, as we could see some tracer over our heads. It was a slow business getting the men forward, but they went; full credit to Hole, now a Sergeant, commanding 10 Platoon. Fire discipline was first class; only the mortars and grenades were used until I gave the order to 10 Platoon to give their Bren a few bursts just before we withdrew.

At 1.45am I gave the prearranged red Very light signal to

withdraw to our fixed rendezvous some five hundred yards back. On firing the light signal we ceased fire and so did the enemy, and then was heard in bad English, "It's all right. You can come on now. They've withdrawn". Taking no notice of this invitation, we moved back to the rendezvous where we re-organized and checked up and found that we were still five men down. We withdrew to the Battalion area at 2.30am and arrived there at 3.30am on 2 December.

By about 4.00am we were back in the Company defensive position having withdrawn through 11 Platoon at the Wet Valley entrance, and then suddenly the silence of this very homely and reassuringly safe defensive position was shattered by considerable firing on Lieutenant Svensson's 11 Platoon's front. This platoon had not come out on the fighting patrol and, as mentioned, were holding the front edge of the Battalion position in an ambush role. The action that followed in their area was very short. By the time I arrived it was over. Svenson told me, "Three of those missing from the fighting patrol came into the platoon position and sat down in the centre of the ambush, followed close behind by about eight Japanese. At first the latter were thought to be Gurkhas, as the leader shouted to the men on the ground, 'Tik hai, its all right, it's Johnny Gurkha'. In a lightning move this Jap thrust his sword into all three, killing one, mortally wounding another, and the third, Pte. Wiseman, my Company clerk, got away with three wounds. This display of sword prowess barely took a second. The ambush Platoon was still standing-to after our arrival, and this started the ball rolling. Corporal Cunningham dived out of the bushes and emptied a magazine of his Tommy gun into the Jap with the sword. Private Rolfe, on the Bren, almost certainly killed two and wounded two more. The rest of the enemy patrol ran away. But they returned five seconds later and hurled a shower of grenades into the position. Under cover of this they managed to get away their casualties, all except the swordsman, who proved to be a sergeant major. He had a very useful watch, a natty wrist compass, sword, marked maps and reports, grenades and a haversack of rice and a bag of biscuits. I saw his dead body, he had been a remarkably tall man, over six foot."

B Company's total casualties, the missing now returned or accounted for, were three killed: Privates Richards, Pledge and Hill, and three wounded: Privates Wiseman, Higgins and Fry. Enemy known casualties were eight killed and at least two wounded. But as grenades and mortar bombs fell fast and furious during that night's fighting patrol on the enemy's position, this is a very conservative estimate.

This being our first engagement with the Japanese in battle and on a very dark night, some interesting facts came out – the enemy panicked and were noisy, firing their rifles and machine guns gave clear indications of their defensive positions; unsurprisingly, the visibility being barely three or four yards, the engagements were at close quarters, which was evidenced by the bayoneting and our casualties from the enemy sword; the control of the company's two platoons, their three sections and individuals was difficult in the dark, but it worked. I later learnt of the Commanding Officer's praise regarding my control of the Company. This was good for my morale! An important lesson came at the end of our engagement; the enemy had either followed up my returning fighting patrol or had followed up our three stragglers right into our Battalion defensive position; finally, and very importantly and absolutely correctly, my 11 Platoon remained standing to after our fighting patrol had returned, in case it was being followed up by the enemy, and in the event dealt with them successfully. But those three poor stragglers should never have sat down outside the security of the ambush Platoon.

In the growing light of that morning, from six o'clock onwards, the noise of battle in C Company's patrol area increased. While enemy opposition had centred on us the previous night, C company got to their objective, became rather too heavily involved on it and were counter-attacked off it in the morning. Captain John Hamilton, commanding C Company, was very seriously wounded. Tiny Taylor volunteered to go out with a few men from his 12 Platoon and brought John and a number of C Company's men back through our position. The total casualties suffered by the Battalion in this double fighting patrol was seven Other Ranks killed, two Officers and eighteen Other Ranks wounded. C Company had a bad knock, taking fourteen casualties. John Hamilton was very badly hit by machine-gun bullets in one leg. He was a very tall man, at 6 feet 7 inches. In many ways he was a larger than life character, full of fun, with a lovely sense of humour and was a very fine artist. He was awarded an MC, and Corporal Wright, who commanded their stretcher bearers, was awarded a MM.

That afternoon the forward slopes of both B and C Companies' positions were spasmodically shelled; we received no casualties, but John Scott and Geoffrey Collins of C Company were wounded, John only slightly.

Late in the afternoon there was continual bombardment by our artillery 3.7 gun-howitzers, followed by bombing and strafing by Hurricanes and Vengeance dive-bombers in the area B and C Companies had patrolled the night before. It was an awe-inspiring demonstration of accurate bombing, as the Vulti-Vengeance bombers dived from about 4–5000 feet perpendicularly over their targets and pulled out of their dives at what appeared to be 200 feet above the target, but was probably nearer 500 feet.

On 3 December the Battalion moved out, the Gurkhas took it over at 5.00am and we moved northwards, farther up the ridge. I saw Lieutenant Colonel Graham Duncombe, our new CO, for the first time that morning. He took over command from George Grimston who reverted to his previous role of second-in-command of the Battalion. He looked a very inspiring, black-moustachioed, six-feet-four-inches-tall colonel, but, if there was any awe in this large frame, it was immediately extracted by a large, warm smile across his face. My diary:

Company's new position is well forward on the south-east corner of the Battalion area on the spur opposite Point 206, some 300

95

to 400 yards from D Company, our next-door neighbours to the north.

Not much of any interest today. All last night and throughout today there is somebody shouting in the paddy, "Help, help," in English. He is believed to be a wounded man of 'C' Company held by the Japs, who have laid an ambush around him for any who may attempt his rescue. This later was confirmed by a reconnaissance patrol from 'C' Company. This evening the Jap positions on the Point 206 feature and to the south, where we patrolled the other night, were again heavily shelled and strafed by The Royal Air Force.

There had been an apparent enemy threat to the east and rear of the Battalion. Joe Mullins, now my second-in-command, had taken out a ten-man fighting patrol to that area. It returned and reported seeing nothing on 5 December.

At 10.00am. Eric Svenson and two sections of 11 Platoon went out on a daylight reconnaissance of the same area and farther in and higher up the slopes. They came back at 2.00pm with a useful report. Positions uninhabited, but alive with trench systems and foxholes, and could have only recently been vacated. Fire places were still in position; Japanese letters, cigarette packets and hats were lying about. All the positions were expertly camouflaged. Svensson and the other men are to go out at midnight to do the same patrol to see if the enemy evacuated it by day and man it by night.

More Hurricanes came over to strafe yesterday's target areas this afternoon. At about 8.00pm Tiny Taylor and 12 Platoon were suddenly warned by me (just been told myself!) to go out as a large but self-contained patrol to the Point 206 area, just to the north of where we had met the Japanese on 1 December. They are to draw the enemy fire and so to disclose their positions. Our blankets came up that evening. My word! even one blanket made a difference.

96

The Company was finding so many two, three and four-man patrols to sniff out the enemy that we had the best part of two Platoons out on patrols. This meant that I had to close up the rest of the Company into a more compact defensive position. The patrols returned at about 5.30am; from their reports it looked as if the enemy had finally left that ridge which our two companies' fighting patrols visited on 1 December.

A rest day was declared for the Company on 7 December and they did need it. Patrols and sleepless nights had been leaving their mark. I read in the Divisional Intelligence Summary that a V-Force B.2 report (fairly reliable) reported that about eighty Jap casualties were evacuated from the village of Ngakragyaung. This must have been the cumulative effort of B and C Companies' fighting patrols on the night of 1 December, but of course the air and artillery strafe would have been largely responsible! Anyhow it was a good boost to morale to realize that our relative few casualties cost the enemy so much. We were learning very fast the great value of all our patrols, the reconnaissance and the fighting, and how they built up a battle picture of the enemy.

My Observation Posts reported on 8 December that villagers, mostly women and children, were seen carrying bundles streaming north through our 'front' from Ngakragyaung and had been doing so throughout the day. They were obviously Burmese refugees, pleased to get back into British-occupied territory.

As the crow flies, it is only 300 yards to Battalion HQ, but as I stumble it is a damn good 600 yards, and the going is so difficult it cannot be done under forty-five minutes! There is water to go through, small precipitous slopes to go up and down, only made possible by clinging and swinging from one bamboo to another; and so to send a runner at night is out of the question. I have two telephones, one for Company HQ and one for 12 Platoon, who are a little detached across a re-entrant on another spur.

During the day we constructed booby traps and panjis, a form of defensive bamboo sharpened stakes in lieu of barbed wire. A number of troops' comforts came up this afternoon: air letter cards, many cigarettes, toothpaste and razor blades, rum and a bottle of whisky for the officers. Wrote a couple of letters to England during the afternoon and distributed more comforts to the Platoons. The theme of my letters was that one day all this will appear just a ghastly dream – the jungle, cold nights, the continual whispering as opposed to talking and the absence of any movement within the positions at night. The chaps often unconsciously start whistling and humming, which I am afraid has to be curtailed.

During the morning the Punjabis advanced along the Awlanbyin East finger to a position just south of Point 206. This advance was presumably working on the useful negative information of Joe's, Eric's and Tiny's patrols. I gather the Punjabis were fired on from the east by an automatic, but their casualties were only a few wounded. Having a drop of whisky in the evening is a grand tonic, especially for me, as I still have malaria in my system.

It was rare that I commented on a particular meal in the jungle, but on 10 December I wrote in my diary that we had a grand breakfast, sausages, eggs and bread, all fried, and then some bread, butter and jam. The food had looked up enormously recently and there was plenty of it, and well cooked. Platoons cooked on their own, as centralized cooking was impossible as we were too split up and it would have involved too much movement by too many people and the noise of cookers in a forward position would have been unacceptable. The jungle was very thick and the dense high trees absorbed the smoke of the smaller fires.

I visited Battalion HQ at about 10.00am to be put in the picture regarding our local war situation. I had hardly returned to the Company when I was unfortunately called back to Battalion HQ to attend an 'Orders' Group conference in the afternoon; this gave us an insight into future operations. I managed to squeeze in a preplanned foot and fingernail inspection before giving out my orders to the Platoon commanders and to CSM Hudson on what I had learned from the CO. It may appear odd that commanders should carry out inspections of soldiers' fingers and feet and it is true the majority would take great care of them, but it is necessary just for the few. By making everyone present them to me no one's pride was upset and I was assured that all ranks could run on all fours! If I had the choice I would prefer not to have to look at some 2,000 digits.

At last Fraser (now the Colour Sergeant) was able to send up what was known as second call kits, which meant a change of clothing and a few odd private articles. And so Kingshott could wash my stinking mud-starched battledress that I had worn for close on a fortnight, and that went for the rest of the company. We all smelt, some more than others, but in reality 'it' was absorbed by the smell of the jungle that included decaying vegetation.

The following day meant that we all had another good breakfast of porridge, beans, bacon and fried bread, all feeling marvellously fresh in our clean clothes. But, like a number of men, I had one or two bamboo cuts which developed into the inevitable jungle sores; these we had to take care of or we would be walking around covered in bandages, as these sores flared up very quickly and spread because of the richness of the soil and the attention of a thousand and one flies.

At 10.30am on 15 December B Company had to stand by at fifteen minutes' notice to move out to the Punjabis' area on the centre of the Awlanbyin feature. In fact the CO ordered us out at 1.15pm and we arrived at the Punjabis' HQ at 2.50pm and took over their B Company position, which had moved forward in the area of another of their companies, as they are expecting trouble just to their east and possibly in their rear.

This new position had been an old Jap one. On it we found quite a number of Jap papers and messages written on English message forms, ammunition, light machine-gun clips and tins of chocolate-coated malaria pills!

We had a most glorious biscuit dough for the evening meal made out of nuts and raisins, powdered milk, sugar, army biscuits, rice and boiling water. It was grand! Tiny Taylor's Platoon went out on a fighting patrol at 8.00pm.

On the following morning at 6.10am the company received a wireless message from Battalion HQ to say that they had moved and would be in our area soon. At 7.30am the Battalion Head-quarters arrived and took up positions on our left. The reason was the same as for our move – there was supposed to be a threat to our left. The CO told me that B Company need not find any patrols and gave us a rest.

> However, at 2.00pm we find out that this is not to be. The Brigadier wants a company well forward on the left of the Punjabis near the banks of the Kalapanzin River. We moved out at 3.45pm. I had waited a little so as to collect a dozen mules for our blankets and food; I always believed that it was worth a little inconvenience at first to ensure comfort at the far end.

12 Platoon escorted the mules and I moved on some fifteen minutes in advance with 10 and 11 Platoons and Company HQ; we arrived in our new positions overlooking Maunggyitaung village at 5.45pm.

12 Platoon had a grand ambush position covering a defile through very thick hillocks. Sent a fighting patrol out at night at two-hourly intervals to the Kalapanzin River, also a listening post, all found from Sergeant Thatcher's 11 Platoon (Lt Svenson went sick with dysentery on the 13th).

The reports from the patrols the following morning estab-lished that there were few or no enemy seen this side of the river, although we all knew of hundreds on our side of the river a mile or so to the south. From the far bank opposite us the Japanese did fire across this 100-yard-wide river in their efforts to draw our fire, but a lesson long learnt is that one does not fire at night, unless involved in a battle. There is no point in giving one's position away.

1. The author as an acting temporary captain in 1940.

2. Mounted tug-of-war team, Waziristan, 1940. *Left to right:* John Smyth, Dick Kensington, the author.

3. B Company HQ on operations near Razmak in the summer of 1941.
From the right: the author, 11 Platoon Commander, Major Tony Lynch-Staunton, Company Commander, Company Sergeant Major Noke, the signaller and four stretcher bearers.

4. 11 Platoon sentry on a camp piquet near Tanda China in Waziristan, December 1940.

5. A camp being set up in Afridi country near the Khyber Pass in 1940.

6. The Officers' Mess in the shadow of the Tauda China Hills. *Left to right:* Bill Watford, Jack Philips and Dennis May.

7. "George", the head Khassadar, whose job was to liaise between the tribes and the government forces.

8. A typical view of the terrain in the Arakan.

9. Corporal Scott of the Queen's Royal Regiment is evacuated from the Arakan by motor sampan.

10. Major General Frank Messervy, Commander of 7th Indian Division.

11. Brigadier Freddie Loftus-Tottenham, who commanded 33rd Indian Infantry Brigade in 7th Indian Division.

12. Kohima: 1. Deputy Commisioner's bungalow and tennis court. 2. Garrison Hill.
3. Kuki Piquet. 4. F.S.D. (Field Supply Depot). 5. D.I.S. (Detail Issue Section).
6. Jail Hill. 7. Road to Imphal. 8. Pimple. 9. Congress Hill. 10. G.P.T. (General
Purposes Transport). 11. Norfolk Ridge. 12. Rifle Range. 13. Two Tree Hill.
14. Jotsoma Track. 15. Pulebadze Peak. (7532ft.). 16. South end of the
Pulebadze Ridge. 17. Top end of the Aradura Spur. 18. Japvo Peak. (9890 ft.).

13. Dug-outs at Kohima, May 1944.

14. Jail Hill in February 1994.

Although we were not involved in any battle none of us had any sleep that night. The Punjabis on the feature next door to us kept up a continuous blaze of machine guns, rifles and grenades from 8.00pm. until 7.00am the next morning, 17 December. We were permanently disturbed as bullets whistled over our heads most of the night, but we never knew whose bullets they were, although I was convinced there were no enemy! Thank heavens we had our blankets; it was very nearly a full moon and was very cold, with plenty of dew.

At 10.00am a message came over the air (the wireless worked 100 per cent in spite of a distance of three miles or so and many intervening features and jungle) to say that we must carry out a thorough search of every house and dug-out in the Maunggyitaung area.

Before beginning this search, I set up a protective base of my rear HQ together with the mules. I sent 12 Platoon slightly forward to act as a stop whilst I beat round the left with 10 and 11 Platoon, covering and searching alternately until we faced 12 Platoon again. Not a Jap in the place. Contacted two 'V' force sections, who said that all the Japs are in the Sinobyin area about 1,500 yards south of us. 'V' Force was an intelligence organization run by rather special types of British officers, who built round them an escort of local inhabitants and agents who operated mostly through the villages behind the Japanese, and brought back valuable information to us. There was no doubt that the Japanese had a similar organization and on occasion employed some of our agents. As with the Khassadar system on the North West Frontier of India, one had to be careful as to how much one said without giving too much away!

The villagers were genuinely pleased to see us and followed us round, offering us rice, ducks, even glasses of milk, but the latter had not been 'decarbonized', so I forbade anyone to drink it. Our job completed, we left our little base at 2.30pm to return to the Battalion. Before we left, Dick Kensington (Adjutant) informed me on the radio that the whole Battalion was moving and that there would not be anyone in their last night's area, so we were given new map references. As always, I reckoned that the longest way round is the sweetest way home. Instead of cutting across to the new area, we went north-west, then south behind Awlanbyin village. We arrived in the new position (in the Wet Valley area again) at 5.30pm, a distance of about six and a half miles, and found that our Company Quarter Master Sergeant, aka Colour Sergeant Fraser, had prepared a most stupendous meal.

The next day proved to be one of the busiest so far. First thing that morning our CO held a conference, followed by his orders for an attack on Point 182 the next day. The Battalion had received a large draft, B Company's share of which was one officer and forty-two other ranks; I gave them a brief concerning the Arakan operations and then reorganized the Company to absorb this welcome new draft, but it was hard on these new young men that they should be swung into battle on the day after arrival. I gave a talk to all officers and NCOs at 4.30pm on general tactics and a brief on the Japanese.

The operations were in outline the third phase of a Brigade operation in mopping up the area and so straighten the divisional line. First we had the code name 'Tinker', then 'Tailor', then 'Soldier', which affected 1 Queen's, one company of the King's Own Scottish Borderers and one company of Gurkhas and artillery in support. To get to the Battalion assembly area by 1.30am B Company had a sort of reveille, a wake-up call, at 10.00pm with a cup of tea and left our position at 11.00pm.

This was a nightmare of an approach march, as the Battalion objective was behind the enemy and there were almost non-existent jungle tracks along slopes on the side of small hills. Each platoon had a few picks and shovels. My heart leaped every time I heard a man fall or his shovel catch in the trees. Once we were off the jungle slopes I made sure we were all closed up in single file. Paddy With, the Battalion Intelligence Officer, moved with me, so there was little chance of our going wrong! We crossed the reinforced bamboo bridge over a small stream without incident. I had anticipated trouble here, as the crossing place had been reconnoitred and the bridge reinforced by us. With the Japanese sitting very close, if they had had a few peep-holes through the jungle watching the bridge this story might not have been told! After crossing, I put 10 Platoon in front of the Intelligence Officer and me to form our own protective bridge-head.

The infiltration carried on, with Lieutenant Uttley, the new officer, and 10 Platoon leading. And then a terrible moment. I went hot and cold when I saw this Platoon not keeping along the chaung as ordered, but heading across the open to a known enemy position. I could not believe my eyes, but fortunately it was a dark night with only a touch of moonlight. I went chasing after the Platoon and brought them back to hug the course of the chaung. This could have been a monstrous catastrophe. As usual, I had thought that my orders had been clear. I vowed to be clearer in future.

Once in the bridgehead position, a very cold and anxious four hours were spent by commanders trying to prevent men going to sleep and snoring. Few of us are trained to keep others awake. To stop soldiers snoring quietly is an art form, to avoid the soldier taking umbrage and making more noise when in this confused, comatose state in the early hours of the morning.

We literally had to hack our way step by step towards our objective with the enemy possibly less than a few hundred yards away. Cutting and navigating when you can just see daylight is not easy and it was a race against time. In the event our timing was quite good. Initially B Company had to form a bridgehead to protect the Battalion as it crossed the bridge. The other companies arrived at two-hourly intervals so that all would be in the assembly area before first light. At first light B Company infiltrated forward and took up positions on commanding ground in rear of the enemy, followed by a bombardment of the enemy on Point 182 by 480 × 3.7 inch shells and 900 × 3 inch mortar shells; this bombardment lasted for five minutes after which D Company passed through us at 8.45am.

We had a grandstand view of the bombardment. Our guns

were naturally firing to their front and the shells were consequently falling towards us as we had come round the rear of the position. D Company passed through, but had a hell of a job hacking their way through this virgin stuff and finally got on top of the enemy at 2.00pm. After a short, sharp engagement; the enemy withdrew, leaving some dead and a wounded private, who was taken prisoner. This was the first prisoner taken by us and indeed by 14th Army.

One of D Company's casualties included Sergeant Rae, a newly appointed and young sergeant who led his section with great gallantry. Although he was killed, he inspired the others to storm the position. B Company then got into the action as the enemy were forced to withdraw across the open paddy and 12 Platoon opened up, killing three and wounding at least three others. More casualties were inflicted by the carrier Platoon's light machine guns. During the rest of the day Jap shells streamed down on their recently vacated position, mostly in D Company's area. Before darkness set in, Colour Sergeant Fraser came up with our blankets and some more rations. I heard later that we were the only company to get our blankets that night. We were fortunate to have Fraser, who was showing intelligent anticipation without a hint from me. Each of B Company's Platoons, 10, 11 and 12, had its own jungle-covered hill to defend, and each had a section established on the jungle edge in cut off positions overlooking the paddyfields; the only discernible tracks on the jungle hills were no more than well-used animal trails, although we never saw any animals except on rare occasions monkeys coming down from the trees to scavenge. Usually the noise of battle would keep all animals away. My Company HQ included two signallers and four stretcher bearers, CSM Hudson, Sergeant Inskip and Private Kingshott. My HQ, as so often, had to take its share in the defensive system and so we had our own jungle hill to defend, this time positioned between 11 and 10 Platoons. Below us and about 200–300 yards to the right was Battalion HQ.

20 December proved to be an eventful day after a fairly

peaceful night, when the only battle noises came from the 4/1 Gurkha front. We had just stood to at 5.30am and were being asked by Battalion HQ for our 'situation report' when, before we could give the answer, there were yells and shots, followed almost simultaneously by heavy small arms fire, some shouting as of the Japanese war cry 'Banzai!', suddenly drowned in a deluge of machine-gun and rifle fire and grenades bursting. Telephone communications and wireless to Battalion HQ had been cut off and at that moment we realised that this was a Japanese counter-attack.

Then, barely five minutes later, in the midst of the fury of firing and explosions, we in B Company HQ heard the sound of running feet. Then Sergeant Major Hudson leaned over to me from his slit trench and whispered that he thought he could hear sounds of hacking below us. I agreed and said, "It sounds as if it is the Japs hacking their way towards 12 Platoon". However, a minute or two later he said, "No, they aren't going there, sir; they're coming up here". He was right; the beating and hacking of trees and scuffing of feet were decidedly coming ever closer to us. Then, in the half-light, we could see them about eight yards away. Not a move, not a word by anyone of us, and then I whispered, "Prepare grenades first". I allowed the Japs to come up the hill towards us and I could see them as they came to within two to three yards from our parapets, then I indicated to roll the grenades among them. On this signal grenades were rolled over the top. We ducked into our slit trenches and the Japs knew nothing of us until the grenades burst literally between their legs. Amid shrieks and moans and some chatter, the enemy fell back down the hill in the direction from which they had come, but the close blasts of the grenades and the smoke they gave off temporarily blinded us. As it all cleared, Kingshott collected the rifle of one, which was left. No bodies were left, but we could hear the groans from somewhere down the hill. I collected another rifle further down and later three bodies were found at the foot of the hill. These Japanese had caught the full blast of our controlled effort. There were pieces of grenade stuck in the woodwork of their rifles. Rightly or wrongly, we did not follow after them, as only Company HQ occupied this piece of ground and there was a possibility of the old ambush trick.

There was still much automatic firing and the dull bursting of grenades and mortar bombs from down below us. Japs shouting at each other were the only human sounds. From Company HQ we could hear digging in the area where we thought the Japs were. With still no word on the wireless or telephone from Battalion HQ and the absence of any British voices for some minutes after the initial outburst, many unpleasant thoughts crossed my mind concerning the outcome of 12 Platoon, Battalion HQ and the Carrier Platoon, which had been protecting the HQ, all of whom could have felt the brunt of the Japanese attacks. I learnt that 12 Platoon had not been engaged. Then from our position, we heard a stampede of feet running away from us across the open scrub country, followed by long bursts of fire from Bren guns.

I contacted Brigade HQ and the Gurkhas on the wireless at about 8.00am, and later C and D Companies. At 10.00am Battalion HQ was back on the air and gave me their new position, which was tucked into the hill just north of us; previously, I had sent runners but failed to find them, as they had moved. In the meantime there was continued firing in the valley below us.

A few minutes later I visited 10 Platoon with Kingshott and a runner, and went on to the section of 10 Platoon that had a cut-off role at the track junction on the open ground below. We intended going on to Battalion HQ by that route, but we had not gone more than a few yards when the Platoon Sergeant (Cozens) beckoned us back. This section had been engaging an enemy post and enemy had been seen to disappear into a clump of scrub jungle in the valley. My little party remained with this section for some twenty minutes; we brought Bren and 2-inch mortar fire down on to this Jap post some 150 yards away. The mortaring was very accurate; one bomb landed right on the position, followed by screams and moans, on which the whole of this section let out a simultaneous and uncontrolled cheer. It was an incongruous sight on a battlefield. I sent another section of 10 Platoon forward to mop up along the scrub bordering the foot of our ridge, where I knew there was another post because of the noises of digging and Japs talking.

Half an hour later the section returned and Corporal Budworth reported that out of a bush a voice had said, "Idhar Ao", which is the Urdu for "Come here", an old Jap ruse. The voice then fired a few shots from a light machine gun. Budworth replied with a burst from his Tommy gun and, rather surprisingly, silence followed. We made our way back and hacked a new way from my HQ to Battalion HQ, which was now separated from us by only 200 yards. Before returning up the ridge we noticed great bundles of our Battalion telephone wires which had been connecting HQ to C and B Companies and to Brigade HQ, but now all cut up and tossed in a heap into the bushes by the Japanese. That was a lesson to us, to try and avoid laying cable openly along the ground, rather easier said than done; fairly certainly the enemy had followed it in.

At Battalion HQ Colonel Duncombe put me in the picture. The enemy, about seventy men, had been seen off by grenades, bayonets and other small arms, in what was very close-quarter fighting, with both sides using bayonets and grenades. They had burst right into Battalion HQ, part of Headquarter Company and the Carrier Platoon. The CO himself had killed at least one Jap with a grenade that he had tossed into a Jap hole. Dick Kensington had thrown a pretty grenade with the pin in, the CO said with a big smile. I could see that Dick would not live this down in a hurry. By the time of my visit Battalion HQ and the Carrier Platoon had accounted for eleven of their enemy dead and already buried, including a Captain and a CSM. Another officer, a CSM and a corporal had been wounded and taken prisoner. This Japanese officer struggled with Jack Sumner, our Medical Officer, who actually knocked him out and brought him in. Jack's story was that he didn't want the Jap; he only wanted his gold teeth! George Grimston, the Battalion second-in-command, leading a party from Battalion HQ, had spent the morning stalking a Jap post in the HQ area, who were beaten off largely by some accurate grenade throwing by George himself; as an Army and Sussex County cricket player he was probably the most accurate grenade thrower in the Battalion!

One of our unluckiest casualties was Sergeant Johnson, the Officers' Mess sergeant, who was bayoneted in his slit trench. He was a well known figure in the Battalion, and certainly a great friend to all officers. By the way he ran the officers' mess before we arrived in Burma, one understood too well how it was that he had become head waiter before the war at the Cumberland Hotel, near Marble Arch, London.

Firm communications to 11 and 12 Platoons were established before noon. The enemy were still around during the remainder of daylight, having been beatened off and driven away from the Battalion, but they had taken up positions on a ridge about a hundred yards way, from where it was doubtful that they could see anything as the jungle was so thick, with visibility no more than three yards or so, but many of us knew their approximate whereabouts, as they made quite a noise. They would fire at us and we returned the fire. Then we discovered that the remaining enemy were constantly changing positions. Before dusk a company of Gurkhas came over to assist us in mopping up the remaining enemy. An outstanding feature of their effort was the bringing up of eight Gurkhas each armed with a light machine gun. They advanced from the paddy on to the jungle ridge rather like a partridge drive, firing from the hip! Those remaining Japanese showed great courage and tenacity and had not been liquidated by nightfall when the hunt was called off. By the morning they had gone away. The enemy artillery continued harassing fire during the remainder of daylight and claimed a few more D Company men.

Apart from some distant small-arms firing and some harassing fire from our own guns, it was a quiet night, only broken by the explosion of a grenade and a burst of light machine-gun fire at about 4.00am from C Company's position below us. I later heard that a voice in English had called out from the bushes in front of them, "May I come in?" C Company replied with the above orchestration. At daylight the answer to the cry was apparent; a Jap crawled towards them wounded in the legs. He was a CSM and appeared not unhappy at being taken prisoner. He turned out to be the last live Jap in the area.

A total of twenty-four Japs were buried by us and four wounded were taken prisoner (five since the attack on Point 182). We later learnt that the Battalion had at that time got the Empire record for taking Japanese prisoners; this was quite a feat as the Japanese always preferred to die in battle rather than be taken prisoner, as that would have ensured they would go up and join their ancestors. A considerable amount of arms, ammunition, equipment and a large quantity of documents and identification were taken from the Jap bodies. From this it can be gauged that it was a costly Jap counter-attack, as the Jap is a master at getting away his casualties to hide the real issue of a battle. Our total casualties were one killed and two officers and twenty-three other ranks wounded. B Company suffered no casualties and we definitely killed three on the 19th and a further eight on 20 December.

Sometime after this battle Jack Sumner told a marvellous story about George Grimston, the Battalion second-in-command: "George lost his patience with one of our soldiers who had acted too slowly, so he grabbed the soldier's rifle, then killed two Japs just like that, and threw the rifle back to the man, shouting, 'Now get a bloody move on'." This was typical of George, who could produce a short fuse at the appropriate moment.

Dick Kensington, our Adjutant, told me the story of this attack as it affected Battalion HQ. There were in fact, he said, three phases to the attack: Phase 1 was the initial attack by the Japs when they overran the forward positions and got into the centre of the Headquarter's defences. It was barely light and, with people running about, it was difficult to tell friend from foe. It was then that George killed two Japs.

Phase 2 was the bombing party led by George on the Jap group in a nullah (a stream bed) about 50 yards in front of us; this party comprised George, Mervyn Mansel and Sergeant Major Danny Reid. This was then followed by Jack Sumner's dash to succour our wounded, knocking out a wounded Jap and taking him prisoner on the way. Phase 3 followed when a Jap light machine-gun party dodged about in the jungle on the left, alternately spraying Battalion HQ from different positions. This was when George (using his captured Jap rifle) and the Regimental Quartermaster Sergeant hunted the party. Then it was George on his own after the RQMS had been badly wounded.

Finally, Dick said, it was typical that the CO, Graham Duncombe, should have been the rallying point and that the attack foundered ten yards in front of him. The Battalion learnt two important lessons from this battle: the first was that the Japanese is no superman and that, when hit or surprised, he panics, shouts and talks; on this occasion he was put to flight on two successive days; the second lesson was one of tactics, that in thick jungle country a heavy artillery concentration to a timed programme is very often valueless, as it may often take the troops hours to cut their way from a start line to the objective.

A large draft to reinforce the Battalion had arrived a day before our attack, but it could not be absorbed in time. It was called forward on 21 December and immediately the Battalion's fourth rifle company was formed, a new A Company commanded by Captain Mervyn Mansel; as a result B Company lost ten Non-Commissioned Officers and twenty-one private soldiers to boost the new company. This was very sad as they were all old sweats who had done me well. They were replaced by a relatively untrained draft, none of whom had been under fire before.

One of my letters to Ma and Pa in December was, with some years of hindsight, amazingly upbeat: "Please don't worry about me. I am fighting fit and feel very confident about everything.

The war news everywhere is really first class, it gives one added confidence with our successes on all fronts."

> The rations are looking up, we had been living on the bare . . . , but now we are all well fed. Had the best breakfast for about a year two days ago – bacon, eggs and porridge, in the front line too. I have been wearing my clothes for weeks now. All this may sound pretty rough and unpleasant but we are very happy. It can't go on for ever; and what a dream all this will be when we come to look back on it. . . . Very much love, your affectionate son, Mike.

I sent out two reconnaissance patrols on December 22, one in the early hours of the morning and the other in daylight: Sergeant Philpot and three men, and Sergeant Cozens with three. Their objective was a hill feature a thousand odd yards to the south, and they must search it laterally for any signs of present or recent enemy occupation.

From 8.00pm until the early hours of 23 December there were the most tremendous noises of battle in the air, which went on some 1,000 yards in our rear. At first one of the thoughts was that it was a large-scale attack in our rear to cut the Battalion off, but it never moved any closer to us, so after an hour it was reasonable to assume that this ceaseless Brock's benefit was merely a large-scale raid.

Later in the day we learnt that it was a Japanese patrol of about platoon strength that had got into Brigade HQ and the mule lines. The Indian mule leaders had fired off pretty well all the ammunition they had. Casualties to us were one mule leader killed, one wounded and one mule wounded. From time to time mule leaders and others who might not be considered as front line troops found themselves on the front line in this jungle-type war. The reality is that all ranks everywhere need training in fire discipline. This incident was not the poor Indian sepoys' fault; that lies higher up.

The patrols I had sent out reported back that their objectives had been clear of enemy and resulted in my Company being ordered forward another 1,000 yards to occupy three pimples on a ridge; so we moved off at 11.30am and after some four hours of hacking and cutting our way in a southerly direction we occupied the three positions unmolested. We kept in touch with Battalion Headquarters on our No. 48 wireless set. We also reeled out a telephone line and tapped in as we moved forward. As we were so far forward of the Battalion HQ and the other companies, I could not afford to give our positions away and so I forbade making of fires. So from now on we had no tea or cooked food in this position. Actually we each carried our own 24-hour ration pack of biscuits, bully beef, cheese, jam, powdered milk, tea and sugar.

I sent a patrol out at 9.00pm to the ridges in front of us. They returned at 0600 hrs. and said that they had been followed. This is more than likely, as the Japs were busy around us, and I heard from Dick's (Adjutant) report to me this morning that there were some perishers in their Battalion HQ area last night.

And again on the following night there was another enemy patrol in the Battalion area. At least one of them was killed. Nothing of importance here today. Sergeant Cozens' and Lance Corporal Dean's patrols that went forward and to the flanks last night reported very thick virgin jungle and almost impassable bamboo, but no enemy. Company fully dug in everywhere by tonight.

25 December brought new orders for B Company to move forward another 800 yards or so; and the rest of the Battalion would move up to our present position. This Christmas Day was heralded with much small-arms fire from the Gurkhas' front. The RAF came over twice as usual, and delivered two dive-bombing attacks this morning.

We moved forward at 10.00am. This time the route took us through chaungs, narrow jungle defiles and up virgin slopes. We waded some 100 yards down this chaung with it swirling around our middle. As we waded through the water I saw an unforget-table sight. There, perched on the far bank of this chaung, which was 2–3 metres wide, was an unmistakable moorhen. For some reason it had not been moved on by the war and indeed it was transfixed by seeing a sight it had never seen before: some ninety heavily laden men, soaking wet, moving through the water with apparently no legs! I forgot my cigarettes in my battle-dress trouser pockets; others, more thoughtful, carried their smokes in their steel helmets. It took us about one hour of sweaty hacking to advance fifty yards in some parts. We finally got on to our positions at 3.30pm. By now the Company was some 800 yards forward and south of Battalion HQ, and we over-looked the Letwedet Chaung behind which, about 200 yards from us, we knew were the Japanese forward positions.

A concession was made for Christmas Day. The order was for a very limited number of small fires to boil some tea. So, whilst the work of clearing the jungle on the inside of our perimeter and the digging progressed, others made the brew. This move today was rather unpopular; for about half the Company this would have been their first Christmas out of England and no doubt their thoughts were with their families, but once the men were here they were perfectly happy and dug in like Trojans.

The CO sent for as many officers as possible to report to Battalion HQ for a Christmas toast. We toasted each other and the Battalion in port. How marvellous this port was, after not having seen a bottle for perhaps a year.

The Battalion was given no patrolling tasks on that Christmas night. The inevitable Jap patrol started its rounds at about 8.00pm going up the west flank of the Gurkhas on our left and then round and down my east, trying to draw our fire. A grenade discharger pooped off at odd intervals and a light machine gun opened up. The grenades fell short of us, and the machine-gun bullets went harmlessly over our heads. But there was no answering shot from the Company.

During the still of the night the Japs did one of their broad-casts, which I can only guess was on a gramophone record for our benefit during the evening. One of the tunes we could recognize was 'Home, Sweet Home.' This was much appreciated by our fellows as we had no gramophones.

Boxing Day we considered was our Christmas Day; although from about 7.00am. until 10.00am there was a hell of a noise of battle some 400 to 500 yards to our left. A Jap patrol was trying to get out between the Gurkha companies.

ENSA artists arrived to the tune of battle at about 0930 hrs; they put on a first-class performance in our Battalion HQ area. A stage was rigged up and organized by the Battalion Regimental Sergeant Major Noke and a party from Headquarter Company that morning. One show was on at 10.30am and the second at 2.30pm, so that as near as possible half the Battalion saw it each time. It was all incongruous and uplifting; our own shells from behind us were swishing over our heads and there was quite an orchestra of small-arms firing from some battle going over on our left. But the accordionist and comedians all but drowned the battle noises. One act was of an impersonation of a woman who 'lives' in a 'flat' in Bawli Bazaar! Most of us had passed through Bawli Bazaar (about 30 miles behind us) and found the thought that an English woman could become a successful Madam in that environment of jungle-type bamboo houses with a dubious clientele; uproarious but . . .

The Christmas grub supplied to us was not only a magnificent effort, it was of a very high standard; a bottle of beer per man, a generous rum issue and bottle of whisky for the three officers; one duck for every four men, sausages (not soyas), tins of peas and fruit, nuts and raisins, some toffees, plum-pudding and a Christmas cake. The latter two delicacies were indescribably brilliant. George Grimston, the Second-in-Command, came up to the position before lunch and saw that our food arrived successfully, and then I took him to our O.P. and to 10 Platoon. The usual noisy, nuisance-value Jap patrol activity during the night. Visited the Platoons and saw them having their Christmas meal; they all seemed very happy. I am afraid I was still only learning some of the names and faces of the recent arrivals. In the afternoon Tom Garrett, our Padre, gave us a visit. We had a rather unique carol service. Owing to circumstances we could only sing them in whispers. But nevertheless it was a great success and was much appreciated.

Sent out a patrol on 26 December under Sergeant Cozens along the Letwedet Chaung and over in front of the Gurkhas to report any enemy movements over a bridge, which it was thought that enemy night patrols must cross.

The patrol reported the next morning that no enemy crossed the chaung at this point during the night, but that two pimple features on this side of the chaung were occupied, as talking and coughing were heard. What proved surprising to us was to know, and not for the first time, that the Japs were not very careful at keeping quiet. Without that patrol and enemy noises in their position, we would never have known that they occupied positions this side of that tidal chaung. And it was satisfying to know that our patrols were moving quietly and close enough to the enemy to be able to listen and interpret the information without being spotted.

I recorded very little of the RAF Vengeance dive-bombers' activities, but since Christmas Day about a dozen or two batches of six came over twice a day to bomb hill features and the village about one and half miles south-east of us in the Sinobyin area. The Japs appeared to put up no resistance to this, except a rather half-hearted small-arms barrage. Every day artillery duels took place but again the Jap was outclassed; to his one shell we put down at least twenty. The Japs have an OP (Pt. 1301) on the Mayu Range south of us, from where they can see everything, especially our jeep road which comes up directly to behind our Battalion HQ.

The Brigadier came up to see the fellows this morning. We went up to the OP and had a good look at the task ahead and the Buthidaung road. The big task ahead for us was the enormous feature, about 3,000 square yards directly in front of my Company position the other side of the Letwedet Chaung, and known as 162 because of its central spot height. On return from the OP we had a pleasant brew of 'char' produced by Kingshott in my HQ.

Tiny Taylor went out on patrol at 8.30pm to the Letwedet Chaung and to the south-east of it, to see what defences, if any, the Japs have on the north-west slopes of the 162 feature.

The following day Tiny's patrol reported back to me: there was much defensive barbed wire which came down the jungle slopes to the water's edge. The Japs would not reply to the patrol's searching fire, although the patrol heard much coughing. A rather typical day was spent in the position, washing clothes and resting after the night, which was never very restful. I went over to Battalion HQ in the morning to draw out some money to pay the soldiers on 30 December.

Threaded my way around to 12 Platoon, which was barely a hundred yards from my HQ, but took almost a quarter of an hour of winding, stooping and climbing, and paid them some of their weekly wages in the morning. Returned and paid out Company HQ and 11 Platoon. Uttley paid out his own 10 Platoon. There was very little we could spend our money on, and so the men don't get their full due but when they go on leave or get repatriated there will be quite a large build-up in their accounts. All that can be bought in the jungle from the Battalion canteen store were cigarettes, razor blades and toothpaste, stamped air letter cards and sometimes a very limited amount of beer, all of which was normally in short supply. We learnt a way to extend the life of a razor blade: hone it on the palm of the hand; well, it made a good talking point and it encouraged us to try to make a blade last another two or three days. At least we tried! The next day Dick, the Adjutant, rang me up this morning to say that the Brigadier had sanctioned my leave and that I could go whenever I liked. It was too late to organize myself that day, so I said I would go first thing in the morning.

I went over to Battalion HQ after lunch as I had three men for Orders for promotion to lance-corporal. I had another small lunch at the HQ Mess. After Regimental Orders I saw Colonel Duncombe and he agreed that it would be a good thing to take my batman with me, so that he could have leave at the same time. Went to the Mess for a drink and said goodbye to the HQ boys, who wished me a good leave. The New Year was not celebrated with alcohol, but with a performance by the whole Divisional artillery. This opened up at midnight and continued for one minute on a target in the area of Sinobyin.

1 January, 1944. After standing down first thing in the morning, leave! Colonel Duncombe promised me some leave before Christmas, and had said I should go as soon as we had finished this phase of operations. I had been having malarial twinges on and off and not actually had any leave for about two years. In a letter to my parents on 27 December I wrote: "In my total war service (about 4 years) I have had 31 days leave. . . . I have had another stretch of three weeks in my boots and the same clothes." And in another letter dated 30 December, I said, "It is so cold at night that a warm drink is required (referring to whisky), we've only one blanket; the dew and the mist is colossal . . . I don't thaw until the sun gets up . . . (at about) 10.0am. . . . The nights are the worst, as everything appears to rustle and move, we all pray for daylight. Our morale is very, very high and we know this cannot go on for ever." I also added in that letter that the Divisional Commander, General Frank Messervy, who had been in five commands during the war so far, did say that the conditions were three times worse than anywhere else he had been.

Kingshott packed our kit whilst I handed maps, codes, etc, over to Tiny Taylor, who will command in my absence. A mule arrived to collect our kit and we left at 8.15am for Battalion HQ. Here I handed over my rifle to our Colour Sergeant Fraser and left for Brigade HQ, where we picked up a 15-cwt truck.

I had not been aware of the many signposts that had been set up in our rear: "Circular Road", "Tattenham Corner", "To Buthidaung and Tokyo", and many other amusing signs along the Ngakyedauk Pass warning people of the precipitous sides to the dry-mud road, such as "Garrett's Cemetery" (the name of our padre), "Charabancs use this at their own risk".

I must say a few words about the Ngakyedauk Pass. By November 1943 the 7th Indian Division was east of the Mayu Range of hills and had been supplied over the Goppe Pass, which was adequate for mules and porters, but there was no way that it could be used by vehicles, guns and tanks, which would be necessary as the Division advanced southwards towards Letwedet and Buthidaung; and this Goppe 'footpath' was inadequate for enlargement.

Reconnaissances found that the Ngakeydauk Pass was also an inadequate footpath, but it was the only possible alternative. The Divisional Engineers carved their way through the Mayu Range in a comparatively short time, with the Japanese barely four miles away in the Letwedet area, and which my B Company overlooked. Before the New Year this unmetalled road was completed and the Division's supplies, tanks and transport were ready to support the advance south.

No one who has not experienced the thrill of coming out of an operational area can imagine how the little simple things of life are so pleasing and give a boost that included the whole body system. On reaching Bawli Bazar, about 30 miles from any battle, one of the first things I did, very surprisingly, although I do have a very sweet tooth, was to buy a carton of sweetened condensed milk which I had seen on a shelf in a bamboo-type-packing case shop that probably only carried about a hundred tins of everything. I just poured this straight down my throat! It was wonderful. I had a glorious hot bath in a tub when we reached the Bawli rest camp. I was able to stand up at night and smoke a cigarette; there were oil lamps and a gramophone was going in the Officers' Mess, where I read illustrated papers from England sitting in an armchair. My bedroom for the night was still a bamboo hut and I slept on the bamboo floor; but this did not matter. The feeling of release and euphoria had taken over.

However, of one thing I was certain by the end of that day; malaria was fast overtaking me. In due course we moved by truck, steamer and then by train to Calcutta, arriving in the early morning of 5 January. After three days of partying and going to cinemas, I had to leave my hotel, the Great Eastern, and go into hospital as the malaria could no longer be held back. I was also run down with jungle sores, and toe rot caused by long periods of wet feet inside permanently soggy boots. In a letter of 16 January I recalled the marvellous noise of trains, the clatter and banging of railway porters, the cackle and bickerings of Indians over money. Then, of course, the sight of white ladies, taxis and large white buildings was overwhelming.

After a week the medical officer allowed me to become an outpatient between 2.00pm and 6.30pm. This was excellent, as it allowed me to visit some of our own sick and wounded officers and men in another hospital, see some films, read many books that included some Peter Cheyney's, G.K. Chesterton and Churchill's *Into Battle*. And as I wrote on 17th, one day I went with two other Queen's Officers to the Calcutta races and saw the Governor's Cup. That was a grand occasion, very reminiscent of English meetings; women's clothes appeared not to have been affected by the war, the bright colours were enhanced by a glorious blue sky and a sun that was not too hot, and we were fanned by a gentle breeze. We had taken tickets in the Grandstand, but seeing an empty box, which was 'owned' by a maharajah, we took possession by the second race. Our neighbours were the Governor and the heads of the Army and Air Force. We would have moved out very sharply if the 'owner' arrived!

While in Calcutta I bought many packets of razor blades to give the men of B Company. Before departing on leave, I made an arrangement with Mervyn Mansel that I would order a pound of chocolates for him and another pound for me to be sent to us once a fortnight from an excellent emporium cum restaurant called Tony's, nearly as good as our Fortnum & Mason in London.

Chapter 6

Surrounded

I arrived back from leave at about midday on 2 February. The Battalion lay-out was exactly as when I left.

Soon after returning I learnt of a magnificent show put up by 17 Platoon of C Company. It was an action that took place in broad daylight on 9 January, when the Platoon, commanded by Lieutenant Halfhide, was sent across to cover the flank of the 4/1st Gurkhas, who were about to put in an attack. To get there the Platoon had to cross a chaung and were up to their necks in water which meant that some of the shorter men had to swim. As the Platoon was struggling to get into position the Japanese fired on them, whereupon the Battalion's 3-inch mortars engaged and the enemy gave up firing. Once in position they dug in, and fortunately very quickly, as when completed they became an object of enemy attentions, first a few shells, and then no doubt the Japanese realized that the Platoon's position was an embarrassment to their intentions, so the enemy began to deluge the position with shells and machine-gun fire. Young Halfhide was severely wounded in both legs and could take no part, whereupon Sergeant Sawyers took control, continuing to engage the enemy and encouraging the men to dig deeper. For several hours the Platoon was under intense shellfire and the enemy attacked them repeatedly, but Sawyers's quiet, calming, reassuring leadership ensured that there was no panic and fire discipline prevailed. By 4.00pm the

Gurkhas had captured their objective and the Platoon was ordered to withdraw. As they did so, one of their corporals was killed. This man and the wounded Halfhide were the only casualties. The intensity of the enemy fire they came under was gauged by the damage to some of their equipment. A couple of lessons from their predicament became evident: the value of digging in, even if it was only six inches of scrape, and secondly to keep calm. It so happened that I knew Sergeant Sawyers very well over a number of years as he had been in the Battalion's boxing team which I captained in the 1940–41 period. He was a small man, and hence was a Lightweight, but he was quite the best boxer we had. His style, serenity and the punch were controlled by a brain that took stock, then went in for the 'kill'. By the time of that battle he would have had about twelve years' service. How lucky we were to have men like him. He received the immediate award of the Military Medal (MM) for his splendid leadership and gallantry. Brigadier Loftus Tottenham sent the following message: "I watched the Platoon of the Queen's in action this afternoon. They were magnificent and held on to their position in spite of terrific fire from the enemy. It was terrible to watch, but it was a very gallant action and a real inspiration."[1]

Japanese shelling of the B Company area had been heavy while I was away. I visited 10 and 11 Platoons during the afternoon. I learned from Tiny and the men of 10 Platoon of the terrible time they had had from enemy shelling a few days earlier when they were fairly pasted and two positions received direct hits, causing 100 per cent fatal casualties.

The next day the enemy shelled our gun area during the day. I visited 12 Platoon before lunch. 2nd Lieutenant Ian Frisby, who had arrived while I was on leave, was now commanding them, but both he and Corporal Sewell were away on a two-man reconnaissance patrol on the Maungdaw-Buthidaung road. The Company area was heavily shelled again just before stand-to that evening. It is worth mentioning that B Company was the most forward company of the Battalion, being about half a mile from our Battalion Headquarters but barely 200–300 yards from known enemy positions.

Frisby returned from his patrol early on the morning of 4 February and was in Battalion HQ when I went round there at 9.30am. He submitted a first-class report on what he had seen. He had gone out in the early hours of 2 February. His report included Japanese movements along the Maungdaw-Buthidaung road. He mentioned that by day they had seen three officers walking brazenly along the road towards the back of the 162 feature, and had heard cookhouse noises, and seen more movement in the area of 'East Finger'. Ian Frisby was about 21 years old. Within two or three days I had found him to be a very impressive, enthusiastic addition to our Company, small in stature but very wiry and fit, with a smiling face headed by a fresh, quick brain.

There was quite an air battle that morning. About fifty Japanese Zeros and 97 type aircraft came over the Divisional gun area. Our Anti-Aircraft guns claimed three, our 'Tropical' Spitfires chased the rest away and gave them a very good run down the Mayu Peninsula. Before the last had left, I watched as Sergeant Thatcher of 11 Platoon gave one Zero fighter-bomber a very healthy burst of Bren machine-gun fire as it passed over us a very few feet up. But we never saw it come down. This was the first time I had seen Spitfires down here in Arakan, although they were used on two or three occasions while I was on leave in Calcutta.

Shortly before dusk this evening 'B' Company were again heavily shelled. We were very well dug in. Stretching 'inland' from each man's alarm post there are dug-outs that go first into the side of the hill for a yard or so and then down some four feet and then in again, so that there is about eight to twelve feet of earth above some of the dug-outs. Today's shelling is the worst I have ever experienced. Trenches filled up with dirt, gravel, branches, etc. I unthinkingly bent down to pick up a piece of shell that had landed in my own trench, but I never did, it was red-hot. Pte Edmunds was very badly shaken. As a member of 10 Platoon he had experienced heavy shelling only a few days ago. Otherwise there were no casualties.

5 February proved to be a very memorable day for B Company, and indeed the whole of 7 Indian Division. Heavy firing began on our left in the Punkori area at 4.30pm and continued until 7.30am. I thought it was a Japanese patrol disengaging itself from the Punjabis. There was also considerable shelling in that area.

Japanese Zeros and 97s were over again at 9.00am hrs. I was sent news that there are supposed to be about 500 Japs about seven to eight miles behind us in the Taung Bazar area. It poured with rain throughout the morning, and this did not enhance the rather disturbing atmosphere given by the now many rumours about the size of the enemy force in our rear. It was clear to me, although I did not mention it to the men, that some of our own guns were actually firing backwards.

A later message gave the size of the enemy force behind us as being of battalion strength (about 1,000), and that it had done considerable damage in our medical Main Dressing Station and the Divisional gun area. At 11.30am the CO asked for me personally over the field phone and gave me a message from the Supreme Commander, Lord Louis Mountbatten. This order of the day he wanted to be passed down to every man, and went as follows: "Hold on at all costs; large reinforcements are on their way". Until we received this message few of us had thought that the situation was serious enough to warrant a special order of the day; this in itself gave me, at any rate, quite a bit to think about.

Continued drizzling in the afternoon. We can hear gun fire and considerable machine-gunfire going on in our rear in two separate areas; one lot of fighting in the Taung area, and the other sounds were considerably closer, maybe about half a mile north of us. But news is limited to rumours only. No one can say exactly where the enemy is.

As a result of being very wet I again felt a touch of malaria on me, but I managed to drown it fairly well with mepacrine and aspirins.

A Jap nuisance patrol was firing at the hillocks on our left for about two hours from 8.00pm. Tiny, now officially my second-in-command (Joe left me to command C Company before Christmas), insisted that I should have the night off all duties so as to sleep off the malaria. Most unwilling, but grateful as it did give me a reasonable, albeit a hot, sweaty and damp sleep.

On the following night there was virtually no sleep for anyone. A hell of a scrap went on over the Punjabi front from dusk to daylight that morning; and the ambush party of six men found from 11 Platoon the night before shot up a party of four Japs who were on patrol. Corporal MacDonald reported to me that he could not confirm whether the patrol had inflicted any casualties, as his ambush party had probably opened fire too soon when it shot them up at 10.15pm. This patrol of Japs was almost certainly that which cannoned from one feature to another between D Company and ourselves, firing off discharger grenades and a light machine gun, trying to draw our fire.

The decision by an ambush commander as to when to open fire, particularly at night, is pregnant with problems which have to be solved almost instantaneously: at close quarters covering a track in thick country at night, and in the misty gloom, a soldier cannot really see his rifle or gun sights, and so to make sure of success, the enemy is invariably taken on at very close quarters. The difference of one or two seconds could be too soon or too late and, if the latter, it could endanger our own troops; if the former the enemy may escape. Like so many acts in war, luck plays an enormous part, and the responsibilities on the young corporal and the private soldiers who have to make the decisions in that instant are very heavy. It is ultimately life or death.

At 2.45am Sergeant Inskip, 10 Platoon commander, (Lieutenant Uttley evacuated sick a few days ago), rang me up.

His platoon was only 50 or so yards from me, but it was never wise to send a runner in the dark, even on a defined man-made track. He had a most important message for me, and to say the least it was a little disturbing. In front of his position there was considerable noise of movement and talking, jingling equipment and neighing mules and horses. He could not make out from which side of the chaung the noise came. But at any rate it was in the Letwedet village and chaung crossing area. I told him that it was quite possibly the supply convoy to the Gurkhas on 'Abel', although I had not been warned that it was going out that night. In the meantime he was to listen hard and report on any further developments. I phoned up Battalion HQ and passed on the message to Dick, the Adjutant, who told me that there was nothing going to Abel on that night.

A few minutes later we in Company HQ could hear the jabbering and rattling of equipment. Inskip phoned to say that the pandemonium in front of his position had increased. These shoutings and jabberings were now unmistakably of Jap origin. I did not hesitate any longer. I told Inskip to tell the gunner Forward Observation Officer with him to get on to his gun battery and put down defensive fire tasks Nos. 13 and 14, which had the chaung crossing place and possible enemy forming up places just in front of B Company (10 Platoon in particular) as their artillery targets, I then rang HQ to tell them of my action and asked Dick to duplicate my request by ringing the RA Regimental HQ. Within five minutes the crumps started. We only heard the initial opening of gun fire; of the rest, all we heard was the swish of shells close over our heads and their explosions that appeared so close that they must be landing in our positions. But the shoot was admirable. Two ten-minute periods of rapid shellfire were put down. At the end of the shelling the panic-stricken noises of the Japanese were indescribable. The discordant sounds included chattering and shouting, mules and horses neighing, the clattering of equipment and a general stampede, as it blasted across the black night and our jungle-covered hills.

During the hours of darkness we still expected to be attacked. In consequence we stood to at our alarm posts. This hubbub continued after daylight until 7.30am, but we could not see anything to shoot up as we were shrouded in a damp, heavy mist which normally lifted at about 8.30am. The noise of Japs shouting and chasing loose animals moved around to the rear of us, just between the Company and Battalion HQ. One might have been tempted to go after this stricken enemy, but in the conditions of darkness and the mist there could have been considerable danger of shooting up one's own troops. The fog of war is always present in close-quarter fighting and does not need further interference from the weather.

When real daylight came we could see kit strewn all over the paddy-fields and on both sides of the Letwedet chaung; we collected in some of the kit. Among some articles that were retrieved was a Japanese lieutenant's complete valise in good condition; in this were found half a dozen of the most obscene postcard-size watercolours imaginable. This was not the first time that we had come across really dirty photos, drawings and paintings among enemy kit or on their persons.

It was quite clear to us now that it was an enemy supply column endeavouring to reach their encircling troops that we had shot up. Two pack-horses and two mules of the enemy were later rounded up and found their way to our transport lines. I do not think any of that enemy convoy got through or round us. The bulk of the enemy transport was caught in the artillery fire while still on their side of the chaung, as we deduced from the amount of stores deposited around the lower slopes of their positions, which were under observation from 10 Platoon.

On this day, 6 February, in anticipation of the enemy threat, the Division's reserve brigade was moved to fill a gap between our 33 Brigade and Divisional HQ and to take on the enemy established on the eastern end of the Ngakyedauk Pass. These troops managed to temporarily hold back the encirclement threat. Latest reports put the Japanese force behind us at about 10,000.

A battery of 25-pounder guns and another one of 3.7 inch gun-howitzers in the Brigade gun area were firing backwards throughout the day. Other guns were harassing the enemy forward of us in the Punkori and Point 162 areas. The enemy shelled our gun area during the day on a small scale. Our Brigade HQ were not apparently in touch with Division during this morning; later in the day we learned that the Ngakyedauk Pass is now firmly closed and that the Japanese in positions astride it. This meant that our land communications to the west of the Mayu Ridge were cut and no supplies of food and ammunition would get through to us over land, nor, of course, could casualties be evacuated. And so it was a boost to our morale to know that we were in contact with the outer world as twelve Dakota aircraft came over and dropped ammunition by coloured parachutes in the Brigade area towards dusk. Colour Sergeant Fraser arrived at the Company with a protection party and with mules loaded with rations and some ammunition that evening. I was not really surprised when he told me that we were to be on half-rations. The lifeline between the company and the battalion administrative area was pretty thin, by which I mean it meandered in and out of the jungle and was barely secure from enemy patrols over its 800 yards' length.

Between thirty and forty Japanese aircraft came over at 10.30am on 7 February and bombed the gun area again, but this time we saw no Spitfires or Hurricanes. Plenty of anti-aircraft fire greeted them and at least two planes were shot down, one of which we in Company HQ and 11 Platoon clearly saw. It was greeted by a cheer from the troops.

There was another air drop of ammunition at 5.30pm. The Battalion and B Company were shelled again towards dusk.

I wrote in my diary that "the air was 'singing' with missiles from an hour before dawn and for the rest of the day over on our left on the Punjabi front" and interminable battles were going on in our rear to the north. My Company was fortunate as it only suffered Jap nuisance patrols firing blindly during the hours of darkness; no material damage was suffered by these patrols, but they affect the nervous system and hardly encourage sleep. To ensure sensible protection, the two-man sentry in each section of five–six was not sufficient, and since the Japanese encirclement, 50% of the Company was ready for action throughout the night. This, combined with a considerable patrolling programme, meant that sleep was in short supply.

We learnt that direct communications with Division were still not established by 8 February, although all three brigades were in touch with each other, and news of Divisional Headquarters did filter down. We heard that the Admin Box was very heavily attacked all that night and that the Ngakyedauk pass was firmly closed. This was doubtless the epicentre for the noises of battles that shrieked across the jungle during the night.

Later that day we heard that the 7 Indian Divisional Head-quarters was attacked and over-run, staff officers and clerks being engaged in the confused close-quarter fighting, with the Divisional Signals taking the brunt of the attack. Among the casualties was one of our officers, David Bullock, who had been a junior staff officer and was killed, but his body was never found. General Frank Messervy led out a part of his staff by wading down a chaung and set up a new Headquarters, that was almost intact, in the tank harbour of the 25th Dragoons at the foot of the Ngakyedauk Pass. Here was formed what was to become the famous Admin Box.

Colonel Duncombe told me that he had ordered out C Company at first light that morning to contact and disperse the Japs who had burst into the Jungle Field Regimental laager in Wet Valley, which was just in rear of Brigade HQ. The weapons of this Regiment were the 4.2 inch heavy mortars whose range extended the infantry battalion's 3 inch from 1,500 to 2,500 yards. The whereabouts and strength of the enemy who were in or around this area were not known. All we did hear from Brigade was that the Jungle Field Regiment had been heavily attacked at about 7.00am in their harbour area. They suffered many casualties (rumoured at 100) and were caught queuing up for breakfast. It was thought that the Japs pulled back into the jungle in the hilly area immediately covering the gunners' mortars and jeeps. C Company were Battalion reserve company and were sent out primarily to prevent the Japs from capturing or destroying the 16 mortars and 3,000 mortar bombs.

The 25-pounders continued firing backwards and appeared to be doing so at very close range on to the jungle slopes not far from Wet Valley and also in the Point 129 area. From the amount of small-arms fire coming from this area by midday, it was evident to us that either C Company had found the Japs or the latter were attacking the gunners again. It had so far been almost impossible to know where the enemy had infiltrated between and behind us; the valleys and paddy-fields were surrounded by the heavily jungle-covered hills, hillocks and ridges; nowhere could one's security be taken for granted; any contacts with the enemy were invariably at close quarters and confusing.

Had two air drops of ammunition, one at 2.00pm and the other during the evening stand-to period. And at about that time Tom Garrett came up to take a Church Service in 10 Platoon's area; only 50 per cent of the Company could attend.

At 8.30am on the 9th I was ordered in to Battalion HQ. I went in with Kingshott, wearing full kit, as Dick had given me the tip that the Company were going to move back closer to Battalion HQ. Saw the CO at about 9.15am; our new position was to be immediately above Battalion HQ. The CO told me that C Company returned late yesterday evening, but had failed to dislodge the Japs, who were in great strength, estimated between 100 and 300. C Company of the Gurkhas were called in from Abel and took up positions on the high ground above Wet Valley, so as to keep an eye on the Japs.

Within the hour I gave Tiny a call on the wireless and told him to pack everything up and bring the Company back while I reconnoitred the new area, which was in very much the same place as that we had left on Christmas Day. The position included two hill features, one of which commanded the entrance to Battalion HQ from the east and the other gave depth and overlooked the ambush position to the west.

I cannot say that I had ever felt too happy with a Japanese force well behind us and we being a damn good half a mile from Battalion HQ and any other friendly troops, with the enemy front-line troops so much closer to us. The line of communication to Battalion HQ had consisted of a long and narrow track bordered by densely covered steep jungle hills, and on the other eastern side there was a stream, with some trees on the far side, then open paddy-fields. It could have been unpleasant and disastrous if the Japs had decided to plant a roving fighting patrol somewhere along this route and so endangered our daily bread, although, to be accurate, by this stage we were on biscuits, for the duration we were told.

As the Company arrived at this new position, there was plenty of digging to do for the remainder of that day, especially for 12 Platoon, which I put on the hill overlooking the animal transport lines and commanding the eastern approach to the Battalion. This was, until now, a virgin jungle position. To get to 12 Platoon was not easy. The easiest way was via Battalion HQ, although the other and more direct route to them from our ridge was to hack a track up and down the slopes; but I quickly dismissed this, as the fewer tracks and entrances we had going in and out of our positions the fewer men would be required to defend our position. So the long way round was to be the recognized route; I had a Don 5 (field telephone set) installed with them that afternoon. Towards the late afternoon I visited 12 Platoon; they had made gigantic strides in their digging. They had dug themselves in around the top of the hill in an oval shape, with communications to Ian Frisby, the Platoon Commander, in the centre. All trenches and communications had been dug below and without disturbing the jungle vegetation; it was very cleverly done, the position was excellently camouflaged.

A Squadron of the 25th Dragoons with its eleven Lee tanks mounting 75 mm. guns, in addition to the Browning machine guns, joined us in this Battalion defensive box. To get to us these tanks had burst their way past the Japanese-occupied positions in the area of the 7 Indian Division's Admin Base. They brought with them some rations to help us out; they also brought us more news of Divisional HQ which just had time to move out of its original HQ, but only after clerks, batmen, cooks and Divisional signallers had repelled numerous attacks as they fought their way out to a new position. Very little kit was retrieved and we gathered there was much blood flowing. Divisional HQ became installed in the Admin Box, which fast became a fortress box. In this Box was the tank regiment (less one squadron), an artillery 25-pounder regiment, Light Anti-Aircraft regiment, and most of the Royal Artillery Medium Regiment. But the Admin Box had to be a fortress; they had been attacked every night for hours on end since 5 February. So far the Japs had not broken through and, after each of their attacks, scores of their dead were left behind.

C Company is also now under my command and is also in position along the same ridge as B Company. Although Joe Mullins is, on paper, second-in-command to me, he does in fact still command the C Company end of the position, which is responsible for the western and southern approaches, and has his own set of company communications to Battalion HQ. Between us we are to find an ambush position every night in the future. I made B Company find it this evening. Corporal Carroll and five other men of 10 Platoon, armed with a light machine gun, went out at 7.00pm; their position was on the track that leads in to the north from our old position. The ambush's main task was to hold up any enemy approach through the bottleneck of the track, and also to give early warning of an impending attack from the south. C Company, incidentally, are about forty men short; they had had a few casualties yesterday in their fierce contact with the Japanese in Wet Valley. Consequently one platoon and most of their Company HQ and Geoffrey Tattershall have gone adrift.

We were to learn that Geoffrey Tattershall's party broke into the Admin Box and became attached to the West Yorkshire

Regiment. In the course of the encirclement, Geoffrey was killed in one of the many close-quarter nightly Japanese attacks. He had been one of the Battalion's earlier and most effective draft reinforcements on the North West Frontier in 1941. Also at that time the Battalion had received Dick Kensington, now Adjutant in Burma, Tiny Taylor, my second-in-command, Harry Haines, the Mortar Platoon commander, and Graham 'Polky' Polkinhorne, our Signals officer. Tattershall had been one of the Battalion's best hockey players. He was typical of that breed of young Englishmen never destined to become a soldier but caught up in the war, and he proved himself to be an excellent young officer, now cut down in his prime like so many others.

D Company were also pulled back this morning. Their position now is exactly similar to ours, but across the valley some 150 yards away on the ridge to the north; this gives the Battalion a stronger, cohesive defensive box, to be known in future as 'Braganza Box'. B and D Companies had to find patrols first thing each morning to see if our old positions had been occupied by the Japanese and, if not, to light fires as we did normally each morning to simulate the cooking of breakfast. And so one patrol to each company area went out this evening to chuck the odd sixty-nine grenade down the slopes; this is a plastic-covered grenade and does not have such lethal effects as the No.36 Mills grenade and is very much cheaper to make. And so we hope to give the Japs the idea of normal occupation. When the patrols returned the next day, we heard that our B Company's old position was not occupied by the enemy, but D Company's old position was occupied.

The news on 10 February was a little rosier. The Japanese plan for their complete encirclement operation has been captured, but that is as much as I knew of it on this date. We are now in wireless communications with Division HQ; this is done through the tank No 19 sets, and so we were able to get a situation report this morning. But news is still scarce of the exact Japanese dispositions and strength in our rear. The most uncommon and cheering news

15. The author's parents at his house at Donhead St Mary, 1970.

16. The author and his father after the Remembrance Service at Donhead St Mary in 1976.

17. 1948. Reunion lunch for officers who served in or with the Queen's Royal Regiment in Burma. *Going round from far left:* Bob Strang, Brian Grainger, Paddy With, the author, George Grimston, Godfrey Shaw, John Mansel, Hugh Ford, John Lane, Hugh Harris, Harry Haines, Tony Hobrow, Colonel Graham Duncombe, Dick Kensington, Ken Potter, ?, ?.

18. 1st Battalion Queen's Royal Regiment marching in column of sixes past the King of Siam and Lord Louis Mountbatten, Bangkok, January 1946.

is that some more prisoners have been taken: this was quite an excellent boost to everyone's morale, and indicates that the enemy had taken a knock. We had further news of the promised reinforcements, they are still on the way!

We are beginning to feel the pinch of the ration situation. The CO has given us permission to send out organized patrols to round up stray cattle. The local villagers, I gathered, would be getting compensation.

I was very amused at the sight of three of our men chasing a four-legged piece of beef around the paddy-fields and driving it into our box; and then to see it dashing past the tanks and whipping through Battalion HQ on its way to the butchery department. Our butchery is just beyond our administrative area and is under the auspices of the Quartermaster, the six company Colour-Sergeants and the Officers' Mess Corporal, who, being a butcher by trade, is the head butcher and kills for the Battalion, Brigade HQ, the gunners and tank crews.

The message went out over the wireless inviting anyone who had a very sharp long knife that could be used as a butcher's knife would they please let the QM's department have it. It so happened that I had a brilliantly sharp Wazir dagger, about a foot long, which I had bought off a tribesman on the NWFP. I just had to let them have it. Sadly, in the turmoils of war I never remembered to ask for it back!

The water in the chaung is not too good these days as there are so many people using it, and also because it is tidal: one minute the drinking water is above the washing and the next it is below the soap suds! At least at the moment we are well above the Japanese as the stream flows into the Kalapanzin River. The Colonel has ordered two wells to be dug in our box; that was a brilliant idea, the water table could not have been far down.

12 Platoon were on a fighting patrol to Letwedet village at 10.00pm on 12 February. Their task was to protect the eastern

flank of the mule convoy that goes to the Gurkhas on Abel on alternate nights. This Platoon had a secondary task to send out a reconnaissance patrol to the west face of the Point 162 feature to find out whether certain positions were still occupied. The Platoon returned by first light and reported that the enemy did hold positions on this very large hill feature as fire was drawn. This vast feature was about a mile long, north to south, and very nearly a mile wide, it was rhetorically called Massif and marked as such on our maps. The convoy to Abel was unmolested by the enemy on that night.

Further Jap prisoners were taken during the night by the KOSB and by the Gurkhas on Abel, who had been attacked again; as also were the Punjabis fairly heavily in all their company areas. During the afternoon American Dakotas carried out a supply drop for the Division. This time I believed some rations were included, as we could see that the parachutes were multi-coloured. Private Wiseman, my dedicated, very small, quick-witted Cockney company clerk, now recovered from Jap sword wounds across his left arm of some six weeks ago, leant over from his slit trench and said to me during the drop, "Sir, 'ere come our reinforcements; they're dehydrated Americans"! There was sense behind his observation as we had been on de-hydrated potatoes for some time.

> There was some firing on our front and rear throughout the night, and there was an air drop at about midnight of 13/14 February. The Dakotas were flying with navigation lights and were fired on by the Japanese as they flew low over the Brigade's dropping zone, which is about 400 yards north-east of us in the paddy-fields between the jungle-clad hills. One could see the enemy's red tracer zipping past their tails. This morning the ground is littered again with thousands of many-coloured parachutes; half-closing the eyes, it looks like confetti.
>
> For much of the day the guns were firing in all directions and the enemy's shells were coming into the Brigade area from all

angles, backwards, forwards and from the flanks during a large part of the day.

Whatever the targets, B Company were not in anyone's sights. We were having a peaceful day, which was enhanced by the church service we had in 10 Platoon's area at midday; about twenty-odd attended. Tom Garrett made a pleasant change: the five hymns were chosen by individuals, mine being 'The King of Love my Shepherd is' (197 A&M). Since we had come back from our forward position into the Braganza Box we were able to sing the hymns, but with a soft pedal!

There was much Hurricane fighter aircraft strafing and Vengeance dive-bombing during the late afternoon in the Punkori and Sinobyin areas and the following day the guns were again firing backwards and forwards during the morning, especially on the punjabi front, where there was much small-arms firing.

The Japanese Zeros and 97s were over at a high altitude. I think they must have been showing the flag to their troops. They merely dropped a few bombs over the Ngakyedauk Pass and were away in under ten minutes. They were kept more than occupied in that short period by our AA guns and the RAF Spitfires.

At 6.00pm a message came from HQ to say that the Division had intercepted the following message sent by the Japanese: "General attack 7.00pm". In the light of this we were all asked to be teed up more than usual. The various Defensive Fire tasks of the Battalion, and doubtless of the Division, went down inter-mittently throughout the night.

Whether the shellfire put them off cannot be answered, but, anyhow, no attack came in. The message was not dated, and it was in clear, so more than likely it was fictitious or merely propaganda, or perhaps a means to establish where were our Defensive Fire tasks.

There was plenty of shelling on the following day and a battle was raging in the Mayu Range on our right. The engineers at Brigade HQ had a fire exchange with the Japanese that night; it was apparently only a small enemy patrol. There was also some Jap patrol activity outside the Battalion west entrances, which melted away after a few grenades had been lobbed down among them by the Carrier Platoon. The night was otherwise quiet but anxious. Several stories reached the Battalion that morning from various sources: they mostly concerned the Division's HQ where desperate fighting had taken place over the last ten days, in and around the Admin Box, which was at Sinzweya three miles or so north of us. Reinforcements and supplies could not get through as the Japanese were astride the Ngakyedauk Pass and the initial poor communications between Divisional HQ and its subordinate units was because all telephone lines had been cut and one of the forward wireless sets was put out of action. 7th Indian Division Signalmen and the company of Indian Engineers were heavily involved and had borne the brunt of the Japanese assaults. The Main Dressing Station was in that area and was mercilessly attacked. The unarmed sick and wounded were shot and bayoneted in their beds and four or five medical officers were taken out of their hospital, tied to trees and shot. This brutality could not be excused on the grounds of vicious close-quarter fighting, which of course it was, for the Japanese had to consciously make an effort to tie the doctors to the trees.

From time to time Colonel Graham Duncombe, our CO, came round the Company and checked our positions and security from both ground and air attacks, and was well satisfied with what he saw: the men and positions were clean and tidy and the arms and ammunition were in good condition. He asked me back to the Officers' Mess at Battalion HQ to have some elevenses on one occasion. Graham Duncombe has only been with us for three months but has impressed all ranks with his sensitive understanding of the myriad personalities under his command and by his sure, firm handling of the Battalion; he really knew the British soldier's instincts. He had taken part in a number of operations before coming to us, with the 2nd Battalion in Palestine, where he was Mentioned in Despatches in 1940, and then served in the Western Desert during the 1940–1941 period, and, more particularly, took part in the battle of Sidi Barrani, and had done some jungle training in Ceylon. He was an impressive figure of over 6 feet with a large moustache. I doubt there was anyone in the Battalion who could match his brilliant sense of humour. There were several officers with us who, in conversation, would unthinkingly throw in the odd word of Hindustani, such as chai (tea) and chota peg (a small whisky). With a large grin and always a twinkle in his eye, the CO would say, "I won't have hurgery burgery spoken in my mess". This was his little joke which he produced whenever a newcomer came into the mess. He wasn't serious, but it broke the ice and produced much laughter. It also ensured we kept to the King's English!

About twenty Japs had dug themselves in on to the end of A Company's feature. Initially A Company could not dislodge them; on the second day the Company attacked again and were supported by a troop of tanks that tried to blast them off a precipitous ridge. During this fight the Company had one killed and six wounded, and, in spite of their gallant effort that earned Private Cornthwaite the MM, the enemy were still there at the end of the day, but they withdrew under cover of darkness, leaving behind one dead Japanese officer, a sword and some maps.

For the last week or so Hugh Ford of Headquarter Company and the Padre, have been running a general knowledge inter-platoon quiz competition. All our answers went in two days ago. I am reminded of this, as today I saw the results of an individual poetry contest which I held in our Company. Private Kent handed in a grand historical effort covering the salient movements and events of the Company since our march down in September. Sergeant Thatcher's effort was a clever, witty piece entitled 'The Men England Forgot'.

Not a very high percentage actually took part in this competition, but it caused great amusement as the poems were passed round for all the soldiers to read.

Ian Frisby took out two sections of his 12 Platoon on a fighting patrol to the Pazwanyaung area at 6.30pm, by which time it was dark. Their task was to beat up any Jap mule convoy that may move that way, and return by first light.

17 February. Another quiet night in our area, except for the guns in the valley just behind us, and they were only spasmodically active. I noted that in the Battalion Intelligence reports for 16–17 February that the King's Own Scottish Borderers and 89 Brigade of our Division, had moved in to strengthen the Admin Box, which was attacked again last night, the enemy leaving behind ten dead.

Frisby reported to me on his return that his patrol had shot up about six mules and their leaders, but total damage unknown. This small convoy was moving north. The Brigade was aware from other unit reports and prisoners that convoys of up to 200 mules moved most nights. Most of their routes were known, and so there was a big plan afoot to cover the whole ground between the Punjabis on the left and the Mayu foothills on the right, both by machine-gun fire and fighting patrols.

The enemy landed three shells that night in the Quartermaster and Colour-Sergeants' area of Battalion HQ. No casualties, but much kit written off. A letter was sent round to all companies signed by the Adjutant, Dick Kensington, to say that reports had come in of dead Japanese wearing British battledress and British steel helmets among other things. These might have been looted when they attacked the Divisional area. But there was a view that they may have preplanned this charade to confuse us; anyhow we were warned.

Intermittent firing and shelling throughout most of these nights. We had a parachute drop on 18 February in the early hours and another one at 11.15am; both rations and ammunition were dropped. All these rations and ammunition and air activity must have made the Japanese jealous, as they were unable to shoot our planes down, and their previous losses to the Spitfires proved that their Zero fighters could not compete with our superior tactics and aircraft.

Although we were still on half-rations, we did not do too badly. Organized scrounging parties went to the village every day and brought back potatoes, beans, fruit, an odd chicken, a few eggs and plenty of rice; we also got fresh meat fairly regularly from local cattle that had been rounded up. Cigarettes were very scarce, in fact they hardly existed. For once the men would do anything even to get hold of a 'Vee' cigarette; this Vee cigarette was a free issue which used to arrive intermittently but in many ways was considered to be the least favoured of all. The leaf was probably cultivated somewhere in the east, propagated with some downmarket dung. In desperation we would smoke them and welcomed them when they were available.

> Many men of the Company have made bamboo pipes, and although they do not last they are temporarily very good. The men use a variety of tobacco, mostly fag ends, some even use grass. I hand all my fag stubs to Kingshott. No mail comes in or goes out, of course. Soon after standing down the Battalion Welfare wireless set opens up in Battalion HQ. From this set British and world news is broadcast and a news-sheet is sent out to companies most afternoons. This wireless set has been with us since we have been in Arakan, and was one of three given to us as part of the Fourteenth Army amenities. These news-sheets and sit.reps. are passed to the Platoons in turn. It was so good to know that the chaps are eager to see how the war is going in the other theatres of war.

The men were excellent over shaving, turn-out and the cleaning of arms. Uniformity of turn-out was perhaps not so easy and not always as good as it might be. However, it did improve a great deal. Quoting my diary of that time, 18 February:

> And we do at least wear the tin hats at about the same angle, and always equipment when leaving the Company areas. Any man

that does manage to creep away from the Company with his braces crossed wrong, or wearing his water bottle incorrectly, does not get very far in Battalion HQ; the Second-in-Command or RSM do not waste time over return tickets! Obtaining a full bath in the chaung is not easy, but one section of a platoon manages to get a wash down nearly every day. This is subject to patrol activities, ration fatigue, and parachute collecting parties.

And of course enemy activity. Some might query why wear the tin hat at about the right angle. Well, if one wears the hat on the back of the head, the head is not getting the best protection. There may be many who do not appreciate the necessity to wear one's equipment uniformly throughout a unit. It is important for soldiers on operations that this is the case: for when a soldier is wounded, whoever goes to his aid must know exactly where the wounded man is carrying his first aid field dressing, likewise his water bottle and food. In a battle area there can be no time to hesitate or doubt as to where things are; similarly many soldiers will become exhausted and tired, and they must be able to turn instinctively to that of their equipment they want, and so bayonets, reserve ammunition and grenades must have their place.

During the afternoon we had another RAF display of air superiority. Vulti-Vengeances (dive bombers) and Hurricane fighter aircraft, mounting two Bofors guns, were over in numbers: the dive bombers taking on targets in the Taung area and Jap positions north-west of the Gurkhas on the Abel features. The Hurricane strafers went farther south to the road and Buthidaung areas.

Whenever the Vulti-Vengeances came over to bomb, to us soldiers this was a mind-boggling event: they did not just drop their bombs whilst flying at a great height, but from maybe 3,000 feet would roll forward to the perpendicular and attack their individual targets with pinpoint accuracy as each plane let its bombs go when it was 90 degrees over its target and then pull away to the horizontal and up when it had reached what looked like about barely 100 feet above ground.

Hugh Ford invited me to tea in Administrative Company Mess, where I met Padre Garrett, and arranged for a service in B Company at midday for the next Sunday. I returned to the Company to visit 10 Platoon which was preparing to go out on a fighting patrol, commanded by Tiny Taylor, who took it out while the rest of the company was at its evening stand to positions.

This 10 Platoon came in at 7.00am this morning, 19 February. There was not a sign of an enemy convoy last night, nothing to shoot up. Very dull, they returned looking haggard and blue with the cold, having lain quietly doggo in the wet paddy and the dank cold dew encasing them for about eight hours.

Tiny reported excellent shooting by our 25-pounders on the Punkori area. This may have upset the Jap convoys.

Saw the CO just before stand-to this evening and he told us present in Battalion HQ a marvellous dialogue, which he could not help but overhear this morning, going on between two private soldiers digging a slit trench: "1st Private, 'Seen the nooze, mite? Churchill says that 'e is wotching ar front wiv intense int'rest.' 2nd Private: 'Yus?' 1st Private: 'Well, wot I sez is, he ain't wotchin' ar bleedin' rear'."

A very sharp battle was fought just behind us at 9.30pm last night in the Brigade HQ area. Red tracer was everywhere and grenades by the hundreds exploded. After fifteen minutes the firing died away as suddenly as it began.

At 4.00pm on the following day there was a fairly large air strafe by our dive-bombers, escorted by twenty-four fighters.

We learnt late this evening that the flare-up in Brigade HQ last night was the mule company loosing off just about all their ammunition at a Jap reconnaissance patrol that had penetrated the area.

At night the nerves are usually more taut, when darkness induces extra fear as noises, real or imaginary, can also give the tired and staring eyes a vision of fantasy figures looming up through the mist when the distance appears to be only a few feet. Self preservation should not, but it can, take over. A man starts to fire and this in turn can motivate another to open fire, and so other defenders join in the firing; once started, the firing, particularly at night, is difficult to stop. The jumpy conditions at night demand a strict regime of fire discipline.

It was a very great surprise to us all to discover that Dr Jack Sumner, our Medical Officer, arrived back in the Battalion on 21 February at lunchtime from leave. He had been due back about a week or so ago, but the Japs had prevented it. Being a very determined man, he picked up a lift in a two-seater Moth, which landed in 114 Brigade area (across the Kalapanzin), and he eventually reached our Brigade HQ by moving with mule convoys. During the time he had been waiting to get back to us he volunteered to go up with the Dakotas and help with the supply drops over our Divisional area. Something I had not previously realized was that all these supplies were pushed out by volunteers, and it was no easy job. Jack had actually dropped supplies to us on four occasions. It was certainly grand to see him back; his presence in the Regimental Aid Post was a great reassurance.

One troop of tanks went out of our Box at 1.00pm to help the Sikhs on Point 182, which is about 500 yards behind us. Ian Frisby took 12 Platoon out on a fighting patrol at 6.45pm to the Letwedet Chaung just north of Punkori, where it is thought he may catch the Japs crossing the chaung from the village, or he may even catch some sampans loaded with supplies going to their positions in front of us.

Private Kingshott came to me this afternoon just as he was going off to dip our clothes into some muddy water to wash them, when he said, "Ever seen these before, sir?", showing me his shirt. I answered that I did not think I had; "these" were lice crawling about the seams of the shirt. I told him not to worry, but just wash it and lay it in the sun, and do the same with mine without looking too closely at it. We have all, of course, been eaten alive with bugs, hoppers and the usual dug-out crawlers. At that very moment I had at least four ticks on me, their heads firmly imbedded under the arm-pits and in the shoulder blades. They had dug in so far that a penknife was necessary to prise them out.

A great deal of firing everywhere last night: the Gurkhas were attacked and beat off the enemy onslaughts, and the Punjabis were also raided by fighting patrols. The greatest noise of firing came from our rear, from just behind Brigade HQ and farther in rear of that.

Twelve enemy 97-type bombers came over with some fighters as escort. I think their target must have been the Ngakyedauk Pass or the Admin Box. After concentrated AA fire they left after twenty minutes at about 10.30am. We had a large air drop towards midday.

12 Platoon's fighting patrol returned this morning, 22 February at 7.00am. Frisby rang me up and said he had reported to the Adjutant and told him all. The men had had some fun, he said, and no casualties. The Platoon sank one sampan loaded with kit and definitely killed one and wounded another Jap. Frisby himself threw grenades into the boat and said he saw the Japs leap over the side. There were some Japs on the far bank ready to receive the sampan, and they opened fire with an automatic and rifles on the patrol.

Small Jap patrol around the Battalion west entrance was beaten off with grenades by the Carrier Platoon.

The Japs attacked most of the battalions down here since the encirclement, but left us alone apart from reconnaissance and probing patrols. Those patrols were trying to find a weak spot and a way in, but met with no success. A couple of days ago 114 Brigade reported that captured documents included a detailed sketch map of the area around the Battalion and our Brigade box. But if the Japs ever did try their hand at attacking the 'Braganza Box' they would have caught a cold. The Battalion holds all the high ground with ambushes in depth at both entrances, and the Tank personnel hold the valley and low ground between D to the north and B and C Companies on the south. The tanks alone have 74 automatic guns between them, and the majority of these are dismounted at night for ground action.

Our dive-bombers came over at 3.00pm and bombed targets in the rear and in front of our positions.

Tiny Taylor took 11 Platoon out on a fighting patrol at 7.00pm to the east beyond Pazwanyaung, to link up the valley between us and the Punjabis. When they returned the next day, Tiny's patrol reported seeing nothing going north or south. He said the Punjabis fired 2-inch mortar and light machine guns at odd moments during the night, but he heard no Jap firing. The Punjabis themselves had a fighting patrol out on the paddy some 400 yards to the east of him. Quiet night here.

In the last week of February Colonel Duncombe held a conference on promotions. I recommended Sergeant Thatcher for promotion to Company Sergeant Major. He has done excellently with us down here and has made his 11 Platoon by far and away the most efficient in the field; it is neater and cleaner in the positions. Thatcher always has things laid on for his men, and he is not above getting them extra things when he can! But by making him a CSM I shall lose him to C Company. He likes our B Company so much, he says, he would rather stay in it as a sergeant. However, orders are orders, and he goes to C Company and comes back to us when CSM Hudson is repatriated.

My Company had been short of officers: Tiny was really my second-in-command, but I had used him to take out 10 and 11 Platoons on occasions. But I had the quite excellent Ian Frisby of 12 Platoon, who could have been born to the task of command in the jungle. However, over a period of four months I had to remove one of my platoon officers who I thought would serve the cause rather better as a staff or liaison officer; I had corporals and sergeants who had the edge on him when it came to command and he proved to be less at home in the jungle than others. Like it or not, we had to make the jungle our home and to make it work for us. And I did have one sergeant during the days of Japanese encirclement who was clearly fearful of this claustrophobic existence, which could be mentally magnified when visibility was down to nearly nil on moonless and misty nights. I was aware of his weakness and had to watch that his aberration did not spread. Added to his mental state, and perhaps it was all part of it, was the fact that he was married with a young family in London. There were a few other soldiers in the company who were also married, but they appeared not to be overly affected. I did have the Sergeant moved on when communications were restored.

The noise of battles at night were getting closer as the Japanese were being driven down towards us from the north. Their movements up to 25 February were almost always at night.

John Smyth, of C Company, took out a platoon on a fighting patrol into the paddy-field to our west on the previous night. They had a colossal shoot-up of a Jap convoy moving south; this ambush patrol captured much kit.

The situation reports were making clear that the general trend of the Japs was southwards; they were apparently short of ammunition and rations and were trying to get out of it. Most night patrols of the Gurkhas, Punjabis and Queen's reported this. At about 7.00am on 25 February A Company saw a magnificent target of between 100 to 200 Japs moving south across the paddy between us and the Punjabis. The Japs had mistimed their movement and were caught in daylight. Vickers medium machine guns and Bren guns opened up on them, and then our artillery caught them. Their confusion was stupendous and their morale so shaken that the Japs were committing hari-kari by placing grenades to their chests.

The Battalion was shelled in the afternoon at 2.40pm, some shells landing immediately in front of our Company HQ. We heard a rumour that the Ngakeydauk Pass was open, but Brigade later this evening sent us definite news that the Pass was only open to evacuate casualties as there were still elements of Japanese in the area. Altogether 411 casualties were evacuated over the pass yesterday. In the last few days Auster aircraft have been landing in the Brigade HQ area and taking off the more serious casualties. A word about the sick: B Company had about eleven really sick men, with malaria and dysentery, but of these only six were prostrate. These fellows couldn't be evacuated and just lay in their platoon areas receiving the appropriate pills.

There was another huge party all last night. John Smyth volunteered to take his platoon out again to have another go at the Jap mule convoys going South. It was obvious that the Japs were no longer using the eastern route, but went west in the Tatminyaungwa area, down the track that ran parallel to the Tatminyaungwa Chaung, and was about equi-distant between C Company and the Gurkhas, whose positions were in the jungle-covered hills astride the valley.

At about 8.40pm the firing started and increased into a crescendo. After half an hour or so we could hear the rattling of equipment on mules. The Battalion Carrier Platoon opened up as did the Sikhs just north of Brigade HQ; the sky lit up with flares, bomb explosions and tracer. This convoy was fully caught and could not get back, and so tried to get forward south to their own positions in the 162 area. As the remnants of this convoy moved on south and got through this devastating cross-fire, they were met by another small ambush patrol we had out just this side of the anti-tank gun troop, which also doubled in an infantry role, on the Letwedet Chaung. This ambush fired at them from the south, so again the Japs were caught in between the two ambushes.

All this firing and cross-firing between the positions of five or six different units and sub-units that took on the enemy that night was a testament to good training and night firing discipline, that no friendly troops became casualties; the positions and arcs of fire were known to those who had need to know. And, as so often can be the case, there was some luck that we did not fire at each other in the dark.

After dawn broke we could see the kit strewn over the burnt paddy; it covered an enormous area. Dead and wounded mules lay around; only eighteen Jap dead bodies could be found. I went out to see what kit there was and found an 81 mm mortar bipod and brought this in, with a few rifles. John Smyth's chaps brought in the baseplate.

It was thought that not many Japs got over the chaung. So one platoon of B Company and one platoon of C Company were to go to an area where it was thought that the enemy might lie up in daylight. Joe Mullins took the C Company Platoon across the jungle-covered slopes, and I took 11 Platoon round the left. We left our old position on our left and went straight on up the narrow and wet re-entrant and chaung-bed, to the source of the stream and up over an almost perpendicular bamboo-covered ridge. From the ridge we then dropped down into a thick but large re-entrant. This was the place all right – clothing, equipment, papers, maps, ammunition, shells and fuse caps, and up the deepest re-entrant we found the barrel of an 81 mm mortar. So now we have a complete Jap mortar less the sights. I dispatched a section through our old positions and told them that if they found no Japs to return to the Battalion area, whilst we gathered in all the documents and kit. There were altogether seven mules in different stages of emaciation and some were wounded. The Battalion were shelled quite heavily this afternoon at 3.15pm; C Company had a few in front of them, and we had some in our area, one landing right in the cookhouse, but no casualties in the Company.

We hear now that the Pass is definitely open for casualties, supplies and mail. Tiny took out 11 Platoon and one section of 10 Platoon on the same job as John Smyth did last night. He took out a veritable little fortress of arms: four light machine guns and two 2-inch mortars and about forty-eight High Explosive bombs. From 9.30pm this evening of 27 February until the small hours this morning, the noise of firing from the ambush area was incessant and huge; the Carrier Platoon again opened up on their arcs from their ambush positions at the Braganza Box west entrance.

147

Tiny's patrol came in and reported to me at 7.15am. He and his fighting patrol had great success against another Jap convoy going south last night. They brought in a wounded Jap as prisoner; only seven dead were counted and three dead mules. Documents, arms and equipment brought in were quite considerable. The story of a Jap officer, who was killed whilst rushing one of the section positions single-handed, was told me by Tiny, and once again goes to show how fanatically brave the Japanese soldiers were, particularly when cornered. They did not give up. Apparently the section of 11 Platoon commanded by Cpl. Berry surprised a party of Japs at about ten yards and had them silhouetted against the sky. The Jap second-lieutenant, in front of his men, stumbled into the ambush position and only then saw our men, who had not yet fired. He shouted, "Tiyro!", (Urdu for "wait") to the Bren gunner and drew his sword, but the gunner gave him a burst and got the Jap in the thigh. The Jap jumped over the gunner and struck round with his sword left and right, hitting the pack of the gunner and just piercing the back of another rifleman. In the meantime the Jap was hit by another rifle bullet and bayoneted in the side, but still he showed fight. Lance Corporal Chamberlain finally put a burst of tommy-gun into him, which floored but did not kill him. The officer was finished off by a couple of men running bayonets through him. The remaining six men were dealt with by others of the section with grenades and the light machine guns.

Our casualties were one wounded slightly by the sword and Pte. Perks got a burst from our own light machine gun as he jumped across its line of fire. He was seriously wounded in the testicles, but I gather from the M.O. that he is going to be all right.

That action could be said to be typical of this close-quarter type of warfare. The anticipation of any action, particularly a night ambush operation, will probably involve someone being killed, and what is inevitably the unknown and at close quarters will in itself induce a state of apprehension of danger that can pump the adrenalin and generate an element of fear as to the outcome of the engagement. One rarely ever knows how many enemy one is likely to meet and how will they be armed, but we always assumed that they would fight to their bitter end and, as I have mentioned before, one could not in the gloom or at night see for certain across the sights of one's own weapon. When the battle begins, it necessitates an immediate reaction to a very sudden situation. How grateful Britain and its Army is and always has been to these stalwart soldiers, the corporals, the lance corporals and so very often the private soldiers, who have to take on a great burden of responsibility and must make these split-second judgements when operating invariably under tense conditions. In this case they reacted and did exactly what was expected of them.

On the next night, the Divisional artillery put down some heavy fire in the Punkori area and east of Point 162 last night. Tiny Taylor took one section of 10 Platoon out as a contact patrol to a brigade of 26 Division, who are part of the relieving force and have advanced south down the foothills of the Mayo, and are now west by north of us. The patrol left at 10.30am and arrived back at 4.30pm, and came under Japanese fire as they went across a little too much to the south; on working their way up north, the patrol met up with the Frontier Force regiment of that Division, who had just put in an attack and were still scrapping with the Japs. Tiny's patrol brought back some vegetables and rice that made a most welcome addition to our bully beef! The last few days have seen a great change in the Japs' fighting. 26 Division had advanced down the coast road from Chittagong in the north, crossed the Goppe Pass and were a matter of four miles from our northernmost troops. We could follow the progress of this Division on the Mayo Range as our Vengeance aircraft bombed from one peak to the next just in front of that Division as they moved south.

We learnt that General Briggs' 5th Indian Division had broken through the Japanese in the Ngakeydauk Pass and had linked up with men of the West Yorkshire Regiment and the King's Own Scottish Borderers, very closely supported by the tanks of the 25th Dragoons which had broken out from the 7th Indian Division Admin Box.

All this had happened a few days before but by 29 February it was clear that our encirclement had virtually ended, as, although there were still large numbers of Japs in our rear to be mopped up, our communications were fully restored. The road back and through the Okeydoke Pass, as the Ngakyedauk became to be called, was re-occupied by our troops; all the forward sick and wounded had now been evacuated and back-loaded over the Pass. My B Company and D Company moved back to our original positions, that is to say once again over-looking the Letwedet Chaung and the northern front of 'Massif' which we had left on 9 February.

The Japanese strategy for its intended 'march on Delhi' had been to coordinate an offensive in the Arakan and force General Bill Slim to draw on the 14th Army's reserves and so enable the Japanese to move in the north in Assam and capture the only supply base and the railhead at Dimapur some 400 miles to the north of us. They were not only the lifelines to the garrisons in Kohima and Imphal, but also, importantly, to General Stilwell's Chinese troops in Ledo. The loss of Dimapur and the railway would have opened up to the Japanese the road, railway, a number of airfields and the broad, navigable Brahmaputra River that led into India. In the event the Japanese did encircle 7th Indian Division and drove a wedge between it and 5th Indian Division that was to the west of us across the Mayu Range. The encirclement forced General Slim to bring out the reserve 26th Indian Division. But General Slim had not been caught; it was the enemy who had overlooked air power. In previous opera-tions against the Japanese, encirclement had generally meant that our troops had to fight their way out. But this time the 7th Division did not give any ground; the enemy lost heavily – a figure of about 7,000 has been given as an estimate of the Japanese killed and wounded – and it became the enemy who were cut off without supplies. They had been cut up and split into scattered remnants. A more lasting morale-booster was the proof that the Japanese soldiers were in no way supermen in the jungle: time and again they were far noisier than ourselves and gave themselves away. In close quarter contacts we always came off best. Once the Japanese had been thrown off their written plan, their command initiatives were invariably limited.

Now that the encirclement of our Division had ended and the Japanese had had a bad mauling, it is possible to reflect on several aspects of that phase:

Some interesting stories and statistics came to light once the battle for the Admin Box was over: Supplies for the trapped troops consisting of ten days for 40,000 men had been set aside and already packed up near the airfields. From the time the airdrop began on 6 February some 60 tons of supplies were dropped daily, and sometimes at night; in a month the supply aircraft made 900 sorties and delivered 3,000 tons on the divisional dropping zones in the battle area. As already mentioned, our own Medical Officer, Jack Sumner, joined many of the crews to help the supply-droppers heave out the enormous crates and bails of ammunition and food. This was exhausting work, as the moment the bales had been pushed out others had to be hauled along the hold of the aircraft to be ready for the next push. Jack Sumner later explained to some of us that the aircrews barely had five hours' sleep or time off in the day before they and the aircraft, which had to be serviced, were loaded and flew off again. It was a tremendous combined effort that involved pilots and crews from Britain, the United States, Australia, Canada, India, New Zealand and South Africa. At the time, seeing this marvellous manna from heaven, without which it is doubtful if we could have defeated the Japanese for the first time in the war, most of us at the receiving end never really gave a thought to all the planning and hard work that went on day after day. The magnificent pilots had a demanding task: the aircraft had to fly in low at a slow speed over the dropping-zones, which were often hidden in narrow valleys between jungle-covered hills; to make an accurate drop may have meant the pilot making a number of circuits, and in this the aircraft were subjected to small-arms fire from the enemy, but only one Dakota was shot down during this period.

Within the Admin Box clouds of smoke rose on many days after ammunition and petrol dumps had been blown up by enemy shelling; it was some time later that we were also to learn that on four occasions the stocks of ammunition fell dangerously low.

And we were to learn of the details of some of the horrors that Divisional HQ and the Admin Box had to withstand during the encirclement. The initial assault, on 6 February, by 200 Japanese fell on the Divisional Defence Force, the Signallers and Indian Engineers, who were attacked many times on that first day. Lieutenant Colonel Pat Hobson DSO, the Division's Chief Signals Officer[2], commanded this force and repulsed these initial attacks, killing at least forty and wounding a much larger number. In time the defenders hacked their way out to join the Headquarters group of officers, clerks and orderlies which had been led out by General Frank Messervy, who was himself dressed in a vest, trousers and carrying a grenade. The General had had to move, as the Operations Office had been hit by mortar bombs and set on fire and all telephone wires had been cut. So he led this party through shoulder-high water to join the Admin Box about three miles away. This had taken them four hours.

Later that day, on the first evening of the encirclement of Divisional HQ, one of the enemy units of about seventy men assaulted the Main Dressing Station, which had been made up of three Field Ambulances and so in reality was the Divisional hospital and was full of sick and wounded, doctors and order-lies. There was a burst of fire as the enemy "rushed through the wards howling like dervishes, cutting down everyone who stood in their way, doctors, orderlies and patients". The Japanese shot and bayoneted every one of the medical staff they could find; the cries of the wounded could be heard far away in the night, but no help was available to them at the time. As a final mockery to any Geneva Convention, the Japanese lined up six doctors and shot them through the ear. This story could only be told because a seventh doctor, Lieutenant S. Basu of the Indian Medical Service, was also shot through the left ear and then, when he realized he wasn't dead, he feigned that he was and eventually crawled away and was rescued by our own troops.

The West Yorkshires carried out a counter-attack on this hospital area and managed to rescue some survivors. A couple of days later a detachment of the West Yorks under its Regimental Sergeant Major caught a large number of Japanese in the misty half-light of dawn making their way along a chaung they were defending. The RSM ordered some men to throw grenades and others to pull out the pins to get them ready, "otherwise we could not get the stuff into the chaung quickly enough". After fifteen minutes the battle was over and in daylight they counted forty-five dead Japanese in the space of forty yards.

Enemy aircraft, artillery shells and nightly infantry attacks hammered the Admin Box over eighteen days. The position was overlooked by the surrounding hills and so the Box was constantly mortared and machine-gunned. It became a fortress. In addition to service troops, it included the repositioned Main Dressing Station for the wounded, hundreds of vehicles, mules and guns. There were also elements of a brigade of 5th Indian Division and the West Yorkshire Regiment.

In time General Messervy told an incredible story about the large number of our Divisional vehicles in the Box. He called it an "Ascot car park", which was in view of the enemy throughout the siege. Outside the perimeter of the Box, in No-Man's-Land, were another 100 vehicles loaded up with pontoons (to ferry troops). The General said, "When I discovered that the Japanese were not destroying them but were using them to sleep in, I decided to thin out the Ascot car park and stick some more of my motor transport into No-Man's-Land! The Japanese stuck rigidly to their orders that these trucks were to be preserved to carry them to Calcutta when the British had been annihilated or driven into the sea. They never fired on them, even to the end."

But to return to my story:

> The KOSB reconnaissance parties arrived at midday on 29 February in our forward position just north of the Letwedet Chaung. Robin Innes, commanding B Company, KOSB, came with the party. I took him around the positions and fixed the party up for lunch. Innes told us of their heavy officer casualties: their second CO was wounded in the Ngakyedauk Pass. They have altogether had about twenty-one officer casualties since they have been down in the Arakan, whereas we have had only eleven. Their first CO, Colonel Mattingly[3], was killed by a shell in January. I knew him very well in Razmak, and travelled backwards and forwards to the Arakan with him in July 1943.

In the meantime Tiny Taylor and a representative from each Platoon reconnoitred an area in Wet Valley, which is about 1,000 yards behind and to the north of what had been the Braganza Box. The Company arrived in Wet Valley at 2.00am.

Chapter 7

The Maungdaw-Buthidaung Road

All company commanders met Colonel Duncombe at 6.00am on 1 March to talk about our new positions in the Wet Valley area, where the Company moved in after breakfast. It will be recalled that this was the area where the unfortunate Jungle Field Regiment were overrun by the Japanese about three weeks before. It had been well fought over. I did not like this 'Valley' at all. It showed all the signs of its recent history; it looked like a dirty old scrapyard where the dust carts had failed to collect the rubbish; the detritus of a putrefying and decaying battlefield remained – jeeps, bicycles, camp kettles and cooking pots, and maps by the score. There were still some unburied Japs and there were others who had been buried, but their feet showed above ground. I had not seen until then such an unbelievable abundance of kite hawks and vultures in one small area; thousands were living off the many unburied corpses. There was no noise of battle close by to disturb the birds as they fed on the carrion. We spent the rest of the day digging ourselves in in defensive positions on the higher ground, away from the valley itself. Even so, we gave the place a good clean up where we could; indeed, we had to.

This was the first time that we had been in a rest area position and behind our own guns since 1 December 1943. All that was necessary here were the normal day and night sentries, but there was no patrolling programme for us. During the last month we regularly found two patrols every day, in addition to the fighting patrols that went out nearly every other day and the routine ambush patrol that we found alternately with C Company. Sleep during that period of encirclement was at a premium, and I myself was on duty as a sentry, OC reliefs and officer on duty all combined every night with very few exceptions; but Tiny and Ian Frisby have had far less sleep than me, as they have borne the brunt of the patrolling.

On arrival here we did feel very tired, but, in spite of everything, we felt very relaxed with no immediate operational worries.

After a day, I began to like this position. It was tidy, compact and undemanding; and we have our own drinking and washing points that were approved by our Dr Jack Sumner yesterday; This water was beautifully clear, as it gushed straight out of the hillside.

At this time we were joined by 2nd Lieutenant Deacon. He, and four other officers to other companies came to us direct from the Bangalore Officer Cadet Training Unit.

These young men had been made fit to become officers but had had very little training to meet the rigours of this type of warfare. One would try and break in new arrivals gradually for fear of cracking them up, but in an operational area this could be difficult.

General Messervy visited the Battalion at 10.00am on 3 March and spoke to the CO, Second-in-Command, Adjutant and all company commanders. He addressed us wearing his new-looking bush hat at a pleasantly jaunty angle, enabling us clearly to see the features of his face. I say "new", as I presumed that he had lost his old one with most of his clothes during the Japanese attack on his Headquarters[1] a month earlier; but I was wrong, as I heard that the General's red-banded bush hat was discovered on the head of a Japanese soldier who was in a party that was ambushed by our troops about two weeks later. General Messervy told us how very pleased he was with our work and fully appreciated the hard time we had had. This time he promised us one more battle definitely, with possibly two or three more, all according to how things went. "You never can tell in war," he said. The General always seemed to be smiling as he spoke. He was probably compensating for the fact that there was not too much to smile about in jungle warfare. He did have a relaxed and kind face, which in itself could encourage and raise spirits, whatever one might think of the prospects of having three more battles with the enemy!

> We received a verbal warning order from the CO on 4 March about our next operation, which comes off not before the 6th, and probably on the 7th. This operation is almost identical to an operation that should have taken place in the first week of February. We could see that our rest period was to become very limited.

But it was a classical military decision that the generals in command had to make: by standing firm during its encirclement, the 7 Division, with the help of 5 and 26 Divisions, had broken up some enemy formations and had heavily defeated the enemy in battle. So this was the exact time to strike again quickly before the Japanese had time to regroup; no victory is complete without instant pursuit. The recent victory in Arakan had demonstrated the future pattern of jungle warfare as being a combined operation of ground troops and air supply.

> On the following day I went over the plan of the operation with my Company Orders Group before lunch and gave them the administrative set-up for the near future as far as I could foresee it. Briefly, the operation was to be in five phases: 1st phase at 7.30pm on 6 March, a brigade was to secure the Letwedet hill and village preceded by a thunderous artillery barrage which would go on for most of the night; 2nd phase, 11 Sikhs assault

and capture 'Poland' and 'Rabbit' features at 11.00pm., after another huge artillery concentration; 3rd phase, the Punjabis secure Point 142, and 4th phase, the Punjabis again assault the north end of 'West Finger'. These attacks to go in at 3.00am on 7th and secured by 5.00am. Finally, 5th phase: our Battalion to attack and consolidate the feature 'Cain' at 8.45am., B Company will be on the left and D Company on the right; each attack in each phase was preceded by an enormous artillery concentration of the whole of the Divisional artillery including a regiment of medium guns. It was reported that the artillery bombardment was carried out by 200 guns: that gave us a gun to every ten yards of enemy front.

At 5.50pm I received an urgent telephone message from Dick to say that the Brigadier had just informed the Battalion that it would be a good idea to send the two leading commanders in the attack on Cain across to the 4/1 Gurkhas on Abel tonight, so that we could spend a day of reconnaissance with them. We left here at 6.15pm and joined the mule convoy that formed up at Brigade HQ. Kingshott and I hurriedly girded up our kits, and I handed over the Company to Tiny before we left. Godfrey Shaw, Commanding 'D' Company, and I found the convoy commander, Capt. Punch Chadburn, Quartermaster of the Gurkhas. Chadburn had made these journeys to Abel almost every other night for the past month, delivering food and ammunition, and any other stores such as barbed wire. Usually the convoy included over 100 mules. I considered that this was a rather eerie trek. I could not understand why the Japs had not ever tried to bust up these convoys. The escort for the convoy is a Gurkha company, and a platoon from one of our Brigade's battalions goes to Letwedet village; but even so I should have said a convoy going across about two to three miles of open paddy, and the last half-hour spent winding along tracks in close and hilly country, would have been worth a try, anyhow, once!

The journey went off without incident and we arrived at the Gurkhas' HQ after about an hour.

We spoke with the Gurkha CO, Lieutenant Colonel Berthon and Pat Thompson, his Adjutant, in their command post. They gave us a spot of rum and dug-outs for batmen and ourselves: these dug-outs were quite beautiful little holes, with plenty of straw to lie on. It was a pleasant experience having a very restful night with no responsibilities.

> After breakfast Godfrey and I were taken on a conducted tour round the OPs by a company commander, Chris Nixon. These Gurkhas must have had a hell of a time. Their whole area had hardly a living tree on it as a result of Japanese shelling. The Jap positions themselves are to the west and north of this Gurkha Battalion, sharing the same hill, being barely fifty yards away from each other in some places. They have had to do repeated counter-attacks, sometimes as many as six in a day; they have had to do these as a result of many orders received to the effect that Abel must be cleared of enemy at all costs by such and such a time!

As Godfrey and I moved around their positions, we saw that little Johnnie Gurkha had built some really first-class communication trenches and dug-outs. We both agreed that somehow the Gurkhas always manage to make themselves more comfortable than British troops, partly, I thought, due to the fact that these marvellous Nepalese troops are experts when it comes to living out.

As I was carrying out my reconnaissance of B Company's objective on Cain, which was south across the Maungdaw-Buthidaung road from this Gurkha position on Abel, I realized that it stretched over some 250 yards of front, but because of spurs and jungle indentations it was actually rather more on the ground. We all knew that it was occupied by the Japanese; if I were to put one of my three platoons of about twenty-two men each on both of the two obvious spurs, they would be 'swamped' by jungle and quite lost in that country, and I would not be able to see or control their progress. So it was clear to me that it had best be a two-platoon front on only one of the jungle-covered spurs. As I was considering this, I then put a very stupid question to Colonel Berthon, who was standing with me in a trench: I asked him, if he were attacking this hill, which spur he would choose. He was correct to say quietly and diplomatically that I had to make that choice; supposing it all went disastrously wrong if I took his choice; I had learned a good lesson.

> Tommy, their Adjutant, realized I had not got a watch for tomorrow's attack (two of mine have cracked up), and so he lent me one of the Battalion's, War Department, pocket watches, an exceedingly thoughtful gesture.

Godfrey and I returned to the Queen's that night. At 7.00am the next morning, 7 March, all company commanders met Colonel Duncombe, when he once again outlined the final plan: D Company right, B Company left; the other companies and Battalion HQ remaining back in Abel. The enemy strength on Cain was thought to be about a company of some 100 men. Godfrey was going to go up the centre of the feature and then on to the right spur and high ground, and I was to go straight up the right-hand element of the left spur and on to the dominating high ground to the left of D Company.

A further artillery concentration was put down between 8.25am and 8.40am. I went round all the men just before we moved out, wished them the best of luck and led the Company out from the Forming Up Place at 8.30am. When we rounded the south-east corner of Abel I had to hold up while D Company shook themselves out across the main road (Maungdaw-Buthidaung), and then the artillery ceased firing. The ground in front of us was open paddy to the road some 100 yards away and just on the far side of the road our objective climbed steeply away to the south, covered in thick jungle with odd bare patches on the top where shellfire had laid it waste. D Company moved on again; when we next moved I pushed 12 Platoon in front of me. Almost as soon as we moved the Japanese opened fire with a machine gun from the direction of our objective, Cain; initially

I could not tell exactly from where it came or where the bullets were landing, but it was in front of us and mighty close. Then, as we moved forward, and it had to be in single file, three men of 12 Platoon were hit barely eight yards in front of me. As they fell I saw the bullets striking the track along which we were moving. I shouted to Ian Frisby, who was next to one of the men hit, and told him to keep the Platoon moving and to cut their way through the thick scrub off the track at the foot of Abel. This took some time, as it was virgin scrub. As I passed I took a quick look at the wounded, who appeared all right except for Vincent, who seemed to be losing much blood and was very pale. But there was no time for me to pause other than to alert the stretcher bearers. I warned the rest of the Company to ease in under the scrub and told 10 Platoon, who were immediately behind me, to open up with their 2-inch mortar; in the meantime I got on the wireless to Battalion HQ and said I wanted 25-pounder smoke and HE put down while we crossed this bit of open ground, and also to give time for 12 Platoon to cut their way in. By now I had more or less fixed the enemy position as being a third of the way up the spur that was my future line of advance. After a minute or so a ranging shell came down and I sent corrections back; it had landed 100 yards plus. After three minutes' ranging and corrections we had four gun salvoes. It was fairly unpleasant waiting for the first salvo of gunfire as the light machine gun was sweeping the track in front of us. As I moved forward again to catch up with 12 Platoon, I witnessed a staggering sight which mentally and momentarily transfixed me. As I hurried down the track I saw myself running into a stream of bullets as they struck and splashed their way through a puddle of water a yard ahead of me. I had no time to think, but my instinct told me to jump over the puddle, and I was very conscious of the mud and water being churned up under my feet by the bullets! As I passed over the top and above the line being taken by the stream of bullets, I was quite certain that no fear had entered my head. I had no time to contemplate the situation. Anyhow, my thoughts were too much taken up with the task in hand – the control of the Company and our impending attack.

During the 25-pounder shelling we got forward and crossed the Maungdaw-Buthidaung road without any further incident; apart from patrols, this was the first time that 7 Division troops had crossed this, perhaps psychologically, important east-west road, which had been in Japanese hands for nearly two years.

After winding through scrub and jungle and walking along the chaung-beds up to our thighs in water, I sent 12 Platoon off to the left and gave them their objective on the high ground immediately above the located Jap post; they had a precipitous climb. I went with the leading section of 10 Platoon by the right-hand route and up the re-entrant just clinging to some of the spur, with the rest of the company following. We got to the summit of the feature after a stiff climb and, surprisingly enough, there were no Japs to be seen or heard. The position was completely deserted; there was plenty of evidence of previous occupation, although most of the trenches had caved in from our own shellfire. Jap grenades were found and two half-buried Japs were discovered in one of the holes later in the afternoon.

In normal open warfare, it would usually be wrong to approach an objective via re-entrants; but, this being very thick jungle country that had no tracks to its summit by the way we approached it, the enemy visibility, like ours, was very limited.

By the time we had reached our objective it was 11.15am. This means that it had taken us nearly three hours to do about 400 yards from the FUP and there were no enemy in occupation as far as I could tell. I placed 10 Platoon in a forward position and on the right, 11 Platoon in reserve in the area of Company HQ, with 12 Platoon on our left. Immediately on our arrival I sent 11 Platoon (Lieut. Deacon) off on a fighting patrol to work round the Company area.

I received a message at 1200 hrs from the CO to say that D Company were in position without opposition and that C Company were coming up to relieve them as D were going on to occupy another commanding feature some 400 yards in front of my present position. There was to be a five-minute medium artillery concentration on to D Company's new feature at 12.15pm. In the meantime all ranks must be warned to keep down during the concentration. After about ten seconds of the concentration it struck me that several shells were falling short; the earth shook and there was a certain amount of blast. I looked up out of the trench and saw that the shells were falling on and around D Company's next feature all right. A few seconds later there was no doubt about it: there were also shells dropping around us. I saw one medium shell burst behind Company HQ in 12 Platoon's direction, and then two landed unmistakably in my Company HQ area after I was grounded by the first. I do not know how close, as I was crouching as near the dirt as possible, but all I knew was that my hole was filled in and I was deaf and dazed. Then I crawled out into the signallers' trench and told them to get on to the Battalion to tell them some shells were falling short. Within half a minute the shelling ceased. The CO told me on the wireless after it had ceased that he had seen this from his OP and ordered the FOO to cease fire at the same time as he got my message. As a result of the medium gun's shelling we had one killed and one wounded in 12 Platoon, one wounded in 11 Platoon, and one signaller seriously wounded in Company HQ. Apparently one of the medium guns had failed to lift on to its second target.

There are occasions in war, fortunately very few, when one's own troops do become casualties from small arms, shells and bombs fired by friendly forces. Regrettably mistakes are made and those who make them will know all about their errors in time and will carry the shame of it.

D Company duly passed through us to the next position and arrived without any opposition on their objective. At 3.15 pm there was considerable firing in the direction where 11 Platoon might be, as at that time they were still on their fighting patrol. They returned at 5.00pm, rather shaken. Deacon, the platoon commander, and three NCOs were wounded, one of whom was Corporal Naylor, wounded in the leg and he was still out there.

Apart from being hit in other parts of the body, all four had been hit by bullets in the face, but Corporal Berry was the only serious case. Deacon had apparently formed a blitz party and ran on to this machine gun at twenty yards' range. Naylor had shouted out that he would crawl out on his own as otherwise any help would attract firing.

> By this time A Company were in position and one of their platoons is only a few yards from the Japs; this platoon is to harass the enemy with mortar and sniping throughout the night and blitz them at first light tomorrow. One of A Company's platoon commanders was killed this afternoon whilst on a reconnaissance by himself in the area of this Japanese position. This young officer, 2nd Lieutenant Geoffrey Highton, only joined the Battalion from his O.C.T.U. on March 2.

This was less than a week ago; poor man, although it was courageous of him, he should not have been on any patrol by himself in that jungle country.

At 6.15pm on 7 March a dead Jap was brought into the area of my HQ. A Jap patrol had been playing about in front of one of our positions and had walked right into one of them, which killed one and badly wounded another of the enemy; the rest of the Jap patrol fled.

> A noisy night of artillery exchanges and small-arms fire. There appeared to be a Japanese counter-attack last night and this morning on Poland. We could hear the Sikhs' war-cry and the Japs yelling "Banzai!" The reason for the counter-attack would be to get back the anti-tank guns the Sikhs captured in their attack on Poland yesterday.
>
> We had a 50 per cent. stand-to last night. I managed one and a half hours' sleep. The enemy post on our left (east) spur withdrew during the night; this was rather as we suspected, as it was completely surrounded. Corporal Naylor's body was found at the foot of the position. In addition to bullets through his legs, it was

evident that he had been hit by a grenade in the chest. By this man's unselfishness in yelling to 11 Platoon not to worry about him, he had perhaps saved the lives of several others.

I buried Private West and Corporal Naylor in the area of 12 Platoon's position at 12.50pm. Our total casualties in B Company to capture Cain were 3 killed and 7 wounded yesterday; Private Vincent died in the Regimental Aid Post. The operation is now complete with the Brigade astride the main Maungdaw-Buthidaung road: this gives the successes of the attacks not only a geographical advantage but must deal a psychological blow to the enemy.

The Brigade's present locations have cut a vital enemy supply link to their east tunnel positions across the road. It is now impossible for the Japanese to supply these positions from Buthidaung along the main road, and neither is it possible from the west from Maungdaw. Their only alternative is by a jungle track running along the temporary dried-up chaung-beds and other low country, which will become impassable when the rains start. This track runs from the south of us to the north-west, not far from D Company's position.

This night the artillery exchanges between us and the Japanese were on a smaller scale. There was still an odd battle going on to the east of us. D Company reported that there were many Japs milling around their positions last night; and the enemy shelled the road that ran behind Battalion HQ between 10.30am and 11.15am.

At 6.30am the following morning, I received a warning order to move at one hour's notice. Where? Forward to attack Inbauk (a mile due south of us, and a focal point on the track to their east tunnel position), or back to . . . ? Many rumours floating around as a result of preparations to move.

At 9.30am the Battalion moved out, leaving one section in each company position. The Battalion concentrated in the low ground astride the main road just below Abel and here we waited all day, not knowing what was to become of us. Everything hangs on the conference at Brigade HQ with the Divisional Commander.

During the day all men had time for a good wash and shave, and numerous mugs and tins of tea appeared. It always amazes me how the troops can put on tea at the drop of a hat. As long as the tactical situation permits they will brew up tea all day long. It is better to be ignorant as to how they obtain and carry the ingredients so long as no one is short! Jack Sumner spent most of the day in my Company HQ, where we talked at length on many topics, especially what the future held in store for us.

At 4.30pm the CO returned from the conference. As a result we moved back to Tatminyaungwa village, less A Company, who relieved the Sikhs on Poland. All moves were done after dark.

B Company moved off at 1900 hrs and, en route, I put 12 Platoon in position on a feature called 'Kidney'. Having seen them safely there, I moved the Company on and we hit Tatminyaungwa tank crossing spot on. The men marvelled at my navigation (it was dark), but I am afraid I had to tell them that I was following a telephone cable that ran straight home. At the bridge I was met by Tiny, who gave the layout. He took 11 Platoon and put them in position himself, as they were to be right up the northern end of the village about one and three-quarter miles from Company HQ. 12 Platoon were a good 800 yards from HQ; 10 Platoon and Company HQ were holding the tank crossing and the southern portion of the village and chaung. We took over from the 4/8 Gurkhas of 89 Brigade, as this brigade was going forward to carry out the next phase of the advance. The relief was completed by 9.50pm.

After breakfast the next day I went up the dusty track to visit 11 Platoon. I had to remember that Lieutenant Deacon, whose wound proved to be slight, was relatively new to the company and he still had much to learn. I had to gently point out some shortcomings in his defensive layout, because, as the Platoon was not in jungle country but on the borders of a track and open paddy-fields, his Platoon HQ and three sections and their slit trenches needed to be mutually supporting and camouflaged more effectively. The Platoon held the northern track junction and one directly opposite Battalion HQ, who were on the other (western) side of the Tatmin Chaung. We were no longer front-line troops in this phase, but a mile or two back in reserve; however, in this type of warfare there is of course no front line, the enemy are just as likely to despatch a fighting patrol and so catch us unawares in a reserve position, particularly at night.

Our company HQ was probably in the most comfortable position I had yet been in. It was flat, no jungle, but had trees in the inhabited village areas. As we were dug in close to but outside the village, we did very well over food, being able to augment our boring 24-hour ration packs of bully beef, cheese, biscuits, jam, dried fruit, dehydrated potatoes, and sometimes a soya link (sausage). We were able to buy from the villagers eggs, the odd chicken, vegetables and bananas.

> The chaung is tidal. I had a very refreshing bathe and swam in two feet of water at high tide. The dug-outs were good and are lined with boosa (grass) in typical Gurkha style. The only drawback to the position was the fact that half 10 Platoon were on the opposite bank of the chaung, and so also lay the route to Battalion HQ; all moves in this direction necessitated wet feet except at extreme low tide.
>
> The 4/8 Gurkhas are to attack and go through Buthidaung with the aid of tanks tomorrow. Our last Brigade operation was such a complete success that the Divisional Commander intends to follow up and keep the enemy on the run.
>
> I had a line run out to 12 Platoon and a telephone installed there. Corporal Davies, one of my two signallers in Company HQ, spent the morning running the line back to Battalion HQ.
>
> A very pleasant and restful night. Nothing of any note occurred today, 12th. Visited 10 Platoon and had a spot of elevenses with them.
>
> Just before lunch I was called in to Battalion HQ. The CO had little to tell me, but that I might have to put in an attack with the Gurkhas on Abel if the latter was not cleared of the enemy.

I visited 12 Platoon on Kidney after lunch. On the map the jungle-covered feature looked like a kidney, but on the ground it was more like a very large five-pointed star and was about 200 yards across. Frisby's Platoon was lost in it, but was concentrated on the home or south-east side and protected the western line of communications to Buthidaung and Abel. The men in 12 Platoon were in bubbling form. They seemed very happy, but lacked drinking water facilities, so I sent the Colour-Sergeant over with their rations and two pakhals of water, about 16 gallons. All were carried on mules.

While in the platoon position I went on to a suitable OP to look at Abel from the north-east angle to view the probable routes and positions of a FUP should we have to do an attack. My task, I gathered, would be to attack from the north with the hope of driving the enemy on to the Gurkhas, who had been on Abel for about five weeks.

After a very hairy journey back during which the enemy had been doing a great deal of shelling of the track behind our position and along the track that connected forward to the Buthidaung road past 12 Platoon, I and my jeep had been chased by two Japanese shells as I sped along the track to get back to Company HQ. One dropped in front and the other behind; the third shell never came my way. Many supply vehicles had been moving down the tracks, supposedly to units of 89 Brigade, kicking up whirlwinds of dust; hence the shelling. My driver and I arrived back in Company HQ at 3.00pm and soon after Frisby rang me up to say that Private Smith (04) had been killed outright by a shell that had sheared off his head. This disaster occurred close to where I had done my reconnaissance. What had I done? Was it my fault? My visit should have boosted their morale.

Chapter 8

The Massif

I heard this morning, 13 March, that my B Company's attack on Abel was off. The Japanese had withdrawn during last night. The Jap really is a tenacious breed of soldier. It was in early February that they had originally been attacked and driven off by the 4/1 Gurkhas; then followed Japanese counter-attacks almost nightly for over a month based on a company of about 100 men. This morning the Gurkhas discovered thirty Japanese bodies and twenty-five graves, in addition to piles of refuse and kit; but we never knew how many wounded they had suffered over this period of attrition. The ratio to those killed is usually well over half. The Gurkhas had put up a tremendous performance to contain these determined counter-attacks, and in consequence had themselves suffered many casualties while sharing that hill with the enemy.

Jack Sumner went round on one of his tours of the Battalion localities and visited us in the morning and had a cup of tea and then chatted to our stretcher bearers, who would normally handle all company sick and wounded before we backloaded the casualties to Jack in the Regimental Aid Post at Battalion HQ.

A 'bombshell' exploded over the telephone at 1.30pm when I was told that B Company was to go to Poland south of the Maungdaw-Buthidaung road to reinforce A Company. This was a blow as we were most comfortable here and everything was well organized. I couldn't believe that we were having to give it all up so soon, but that is often the way in life.

After giving the routes and final destination to platoon commanders, I left at 2.00pm with Kingshott and platoon representatives to reconnoitre their new positions. The administrative arrangements produced certain difficulties: all stores, reserve ammunition and rations for tomorrow had to be ferried up to us in the Bren gun carriers after dark. This meant that the balance of today's food has to be carried on the man for supper. The carriers have to be escorted and then, in the dark, all the kit will have to be unloaded and man-handled to the positions; mules were out of the question, as they are too slow and more sensitive to enemy shelling.

Sitting back many years later and reflecting on some of the words I chose to use in my diary on that March day in 1944, the word 'bombshell' in connection with what was another quite ordinary company move appears a little over the top; but in the context of the time when one was tired and then found oneself relaxing in a comfortable reserve area a sudden order to upsticks came a little hard. However, there was always the realization that the order came because of an operational necessity; so that's that; get on with it.

I met Mervyn Mansel (OC A Company) on Poland and between us we worked out the positions that the two companies were to occupy: A Company were to concentrate on the northern end and cover the road, and B Company to occupy the forward end, which had very much thicker jungle, with one platoon on the rear end of Rabbit, which was not occupied by anyone.

The Company arrived at 5.00pm and we had no casualties from enemy shelling; this was surprising as it was daylight and their artillery is forever active on the tracks and anyone seen in the open paddy between the road and Tatminyaungwa very soon became a target. I sorted the Company out into its new positions: 12 Platoon in rear of Company HQ, 10 Platoon on the next bump beyond, and 11 Platoon on Rabbit. I went over to Rabbit with a reconnaissance party before the arrival of 11 Platoon to make certain that no enemy were lying up there; the only things we found were a heap of equipment in the cutting between Poland and Rabbit, such as anti-tank gun ammunition, saddles, clothing and mess-tins, etc, which were all Japanese.

As always, platoons were connected to me and each other by wireless, as I was to Battalion HQ, but it was an excellent back-up and more personal to have communications duplicated with telephones and so lines were laid to 11 Platoon, and our Company HQ was connected by line to A Company.

When the Company were settled in I accepted Mervyn's invitation for some hot supper in his HQ and this meant that my batman and signaller came too.

At 10.00pm we heard the carriers rumbling along on the track, but decided to leave the kit there as it was too late to get the men out; it would have entailed half the Company on the move to bring up five carrier-loads of kit, and in the complete darkness would have taken maybe three hours up our narrow, winding and steep tracks.

In the morning we found that all blankets, rations, ammunition and water pakhals had been unloaded by Colour-Sergeant Fraser and his escort last night and placed under guard in the bushes. It took the chaps about one and a half hours in daylight to get all the kit up to their positions.

How lucky we were to have Fraser looking after our administrative affairs. He never failed to look ahead and make things easier for me. I hardly needed to tell him anything, other than when and where I needed it.

I saw much of Mervyn and Pat Wylde, second-in-command of A Company, in the morning and had some midday tea and chocolate sweets. Mervyn had done the same as me; he receives two pounds of chocolates about every fortnight from 'Tony's' in Calcutta.

During the last days of our encirclement in February, on one occasion I received my two pounds of chocolates with the other mail that had been dropped by parachute; that really was a red-letter day for me, and a few others in the HQ were able to join in this treat.

> Terrible nights in this place. Small battles went on around us and behind in the 162 feature. Jap shells, aimed at the road and track just behind us, fell short and did not always clear these features, but land very near our positions. The monkeys at night appeared to be playing at being noisy soldiers as they simulated the movements of humans. There was no doubt that these noises could have been humans but from time to time they jumped from tree to tree and scratched about in the undergrowth and so they were probably not. During those nights there was also a continual pitter-patter of dew falling from leaf to leaf, and a mist which formed at about midnight and did not completely lift until 9.00am. During the hours of darkness the visibility was down to about three or four feet.

Those combinations sowed seeds of concern and doubt, which possibly excite the nervous tensions of tired sentries into thinking the worst, and was quite a drain on the system, and the more so as it went on just about every night, and was not just confined to this position on Poland. I wrote in my diary that it was "all very eerie". This was apt to make some of the men jumpy; one would sling a grenade, and then perhaps two or three others would start, followed by a stand-to. This was precaution in the right direction and meant that the men were on their toes, but at the same time a burst of ammunition at close range in an otherwise quiet night was a little unnerving to some. One thing I will say was that the men, whatever the state of their nerves, never fired any small arms weapons at night without orders.

More rations came to us last night and were collected this morning. I received some letters and papers and it was my turn to receive my chocolate 'ration' on 16 March. We had a fairly quiet night. A few grenades were being thrown in the 162 area, probably C Company patrols on the north-west face. Also some shots from south Cain. Our artillery were sending over concentrations and harassing fire to somewhere south of us for most of the night.

I visited all the platoons in the morning. Mervyn came over to us at 11.00am for a cup of tea and chocolates; Tiny was also present. I made the most of our chocolates, which understandably only showed up the once during our encirclement. Mervyn stayed for lunch and the Padre joined us, as I had arranged a church service for the Company at 1.30pm in 12 Platoon area. After that I took Padre Tom Garrett to 11 Platoon on Rabbit for a service with them.

These non-denominational church services were well attended, perhaps about 90%, but of those that do not, there are probably three or four men in each platoon serving as sentries who are protecting the rest of us.

During the morning our artillery put down an enormous concentration of shells at 10.00am, and a squadron of tanks of the 25th Dragoons were shooting up the bunkers at close range on the south-western features of Point 162. C Company of the Queen's and the KOSB assaulted and took the northern and north-west features of Point 162.

This hill feature in general only reached about 150 feet in height and was covered in dense virgin jungle for the most part; but it was a huge feature nearly two miles long and a mile across, and hence it was always known as the Massif. Company commanders knew that it was occupied by possibly a large number of enemy. The fringes of the feature had been well patrolled and tracks and evidence of Japanese occupation had been long established, but details of how many and where were not known.

On this occasion the noises off were terrific and from this position we had a grandstand view of the concentrations and the tank poundings. From what I gathered from Dick over the phone, opposition was negligible on the KOSB front and the enemy had altogether flown from their positions on C Company's. Nothing could have survived the pasting the objectives received.

But, however successful this operation had been, we were to learn that the battle for the Massif was far from over.

The next day, 17 March, Mervyn and I were called in by the CO for some new orders at Battalion HQ, which was some two and a half to three miles farther back. We had lunch in the Headquarter's Officers' Mess. Briefly the Battalion had been ordered to clear the Massif of Japs tomorrow. C Company were to feel forward to a line by 7.30am, and B Company were to take on and move across the line by 8.00am. Our piece of country actually took in the centre piece of Point 162 and beyond, which meant we had to cover about 1,000 yards as shown on the map. From here D Company would take over and move to the eastern edge of Massif, the KOSBs moving parallel to us to our north. The operation was to be completed by 2.00pm.

Nothing is known of the Jap strength or their positions, beyond the outer rim of the Massif, as no patrol has ever been inside this feature. The whole operation was to be rather in the nature of a partridge drive. One battery of 3-inch mortars are in direct support of the Company.

With its high trajectory the mortar is ideal for hitting an enemy entrenched in jungle.

On our way to the Battalion HQ and back to Poland, Mervyn and I ran the gauntlet of enemy shelling as we raced along in the jeep as fast as we could. This, I thought, was so far one of my worst experiences of shelling, rather more so because we were the enemy's individual target, being in their sights for the best part of two miles, and no doubt the Japanese were placing bets on it as to how many shells it would take and which gun would get us before we became a statistic! The track was plastered behind and in front of us as we moved forward, and we passed several 15-cwts vehicles and the odd Bren gun carrier still burning or immobilized by the side of this much-pitted track. There was only one thing to do: we had to keep going through it, as the enemy could plainly see us all the time in the open. I suggested to my driver that we moved off the track over the paddy-fields. The going was rough and tortuously slow, but at least we got out of the line of this shellfire. On the way into the Battalion the enemy were using 75 mm, but on the return journey they were using the larger 105 mm shells, some of which exploded within thirty yards of us. I got back to the Company at 4.00pm. Tiny had guessed what was billed for us on the next day.

The next morning the Company left Poland at 6.30am, wearing fighting order, less packs, and carrying a day's food in our haversacks. C Company were in position and we passed through them as planned. Major George Rothery, (C Company commander) showed me the extent to where they had patrolled. The artillery efforts of yesterday had certainly devastated the near slopes and re-entrants in front of C Company, but very little damage was evident beyond them inside the Massif proper. Along the jungle track that moved into the feature I noticed several signposts and arrows that were obviously of Jap origin. We saw the old gun-pit on one of the highest hillocks, a well-barricaded site with colossal dug-outs around it. This was the gun that fired at us at very close range and used to go zip-bang when we were positioned north of Letwedet Chaung (the bang being after we had seen the explosion). Along one of the deep re-entrants, almost a gorge which had precipitous sides, there were dug-outs every five yards. Much of this hinterland had knife-edge ridges, along which we had to move to make any headway; the ridges had perpendicular drops on either side in some places. What track there was, was more like a game trail.

If there were any Japs here we should have had it, as there was no possible way out. In order to get along some parts of the track we had to slide down some twenty feet of sheer drop which was only broken by clutching on to bamboo. Then there had to be a climb up so as not to lose height. We passed some piles of Jap and British small arms rifle ammunition and grenades, and other discarded equipment, all in fairly large quantities.

Navigation through all this was most difficult, and the country was not exactly as per map. I led the Company in for some few hundred yards; on arriving at what I thought was the spur climbing up towards what I considered to be the Point 162 itself, I handed over the lead to 12 Platoon, which had been immediately behind me and told Ian Frisby to send a section patrol to what I called our first objective. All of this was absolutely blind country with visibility of three to five yards. Before sending off this patrol, I asked the artillery Forward Observation Officer to get his 4.2 inch mortars teed up and ready to fire on to this objective, which was Point 162 itself, as it was here, I said, that if there was any opposition we would meet it. I intended this position to be a pivot if necessary for any operation. I had already sent off 11 Platoon on a patrol to the left of us to try and cover some of the ground between us and the KOSB.

11 Platoon returned and reported nothing seen just as the 12 Platoon section went off in front of us. About twenty minutes after the section moved in front, a hail and whistling crack of bullets screamed across us, and then came an agonizing cry and whimper obviously from one of our men of that leading section. As a result of this contact, I sent the rest of 12 Platoon off to join up with its section and see what could be done to eliminate this Japanese post. Then they were also heavily fired on by another light machine gun farther to the left. Grenades were exchanged with the first Jap position. I got a message back from Frisby, which told me of the above. The man who let out the scream was the leader of the foremost section who was killed about ten yards from the Jap position that was up on higher ground. From where I was in Company HQ we could see the smoke and dust

from the firing from that first position; there was no clue as to where the second enemy position was except that it was 50 or 80 yards away across a ravine; if we went down there and worked our way round, we would then have a stiffer climb up to the enemy, who could have rolled grenades onto us; but then we had no idea of its exact position. In general the ground was densely covered with bamboo and virgin undergrowth. Hacking through this would alert the Japanese of our entire progress.

12 Platoon was now just ahead of me and my tactical HQ, and all of us were tucked into the cover of the jungle slope, while I had the enemy position plastered by Harry Haine's 3-inch mortars for ten minutes. This was a big risk. I was just a little dubious; although I was pretty certain I knew where I was, I could not really be sure that the map was all that accurate as regards distance. We heard the initial salvo come whistling over mighty close. What shooting! It was grand, right in the target area first time; made us wince a bit, but we had no casualties.

Time was now about 11.45am. When the mortars had sent their last bomb, I sent off Sergeant Butkas's 10 Platoon to go feeling round the right flank where possible. Much the same happened to this Platoon as happened to 12 Platoon. First the leading section and then the whole Platoon had to advance along this one and only narrow track to the summit, as 10 Platoon's track led back again into the other one. To move off the track and assault was impossible; the slope was too steep and entailed scrambling on all fours, and the jungle was well-nigh impenetrable. This Platoon's 2-inch mortar and one Bren light machine gun were smashed and blown out of the men's hands. Sergeant Butkas had his tin hat knocked off by a bullet, and Private Woolridge, another machine gunner, had a grenade bounce off his helmet and explode; he also got a bullet in his back. We were also sprayed by light machine-gun fire in Company HQ while I was on the wireless set to Dick in Battalion HQ. I had to shout, "Wait!" and picked up the wireless set and dash to some further cover. Sergeant Major Hudson was hit in the wrist. Corporal French, one or my stretcher bearers, received a ricochet in the side, the bullet wedging itself in the scabbard of his dah and resting against the steel blade. It was interesting that these two men were hit, as they were five yards behind me. That was the second time French had stopped a lucky one. Frisby, 12 Platoon commander, had a clean wound through the upper left arm.

In our part of the Arakan there was no jungle on the flat, which was mostly open paddy-fields intersected by streams for irrigation and drainage, but always the slopes of all the hills, even the smallest, were covered in jungle, and so, when advancing, the physical nature of these dictated the formation we adopted. Hence many of the contacts with the Japanese was in single file, and these section files of men were sometimes led by an officer, or a corporal, and on occasions a scout in front. The casualties among them was proportionately higher. The unwavering acceptance of their dangerous responsibilities was carried out without hesitation and with great courage. The men just went and took them on.

With all these small platoon attacks, there was in reality no room to manoeuvre more than a few men or a section at a time. We had not got much farther, although we had established that the enemy had a strong position on ground that favoured defence. In the light of this I got on to the set to the CO and told him the position in detail, and said that hammering away like this only gave us further casualties. As we knew nothing of the enemy's real strength, width and depth of his dispositions, we had merely scratched the surface. In my opinion any further effort on our part would have wasted valuable men to really no constructive purpose. The original orders said "Clear"; there was no intention to carry out a set-piece attack, which was physically not possible, and there had been no plan for an artillery programme; additionally, our own lines of communications were very stretched. There were about 300 unprotected map-yards between us and 'C' Company, and the route was up and down, and through water. The distance we actually covered was more like 600 yards.

The CO got in touch with the Brigadier, who okayed our

withdrawal some five minutes later at 2.00pm, and so I rolled the Company up, 10 Platoon and then followed by 12 Platoon which I placed under command of Tiny Taylor (my 2iC). Although Ian Frisby's wound was slight, I had pulled him out of his command as I felt he was drained; then I left with 11 Platoon as rearguard. The going was very slow as we had to roll up the telephone cable as we moved. Just before we left I gave the Japs another five minutes' mortaring.

On the way back I exchanged a few words with Dick and the CO, who said, "Well done" to us as we passed. Godfrey Shaw (D Company) had heard our conversations on the wireless and phone, and very much agreed with my decision.

Arrived back in Poland at 4.30pm and briefed Mervyn (A Company). Soon after arrival I had occasion to become annoyed with my platoon commanders for helping themselves to tea from A Company before seeing their own men back and settled into their own positions. We had had a very hot and fairly exhausting time since about 5.30am, and consequently we were all very, very thirsty.

The relieving unit of 26 Division arrived at about midnight. They took over and I moved off with B Company at 4.00am, 21 March and arrived back in the old Braganza Box positions at 5.30am. After reporting our arrival to the CO we then moved forward to our original position overlooking the Letwedet Chaung.

We noticed two striking changes: one was that the old jeep track had been continued almost to the foot of Company HQ, and the other was that all the re-entrants that faced south were now filled with 5.5-inch medium guns, trucks, ammunition and vast 10-ton lorries. The gun sites were fairly well camouflaged and were all surrounded by double-apron barbed-wire fences and trip wires; it was really rather amazing to see these guns right up here, for although we had occupied the northern slopes and the near centre of the Massif, we knew that the Japanese were on the feature in some strength; they might just be able to see some of this array of artillery guns.

C Company did not move from their positions on north-west of Massif. Had a good sleep last night; I was very tired. Got the present position more organized and cleaned up. These medium guns shook the earth like a mini earthquake and the sound echoed and reverberated around the hills; they fired one-gun salvoes throughout the day and night every five minutes. The Japs shelled these guns on a small scale.

It rained from 4.45am hrs. until 1.00pm on 23 March. Moved my bed into the large dug-out near by; this had been made by the KOSBs and was certainly a well-appreciated work of art.

The enemy shelled the Battalion on this day; it was not so pleasant going to and from Battalion HQ. Several shells landed in the paddy near our company ration unloading point. I went to Battalion HQ at 1.30pm for CO's orders at 2.00pm. I had several men on charges: sentries smoking and the odd man not alert at stand-to's, for which they received stoppages of pay. It is a pity we had these odd offences; the men are magnificent in the work they do and the difficulties they overcome. Those that have joined us since December have not had the real length of training that the majority of the Company have had and who have been with the Battalion about one and a half years.

By the end of March 1944 there were only two regular pre-1940 soldiers left in the Company, and I found it hard to believe that I was the only one to have weathered four monsoons!

Ian Frisby, whose wound was not serious – his left arm was clean and well bound up – and five men of 12 Platoon, Clive, Anstiss, Downes, Compton and Wilson, went off at 6.45pm on a very tricky fighting patrol to East Massif, that is to say on the far side of where we were a few days ago. This was the first time that any patrol has tried from the east side. They were not due back until after darkness the next day, 24 March; they had to get into the feature and then lie up and observe all day on the 24th, then knock out and kill the occupants of any post they saw. Tiny liaised with the gunners and arranged that we sent the patrol's blankets, food and rum to them so that the patrol has something on their immediate return.

Spasmodic artillery duels during the afternoon until 1900 hrs. Fierce fighting to south-west of us, on south Cain I thought.

Ian Frisby and his patrol returned to us after our morning standing-to. They had had a very sticky, hairy patrol. The night before their return they bumped into an enemy position of unknown strength; the result of the fire fight was that Frisby killed a Jap at very close quarters, after which the patrol withdrew, but Private Downes was missing. Two other companies also had patrols in that Point 162 feature, and each one had also killed a Jap without loss to themselves.

As planned, Frisby's patrol ate some food and bedded down in the gunner's position. From all accounts these gunners did them proud and gave them a very comfortable night and told Ian Frisby that they thought the infantry were the tops!

Chapter 9

Behind Us Again

During this period when my Company and much of the Battalion were across the Maungdaw-Buthidaung road there had been considerable activity by 89 Brigade of our 7 Indian Division in the Buthidaung area. In early March, the 1/11 Sikhs riding on 25th Dragoon tanks swept into Buthidaung and found that the Japanese had withdrawn from this battle-scarred town, and so the Sikhs occupied the commanding nearby hills. However, a force of about forty enemy infiltrated behind them during the night and had dug themselves in overlooking the road into Buthidaung. The enemy had to be driven off their entrenched position on the top of a knife-edge ridge. The Sikhs put in an attack. The leading section was commanded by Naik (corporal) Nand Singh. Coming under fire, he was wounded in the thigh but took the first trench with his bayonet; he was then wounded again in the face and shoulder by a grenade. He stormed a second position singlehanded and killed all the enemy. By this time most of his section were killed or wounded, but he took on a third position, again with the bayonet, and killed all the enemy. This very courageous Sikh was awarded the first Victoria Cross[1] in the Division.

Letters from Ma and Pa were very cheerful. They had managed to visit our old haunts and friends in Berkshire. Uncle George was a Home Guard commanding officer and did his work from the very comfortable surroundings of his own

Finchamstead House. In my letter home dated 23 March I mentioned how the days were becoming very hot, although the nights were still chilly, even under a blanket; when the dew had dried off, the tracks gave off clouds of very thick dust whenever transport wove its way across the open paddy-fields.

A hectic day; there had been a plan for the Battalion to move on to Massif and from there to liquidate the remaining Japs on the feature, hoping we could assault their known positions and winkle out the many unknown ones hidden in the craggy, precipitous hinterland of this feature. However, an hour or so after dawn on that 26 March I heard much firing and mortaring going on, maybe a mile behind us. I put this down to the continuation of 26 Division's live firing exercise which they had been doing yesterday, so we were told.

A little later Dick gave me a ring to say that the Battalion move onto Massif was postponed. This set us thinking that the firing in our rear was a little more than a mere own troops exercise. I wished to get more information and so I visited Battalion HQ. D Company, I learnt from Godfrey, had received orders to move back to the Divisional Admin Box, which had remained in its old position, as apparently about 400 to 500 Japs had once again infiltrated behind us in the Wet Valley area and taken up positions on the hill features south of the road opposite the Admin Box at the eastern end of the Ngakyedauk Pass.

And here the 11 Sikhs were engaging the Japs. As I wrote in my diary: "Once again our lines of communication are threatened".

B Company were to move out as soon as possible to Brigade HQ to pick up MT and then move to 11 Sikhs. I raced back to the Company to get them packed up at breakneck speed. There was a hell of a lot to pack up, rations in bulk had to be split, reserve clothing, blankets and so on had to be man-handled some distance to the jeep track. Dick rang up again at 9.45am to say that there was now no immediate hurry as the whole Battalion are to move back at 11.00am. I saw most of the kit packed up; the Colour-Sergeant again did some mammoth work getting the jeeps back and unloading them at a Company dump at 10.50am hrs; but 11 Platoon for some unknown reason had been atrociously slow and were not immediately ready.

Because of enemy intensive shelling on the alternative western route, I led the whole Battalion by a very roundabout route to Brigade HQ.

It was an incredibly hot day and at the last minute I decided that we would carry our own blankets across and round our packs. It would be another chilly night. The reason for this was that the mule and motor transport were limited and would have to be used for rations, ammunition, water, etc. It was unlikely that any less important stores, such as blankets, would move today. I met Brigadier Loftus-Tottenham on the track, who said there was no motor transport for moving the Company on in advance, and he gave me another route to Brigade HQ. The usual route might have been tricky, as it was uncertain as to where the enemy had taken up their positions. Three minutes after the Brigadier left, Sergeant Smith (Intelligence Sergeant) came up with a message from our HQ giving me another route! Anyhow, I followed the Brigadier's instructions.

Arrived in the new Brigade HQ area. I gathered from the Brigadier that the whole Brigade was moving back to the Admin Box locality: the Punjabis were moving out first to attack hill features immediately west of us across the paddy. This means that the Japs opposite the Admin Box are faced with the 11 Sikhs to the north and the Punjabis in the south. Queen's, with B Company leading, followed after the Punjabis, then to strike north to the Box itself, and wind our way between the battles. (The Gurkhas are not now part of the Brigade; they had crossed the Kalapanzin River after their relief on Abel and came under command of that brigade about five days ago.)

The amount of transport milling around this valley, including tanks, was enormous. The dust and heat made heavy going. I was given an approximate map reference to go to; I was not absolutely certain what features our troops were on, or the Japs. Brigade HQ moved behind the Battalion, and then the Advanced Dressing Station behind which I put 12 Platoon as an escort to these potentially soft targets. The exit west of this valley was being continuously shelled; the Punjabis moved out of it at about 1.40pm and I followed five minutes after they were all clear. In the meantime the tank regiment, 25th Dragoons, had moved out to picket the flanks of the open paddy-fields, through which we would have to move.

The tank 75mm guns and their Browning machine guns would keep the enemy's heads down as we progressed. The Brigade transport, headed by our carriers, had also started to move out up the track.

As B Company moved we were met by a number of wounded men coming back. They had had direct hits on their vehicles.

And so as expected, the enemy immediately started shelling us when we got into the open, which resulted in some of the troops going to ground, but naturally we had to keep moving; it was more suicidal to remain on the ground than to move quickly and disperse; with the first signs of this I immediately pushed the men on again. We could see where the shells were being ranged on us and the tanks in anticipation of our advance, and so I made several detours around the shelled areas. The transport just had to be on the tracks. Guns of all types, including 5.5-inch mediums, 25-pounders and the 3.7-inch gun-hows and their ammunition vehicles, were having a hell of a time. I saw several receive direct hits and others blown over by the blast with bodies flying out of vehicles. Throughout this move we also came under fairly heavy sniping from light machine guns and rifles at about 600 yards' range. It was impossible to pinpoint from where the sniping came, and our own troops were engaging the enemy east and west of us as we moved.

185

So, with small arms fire racing across our front and flanks, both Japanese and own troops, it was a muddling battle that scraped around us but of which we were not a part, but we continued our sweaty march northwards as the sun beat down on our steel helmets and the white salt from our bodies, as so often, oozing out through our clothing and equipment. The tanks were firing repeated long bursts of machine guns and quite frequently we could see their 75 mm guns fire salvoes, perhaps ten or a dozen in quick succession at forty to fifty yards' range into the jungle-clad hillside, where the unseen enemy positions must have been.

On entering what I later gathered was the Admin Box area, we were heralded with a shattering din of shellfire only a few yards away around the corner of a hillock. We could not see the gun or guns, and my first impression was that we were being shelled by the Japs who had captured some of our guns, as bits and pieces appeared to be flying around us, and a number of 'whooshes' seemed to be going over our heads. I halted the Company for a minute to have a look-see around the next jungle-covered hillock and then I saw an unbelievable sight in front of me and behind some bushes: there was a Bofors Anti-Aircraft gun and three very sweaty British other ranks firing for all they were worth at the Japs on the hill across the road at point-blank range over open sights! That was a great relief, and what an incongruous sight it was to see these British Anti-aircraft gunners firing their gun with its barrel all but parallel to the ground.

Battalion HQ and those behind them, for some reason, had not followed by deviations through the shellfire. They moved over to the left under the lee of the hills. I had done my best to avoid this as there was a sharp battle going on there. By the time the mules had reached this point the enemy had this area well taped with mortar fire, and resulted in a few casualties in rear Battalion HQ and some of the mules had been hit and they and their loads became very scattered. I gathered that Frisby's 12 Platoon did sterling work carrying casualties and salvaging kit under fire. We arrived in the Admin Box area at a few minutes to 3.00pm. I personally was dead tired and terribly thirsty, and Frisby's Platoon looked completely exhausted when they arrived an hour or so later.

On passing that Bofors gun I realized we were in the Box, and so I laid the Company out, awaiting the CO's arrival to give us our final positions. The Company was all in position by 5.30pm on the most eastern spur north of the road. C Company were above us and to our right, D Company on the right, and A Company on their right again above Battalion HQ, the latter being on the inside of the box. From our position we had a grandstand view of the Japs on the hill opposite us, with the Sikhs clinging on to the spur. Our task was to guard the road and eastern approaches to the Admin Box. 10 Platoon's positions were on a bank about fifteen feet above the ground level of the Pass and with a sheer drop to the road. All guns were beautifully locked with a cross-fire capability.

During this withdrawal, I later learnt that eight men of the Battalion were wounded and Corporal Potter of the Carrier Platoon, which had been escorting the Battalion and Brigade soft vehicles, was killed. This exceptionally brave man was in the leading carrier when it ran into an ambush; Potter immediately jumped from his carrier and, seizing the Bren gun, charged the enemy post and killed all the Japanese in it, and in doing so he himself was killed. Lance Corporal Jordan of the Regimental Police was awarded the Military Medal for gallantry shown throughout the day.

The Company managed to get a quick supper and a mug of tea before stand-to. The company of the Punjabis of another brigade, whom we were relieving, moved out after their supper and very kindly gave my HQ and myself much of their chocolate ration. We were very grateful for this, and it was interesting that the Punjabis don't appear to have the same craving for chocolate as do the British.

The Japanese and our own troops across the road punctuated the night with machine-gun fire crackling every few minutes throughout that night of 26 March. As we expected an attack at any time the Battalion had a 50% stand-to throughout this seemingly longer night.

At 11.00am the next day a tank squadron of 25th Dragoons engaged the enemy with heavy fire on their positions barely fifty yards away on the feature opposite us. After the fifteen-minute barrage, the Punjabis attacked: it was a great success; all positions were taken and fifty-three dead were counted. My view from 11 Platoon's position was first class; the Punjabis were crouching barely fifteen yards from the crest of the hill which the tank 75 mm. guns were pounding.

It became evident that the Japanese had sent in a 400-strong suicide party to hold up the Division's successful advance southwards.

Tiny Taylor took 10 Platoon out in the morning to Schwechiang, some seven miles to the north of us. This was another possible route and assembly area for an attack on the north entrance of the Admin Box.

> Deacon and 11 Platoon go out on a fighting patrol to Laung Chaung at dusk this evening. Laung Chaung is the area where the old Divisional HQ was when the Japs overran it last February. It was thought that the enemy might adopt the same route to come into our rear again.
>
> After lunch today we heralded the return of one of our very precious soldiers, when the missing Private Downes suddenly arrived back in Company HQ. We were overjoyed to see him as we all thought that he had been badly wounded and possibly had been captured by the enemy.

He had been missing since Ian Frisby's very exciting 12 Platoon patrol confronted an enemy position three nights ago. In the exchange of fire, he had apparently jumped to cover in the darkness and fallen down a steep slope, missed the rest of the patrol and lain up in the position until the night of 24/25 and then made his way to the Punjabis of another brigade. The CO of that battalion had treated him royally and he had been fed in their Officers' Mess. Downes was quite dazed and overcome at being back and safe again, but he was very, very lucky. The Battalion mules delivered some wire, reserve ammunition and rations to the Company that morning.

A large draft of new soldiers arrived at midday; forty-nine of them came to B Company. Sergeant Major Hudson and I gave these new men a short talk, summarizing a few of our experiences in Arakan, and hopefully not making it sound too terrifying an introduction.

Most of the men arriving in the various drafts to reinforce us had not been in action, but there were a few who had recovered from sickness and their wounds and rejoined us, and others had been at Dunkirk. My batman, Private Kingshott, who came to us a year or so ago, had in fact been with 1/5 Queen's Territorial Battalion, from the Guildford area, and had been engaged in the fighting during their epic withdrawal through Dunkirk. And so both the CSM and I could never assume we were talking to untried men. Kingshott himself and two or three others of the Company had probably come under more shellfire and aerial machine-gunning than most of us.

A party of Japs came into the Box area and probed the Punjabi and our Company positions last night. They got no change out of us; they were merely a great nuisance that made sleep almost impossible as this Jap patrol fired at us for much of the night between 8.00pm and 4.00am this morning.

Tiny and 10 Platoon rejoined from their patrol this morning, 28 March, at 9.15am. The patrol had actually arrived back in the Battalion yesterday evening, but rather than alert too many in searching for us in the dark, and they were dead tired, they had supper and dossed down in our mule lines. Schwechiang was seven miles on the map, but they said that, with all the wandering around in the elephant grass, it's a good twelve miles there and another twelve back over the most shocking country.

About a mile from their objective they met a patrol of the Royal

Scots Fusiliers of 36 Division, who were on a similar mission from the top of the Mayu Range. After ten minutes of stalking each other (neither knew of the other's identity), what might have been an unfortunate incident ended in a cup of tea all round provided by the Jocks.

On their return the Mule Company provided blankets, tea all night, and cigarettes for them all. 10 Platoon appreciated this very much. There had grown up a marvellous spirit of camaraderie and respect between units of the Division; frequently our troops had been looked after by other units.

Ian Frisby went sick with dysentery and was evacuated on 30 March. He has done very well indeed with us. Excellent with men and first class on patrol, he had proved a born leader. His stern rebukes of matters not up to his standards were evinced with a boyish charm that went down well with his men who were mostly Cockneys, and who always responded brilliantly to his good leadership.

One of the lynchpins of a rifle company is its company sergeant major. Our CSM Hudson's time was up, having completed some seven years' soldiering in the Far East with the Battalion. He originally joined the Battalion as a member of the Band, and so he was also trained in First Aid and as a stretcher bearer. Then he came across to B Company on the North West Frontier at Razmak. He was an intelligent, thinking, very smart soldier, probably three or four years older than me, but whose wise counsel I admired. He was not a firebrand, which is sometimes a quality in sergeant majors. His easy manner and equanimity were going to be missed.

Some months before, I had made representations that one day I would like to have Sergeant Thatcher back in the Company as my CSM. And so it was that I was able to welcome him back to B Company as my Company Sergeant Major. He had always done consistently well as a platoon commander, a position normally held by an officer if one were available. He was tough and resourceful, had an ebullient personality and was very much respected by the men; he had never been a regular soldier but had had some years in the merchant navy. He was the only man I ever knew who could roll his own cigarettes with one hand; it was a masterly performance and the more so as he was probably tying a boot lace with the other hand. In a quiet moment or two he taught me to roll a cigarette with two hands, which I found more than a fistful!

> From today, 1 April, for the duration of our stay in the Box, there are four Battalion patrols day and night, which is organized so that each company finds one every day, and in addition perhaps another small reconnaissance patrol. And then I learnt from Dick, the Adjutant, over the phone at about 12.15pm, that all patrols will cease from 7.00am the next day. Another move was in the air. All sorts of rumours from the men in the Company: is it backwards, or forwards to finish off Massif?

We had understood that the Divisional Commander had decided to bypass the Massif, as our own troops were on all the hills around it and were effectively starving the enemy out. I later learnt that two other battalions had had a go to tackle Massif, but had found themselves in a similar position to my B Company's attempt. It was generally considered, and hoped, that we were going backwards and out of the Arakan!

We heard that Wet Valley had once again been cleared of Japanese. The situation concerning the Jap encirclement was becoming clear: they had been expelled from all features west of the Kalapanzin River with very heavy losses. This Jap encirclement was proving another military fiasco for them; the remnants of their last February effort had apparently been sent back again in the form of a punishment in a do-or-die attempt to hold up the Fourteenth Army advance down Arakan. There were now left only a few isolated pockets; the bulk of them, according to sit reps, are stagnating in the near foothills of the Kaladan Range.

Although it was certain that this mini-Japanese encirclement had now fizzled out, there was a general surmise, although we could never be certain, that there was a clutch of Japanese who had perhaps not got the message to pack it in, or maybe there was a suicide stay-behind party lying in wait to inflict the maximum casualties on us. Whatever was the situation, we knew by now that this enemy would fight to the death. He would always die rather than be captured and so we could not relax and assume that this party was over!

Colonel Graham held a conference at 5.00pm. The cat popped out of the bag with quite a thump when we were told that we were for Assam, although in the past few days Mervyn and I cogitated on the prospects of going up there to help IV Corps to evict the Japs, who had recently invaded Assam and threatened India from that front. The news of our being transferred from one front to another surprised the troops, but they were philosophical about it, and I rather thought that the idea was quite well received, as the constant patrolling in Arakan might possibly have induced an element of staleness. B Company had fewer officers than any other company, so from that evening we welcomed Lieutenant John Cato from D Company.

I managed to scribble off a letter dated 2 April 1944 to Ma and Pa, written in green ink. We may have been surrounded by everything green, but wherever did green ink come from? I enclosed three drawings done by Tiny Taylor, of a British soldier with a bloodstained bayonet and a bloodstained kukri-type broad knife with a decapitated Jap's head thrown at the soldier's feet. I noted that the man portrayed was wearing a beard; this was a trifle misleading, as the men of this Company were excellent at shaving, every day if possible; none of us actually had a beard. Until I re-read my letter, I had forgotten that in addition to the two pounds of chocolate I received each fortnight, on alternate weeks I received a two pound fruit and nut cake. Although that had been the idea, it never really worked out with such tidy regularity and, like many important decisions in war, the chocolate and cake diversion was overtaken by events. I never stopped them coming when we left the area, so presumably acres of cake and chocolate were gumming up the works somewhere.

One event that occurred at that time was recorded in a letter I wrote to my parents and which I remember very clearly, but it never found its way into my diary. This was when 12 Platoon were positioned in a nearby village when we were protecting the Admin Box. That Platoon was almost overwhelmed by several hundred refugees who had returned to their empty village. Just before Ian Frisby was evacuated he and some of his men took compassion and felt that they had better nurse the villagers and patch up some who had been wounded or had septic sores. Then, suddenly one afternoon, coming out of the village was a jeep with Corporal Sewell escorting two beautiful young Burmese women in the back who he was taking for treatment to our medical set-up. What was so lovely was to see Sewell and the women with marvellous grins across their faces. They all looked as if they had just swallowed the cream, or perhaps hoped that they were just about to! I should mention that Sewell was a very good looking young man of about twenty years. This was an uplifting sight for all of us who saw this attractive jeep-load pass by barely 20 yards in front of us.

I have mentioned how fortunate the Battalion was to be brigaded with the 4/15 Punjabs and the 4/1 Gurkhas in our 33rd Indian Infantry Brigade. Throughout our training for the best part of a year before arriving in Arakan in Burma, and then followed by some seven months or so of operations, we had learnt a great deal about each other. The Punjabis had a great record and a very proud tradition; their junior Non-Commissioned Officers had seven or eight years' service, and their Viceroy's Commissioned Officers (Indian Officers) and their Havildars, or Sergeants, would have had longer. They had of course been recruited from the Indian Punjab, and included a Sikh Company, and a Mussalman company whose men would have been recruited from what became Pakistan in 1947. Later in the Burma campaign two members of the Sikh Company of that Battalion were to earn Victoria Crosses. Then our Brigade was blessed by having the Gurkha Rifle Battalion included. These marvellous little men from Nepal had proved to be legendary fierce soldiers, whose impish sense of humour appealed naturally to the British soldier. That Gurkha Battalion gave the Japanese no quarter.

I have already referred to our Brigade Commander, Freddie Loftus-Tottenham, always known as Loftus. We were very fortunate to have him as our commander. He was well over six feet tall, with a fine athletic frame and a good strong-looking face, beetle-browed and with a proportionately large moustache. He had a lovely sense of humour and a packful of risqué stories; he really looked a tenacious and dashing commander. I had already met him on operations when he was commanding a battalion of Gurkhas back in Waziristan in 1941 and was so impressed to see a colonel, of all people, running up a craggy hill with his men! He had also experienced battle during the First World War.

Loftus was marvellous to watch giving out orders as we looked over his shoulder while he indicated with a circular motion of his thumb on a map where he wanted us to go; the exact position we would have to clear with his staff, as his thumb would have covered about a square mile. Whilst his orders were never in doubt, we would invariably refer to his forays on the map as Loftus's rule of thumb!

Chapter 10

The North East Frontier, Assam

Following the warning order that the Battalion would move to the Assam front, we were addressed by the Divisional Commander, General Frank Messervy, on the evening of 3 April, who thanked us for our hard and gallant work and wished us all the best wherever we might be required.

We marched out of the Admin Box at 7.00pm on our way across the Ngakyedauk Pass to the west of the Mayu Range and onto Wabyn, just north of the entrance to the Pass and arrived there at 10.40pm.

Tea had been previously organized by Colour-Sergeant Fraser and platoon representatives who had gone on in advance. I personally found the march through the Pass, now a mud road, rather tortuous and trying to the feet after of months of jungle movements.

The Battalion was out of close contact with the Japanese, so we could smoke at night, show lights and talk in normal voices during the long hours of darkness. On the following morning most of the men, including myself, managed a flounder, bathe and bath in the chaung's salt water. This was a marvellous pick-me-up for tired and dirty limbs. The bars of army issue soap worked overtime.

The Commander of XV Corps, General Philip Christison,

visited the Battalion at 3.00pm, inspected us and said some encouraging words to several individuals of the Company on his way round. In his short talk to the Battalion afterwards, he was most praiseworthy of our work.

On return to the Company area I gave a pep-talk and generally put the men in the larger picture as to what was the overall situation, which in outline was: The Japanese had invaded Assam some 400 miles to the north of us in Arakan. In consequence the very large supply depots and the railhead at Dimapur in the north were threatened. These were the lifelines for Kohima and Imphal, and the American General Stilwell's Chinese troops in northern Burma. In addition, the Brahmaputra valley, with its airfields and railway lines, would have opened up communications for the enemy and helped their progress into India.

Our 33 Indian Infantry Brigade was to move up to Assam to reinforce the garrisons, to be followed later by the rest of 7 Indian Division.

The Battalion left in motor transport at 5.00pm for Dohazari airstrip, where we arrived the next morning, 5 April at 0625am. I don't travel well at night and consequently I had no sleep.

On arrival at the camp I read out General Messervy's Special Order of the Day to the men. We then proceeded to sort all the kit into plane loads. This was a good camp. Everything was fairly well laid on and included a cinema and baths. I was very pleased to see Lieutenant Uttley again who rejoined us from sick leave that evening. I reposted him to 12 Platoon.

The following day the Battalion was ferried from the rest camp to the air landing ground. We spent a very pleasant and restful afternoon after arrival in our corner of the plantation, just off the airfield.

Before leaving Dohazari, my batman, Kingshott, had to go sick with malaria and was admitted to hospital. He had done extraordinarily well with me; he was a quiet man, and, being naturally tidy he was able to keep me tidy. He dug excellent slit trenches and worked marvels with bully beef and dried biscuits.

I never had to look for him as he shadowed me; he was always there. Fortunately he had a typical soldiers' sense of humour and his was a difficult act to follow. I replaced him with Private Sear from 11 Platoon.

Reveille on 7 April was at 5.00am and we had breakfast at the same time, as this invariably motivates the men to get a move on. The reason for telescoping the two together was because we were to emplane that morning. However, the airstrip was not an all-weather one and it was still raining at 6.15am, so the take-off time was put back and we were put at ten minutes' readiness to move. In the meantime the rain continued very heavily until 10.00am, making the ground too saturated for landing or take-off.

The drinking arrangements at this very temporary camp appeared to have been overlooked. I pitched into the Quarter-master about this and spoke the minds of the other company commanders. Paradoxically the water in the river gave all those who wanted one an excellent bathe in the late afternoon.

A first class impromptu concert was given to us by the Royal Air Force and some United States airmen. It relieved our minds as regards the important things that might or might not happen. I took my mind to bed at 11.00pm, but it was some time before I could get it into a neutral gear!

The following day we got up at 5.00am. The ground still not fit and it rained again during the morning. The conditions at Chittagong we learnt, were easier (tarmac runway) and so the Battalion left by train at 10.00pm from Dohazari for Chittagong where we arrived the next morning at about 2.45am and were then embussed in motor transport, reaching the airport at 4.15am.

We were all carrying our full equipment that included the two-pint water bottle, two days' rations, a mess tin, a knife, fork and spoon, a first field dressing for a wound and some clothing such as a pair of socks, canvas shoes, towel and soap, a house-wife (which sadly was not of the flesh, but is a small pack that includes a needle and thread to keep the clothing together), a jersey pullover, mosquito gloves and veil, washing and shaving kit, and a ground sheet. And then the important weapons: the riflemen carried 50 rounds, the Bren light machine guns each had 900 rounds in filled 30-round magazines which were distributed down the section of five or six men, and there were entrenching tools for digging slit trenches and latrines. All this would have weighed the best part of 50-60 pounds; some would be carrying more. The getting in and out of a variety of transports in the middle of the night, and everyone checking that he had his correct kit, was wearying in itself, but these occasions usually mean that a night's sleep was impossible, so all of us were very tired.

We slept in our dispersal areas until 6.00am, when a mobile canteen with tea arrived and revived us. The whole Company washed and shaved and the arms and ammunition were inspected by 8.00am. Vehicles were then loaded, each with a complete plane load, and those men on that particular plane travelled with that kit to the air landing ground. To save time, the aircraft took off as soon as a complete load arrived, and this often meant that sometimes a unit and part of another one was loaded onto an aircraft. In my Dakota we were all complete except for a jeep, but, as this was busy carrying kit, I agreed to take about 3,000 loaves of bread, which were loaded and neatly stacked up down the centre of the aircraft. Sergeant Major Thatcher and I could just see each other over the top of the pile; with a broad grin across his sunburnt face, he looked at the loaves and then at me. As well as the bread, we had cooking pots, tools, wireless sets, one pakhal of water (8 gallons), a stretcher, the CSM, two signallers, four stretcher bearers, Private Sear, my batman/orderly, and myself, that is to say nine very good men who made up the forward element of my Company HQ. Jim Cato had managed to collect his platoon load together before I did and consequently took his men off first. Our DC47 (Dakota) left the ground at 11.20am on 9 April.

A fairly bumpy flight followed, which entailed going through some heavy clouds. We flew at an average height of between

8,000 and 12,000 feet, so the pilot told us. Most of the journey was over very thickly covered hills of about 4,000 feet. The men were very tired and slept most of the way. I slept for the last hour and was woken by Sergeant Major Thatcher to find us circling over the airfield; we had no knowledge of where it was until we landed. The landing was excellent; in fact, we did not realize we were grounded until the plane slowed up at about 1.45pm, having covered some 420 miles.

Here we were at Dergaon, and there were Tiny Taylor, my Second-in-Command, and Godfrey Shaw of D Company and a few American ground staff in control of the air landing ground awaiting our arrival. Tiny and Godfrey had gone over in the first aircraft to organize our reception.

No time was wasted here. We were quickly whisked away in motor transport and after a forty-mile journey came upon our new camp at Hautley Tea Gardens Estate. B Company were given a nice, compact area, but before we could set up any bivouacs the virgin undergrowth had to be dealt a few sharp blows. By evening only two officers and forty-six men of the Company had arrived, the remainder arriving on 10 April.

We were now in Assam and about 60 miles from any known enemy, who were in the Kohima area. The XXXIII Corps Commander, Lieutenant General Montagu Stopford, briefed Colonel Duncombe on 11 April, and told him the following: The Japanese had by-passed Kohima and had reached milestone 32 on the Kohima-Dimapur road. One of the enemy's aims was to cut the railway that ran between Dimapur and Ledo. This was the only supply line to General Stilwell's forces and it was vital that the railway line remained open.

As a result of the latest information regarding the enemy, the CO's previous indications of our next role were overtaken at 4.00pm when we heard that the Battalion was to move to Dimapur first thing the next day, the 12th. This was some 40 miles from Kohima. Jim Cato, a tall, elegant and intelligent young man, went off that night to reconnoitre the Company area at Dimapur.

We were roused the next morning at 5.30am and left Hautley at 8.30am. It was a very hot and dusty journey, although I must say the road was better than we had struck for months. It was tarmac most of the way. The convoy was very slow, with many halts. We finally arrived at a camp which was adjacent to the Manipur Road railway station at Dimapur at 3.00pm, having averaged about 7mph.

The CO gave us our future roles that evening. We were to become a mobile column for the protection of the railway line between here and Golaghat to the north and Lumding to the south. For this role a special armoured train had been put together for us; under command of the Battalion was one Battery of a Mountain Regiment of 4 × 3.7 inch gun-howitzers, one section of Royal Engineers and one company of the Medical Field Ambulance. On the assumption that, once the Battalion Group deployed off the train to take on the enemy, it was probable that it would be operating across country through jungle-covered hills, this meant there was a requirement for a large number of mules. The total number of mules was of the order of eighty-four and this included sixteen for the Mountain Battery and five for each rifle company for its water and reserve ammunition. One can imagine that it was quite a sizeable armoured train as the mule load was fourteen trucks with six mules to a truck. In the meantime the whole Battalion was put up in the rest camp, which was strategically placed on the railway station.

As we arrived, one noticed colossal activity in this base area – preparing for a Japanese assault, the erection of barbed wire and bamboo panjis to help in its protection.

One gathered from the CO, who had seen the lines-of-communication commander and area commander, that a Jap attack on the base area itself, or an attempt at cutting the metre-gauge line, was imminent. There were many rumours of Jap reconnaissance patrols visiting villagers in the vicinity of Dimapur; we were to do a reconnaissance the next day.

And so we left on this special train soon after 6.00am on

13 April with the Battalion's Reconnaissance and Orders Group, consisting of all our company commanders, the Intelligence Officer, and the commanders of the Engineer and Artillery units, with 12 Platoon of B Company, commanded by Bill Uttley, as our escort. We stopped at all the little stations and any other spot that looked suitable for detraining a battalion. The reason for the reconnaissance was to try and forecast possible enemy objectives along the railway line where they might infiltrate and then set up defensive blocks, and, as a corollary, the possible places where the Battalion could detrain and deploy. We had visions of the line worming its way through defiles and overhanging trees, but fortunately it was not as bad as all that for 80 per cent of the journey. The jungle for the most part had been cut back for twenty or thirty yards, but even so that is quite close enough. The route to Lumling lay over a thousand and one little culverts and iron bridges; nine out of ten of these were unprotected.

These presented a problem. Initially there was nothing to prevent a few men of an enemy fighting patrol blowing one up, or even several, or perhaps the enemy might hold a vital bridge area in strength, covered from the jungle hills.

Arriving at Lumling, we were surprised to find that the Americans controlled that railway junction; but in time we understood that the American General Joe Stilwell and the Chinese were operating from Ledo station at the end of the line in the far north. We returned to Manipur Road Station, Dimapur, at 4.15pm. It had been an instructive but operationally quiet day, which really was just as well, as we had to switch our thinking and learn some new drills.

On 26 April the air-raid alarm sounded at 10.20am, the alert lasting for half an hour. We could hear the bombs explode some miles away.

I noted in my diary: 'My pencil has been idle for a number of days now. There has been nothing of importance to recount.' Each day had borne monotonous repetition, punctuated with unfounded rumours and unnecessary flaps. Some of the things done included plenty of football, basket-ball and tombolas for the men, plenty of saluting and foot drill, training, including battle drills, such as debussing from transport and from an imaginary train, short-notice practice turnouts, rehearsing counter-attacks in several of the defended boxes of the base area. Malarial parade and weapon inspections were carried out by platoon commanders at 6.30pm every night. In this period I received a magnificent parcel from Ma and Pa that contained a variety of useful things such as razor blades, toothpaste and writing materials, an excellent photograph of Pa and an obituary of Uncle Frank who had recently died of cancer. He had married Pa's older sister. He had become Director of Research of Boots Pure Drugs Company and I noticed that, among many academic awards, he became a Fellow of the Royal Society in 1922 at the early age of 40.

The route march scheduled for 27 April that morning was off, another flap for which there was no apparent foundation. The Battalion was on intensive wiring of all its defensive area and improvement of alarm posts (dug on first arrival). All platoon positions now linked up and a single apron fence (wire for this only arrived at the camp yesterday evening) was erected by the end of the day. The men worked like Trojans all day to complete the task in considerable heat.

The 10 Platoon basketball team, of which I was an honorary playing member, beat the Battalion's Animal Transport Platoon 3–2 so that we were then in the finals. These games were quite exhausting, although we were all very fit.

D Company, who had been stand-by company, were called out at 11.00pm that evening, and the other three rifle companies then stood-to. A few tanks and a cavalry regiment were also called out. The Japs were apparently on or near the road at Mile 18, so villagers had said, and the driver of an ambulance reported that he had been shot at.

D Company returned the next day at 5.00am. No Japs were seen and the road was clear. But information was firm and definite that the enemy had been in a village in the eighteen-mile area, and so we remained on our toes at one hour's notice to move. By then there were two trains always made up in the station with the engines standing by with steam up ready to take the column out in either direction immediately any Japanese were known to be in the area. However, the Japanese never did reach the railway line.

Our 10 Platoon won the final of the inter-platoon basket-ball competition against the Motor Transport Platoon on the afternoon of 4 May. It was a very tough and exhausting game. The tallest man in our team was Corporal Aukett who so often had possession. I would always feed the ball to him when possible. I was almost all in at half-time and by the end of the game, after five minutes' extra time, I was all in. A damn good prize was presented by the CO, consisting of a tin of fruit, milk, jam, cake of soap, bottle of squash and 100 cigarettes for each player.

As we were far from the battle area, we had been living a near normal life in Dimapur, although taking full protective precautions with sentries and patrols. This meant we had been operating Officers' and Sergeants' Messes for our feeding arrangements. Almost every night the fun and games in the Officers' Mess was initiated by the CO, Colonel Graham Duncombe, whose fund of stories hardly knew any bounds. His anecdotes were probably overtaken by the laughter caused by his monstrous sense of the ridiculous; his leg-pulling was sheer cabaret and never hurtful. We played the game of Ludo on many nights and he would give the various moves impossibly funny names, although I would add that it was wartime soldier's humour and not meant for any drawing room, even after 9 o'clock. But the result of all this were hilarious evenings which were instrumental in drawing us, as a team, closer together. Colonel Graham was a tall impressive man, with a large square face and jaw; his moustache was perfect for his large frame and always appeared to be immaculately groomed. He had the ability to reduce seemingly complicated problems to basic essentials. And when necessary he would ensure our Battalion got a fair deal. His qualities as a man and a commander had a great deal to do with the Battalion's high morale.

Of the thirty-five officers in early May 1944 only four, Colonel Duncombe, Major George Grimston, Captain Mervyn Mansel and myself, were regular army officers. The others were a marvellous mixed bag of bankers, stockbrokers, solicitors, men from the oil industry and commerce, accountants and an architect. Some had just completed adult education.

We held the usual morning parades, various operational battle drills and some map reading, and as a change I got our ex-sailor Sergeant Major Thatcher to give a talk on watermanship, knots and lashings. At some stage we were going to move up towards Kohima. It was put off twice and finally postponed until the morning of 6 May. This delay proved a great asset to us all, as the Battalion's own concert party, under the direction of Godfrey Shaw, was able to go ahead. Corporal Mollett of D Company was brilliant as a costermonger; his wit and his singing made him the undoubted star. Godfrey himself and John Scott, with his monocle, were quite superb taking off two colonels. The logo for the Lines of Communication for these parts included an elephant. Needless to say the two 'colonels' had to incorporate a dialogue that included 'the higher the formation the bigger the balls'! The whole show was exceptionally good and the more so bearing in mind that the players had only a week to get it together.

That evening was spent in the final packing of all kit that was not to go forward into battle. The hurricane lamps, as usual, presented difficulties. They had to be really emptied of oil and the glass protected by something. Private Sear stowed mine away with the Officer's Mess kit, probably, as I wrote in my diary, never to be seen again! I packed up the chess set myself and stowed it in a yakdam (a leather box that could be hung from one side of a mule), that was going to the Battalion dump in the morning. I was in bed by 8.30pm; my mind was preparing for Kohima.

Chapter 11

Kohima

The road from Dimapur starts from a height of about 500 feet and twists its way up the valley through jungle-covered hills for most of the way for 46 miles to the south-east, where lies, at some 5,000 feet, the saddle called Kohima Ridge that runs in a curve and is itself about two miles long. The town of Kohima had over time become a staging post between Dimapur and Imphal and had expanded to include army barracks, a re-inforcement camp and an Indian General Hospital. There are hillocks on the Ridge on which are some army buildings such as the Field Supply Depot (FSD), where there was a bakery, and Detail Issue Store (DIS). Then there was Jail Hill that was a little higher and commanded much of the valley. DIS, FSD and the hillock Kuki Piquet ran off to the north of Jail Hill towards Garrison Hill. Further north still were the Deputy Commissioner's Bungalow, Treasury Hill and Naga Village. To the south of Jail Hill and on the other side of the road to the west was General Purpose Transport (GPT) Ridge and a further mile to the south was Aradura Spur, also on the other side of the road.

While our Battalion was moving out of Arakan on its way to Dimapur the Japanese 31 Division had cut all the roads that led into the town of Kohima and that included the road running to Imphal about 80 miles to the south, which at this time was also under considerable pressure. Initially there was a small garrison in Kohima of about 3,000, consisting of the Assam Regiment,

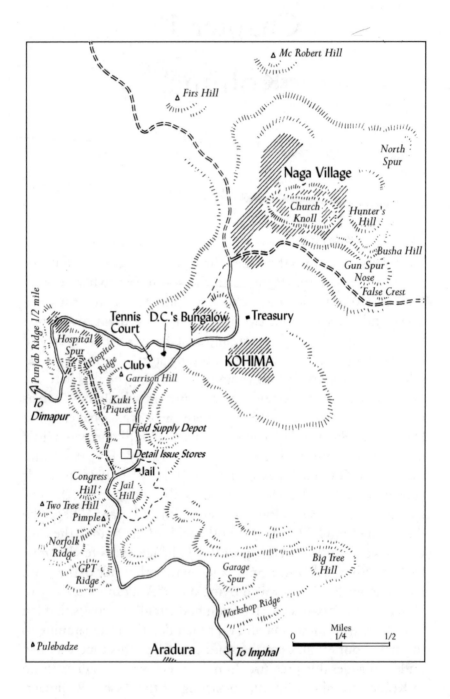

Mc Robert Hill

Firs Hill

Naga Village

North
Spur

Church
Knoll

Hunter's
Hill

Busha Hill

Gun Spur
Nose

False Crest

Tennis
Court

D.C.'s Bungalow

Treasury

Hospital
Spur

Punjab Ridge 1/2 mile

Hospital
Ridge

Club

KOHIMA

Garrison Hill

To
Dimapur

Kuki
Piquet

Field Supply Depot

Detail Issue Stores

Jail

Congress
Hill

Jail
Hill

Two Tree Hill

Pimple

Norfolk
Ridge

GPT
Ridge

Garage
Spur

Big Tree
Hill

Workshop Ridge

Miles

0   1/4   1/2

Pulebadze

Aradura

To Imphal

206

the Assam rifles, the local police force, a raw battalion of the Nepalese army and a battalion of the Burma Regiment, which was the only major fighting unit; there were detachments of some Indian regiments and the Indian Army Service corps; there was also a large number of hospital patients convalescing.

These units formed this scratch Kohima Garrison and were initially the only troops to confront the enemy; most of them had at first been deployed some few miles to the south-east in front of Kohima and consequently took the full blast of 15,000 Japanese troops of its 31 Division as it advanced from the south-east. General Slim reported later that the Assam Regiment, the local police and the Assam Rifles had put up a magnificent defence and the delay they imposed on the enemy was invaluable. By early April the Japanese were in possession of much of Kohima Ridge and, in particular, had captured Jail Hill from the Assam Regiment on 6 April; this Regiment put in an immediate counter-attack, but their attack was broken up. The loss of Jail Hill was to prove very costly as it dominated the DIS and FSD features.

161 Brigade of 5 Indian Division had been flown out of Arakan, left Dimapur by motor transport and moved on towards Kohima. On their way the Brigade successfully fought their way through two road blocks and its Brigadier established a defensive box with two of his battalions and two batteries of 3.7-inch howitzers (8 guns) across the Dimapur road at the road junction at Jotsoma, only two miles from Kohima. The other battalion from that Brigade was the 4th Battalion of the Royal West Kent Regiment, which moved on and joined up with the exhausted Kohima garrison that had had to withdraw into a contracting perimeter as it gallantly endeavoured to halt the daily and nightly Japanese attacks. The enemy assaults were invariably supported by devastatingly accurate mortar and artillery fire.

The Royal West Kents took up positions on FSD and Kuki Piquet and were just able to stretch themselves to complete the perimeter defence on what came to be known as Garrison Hill. Within hours that Battalion successfully attacked the Japanese who had got into some buildings on DIS Ridge. Then, soon afterwards, their D Company came under fire from a further bunker on DIS Ridge. While the company commander was making his plan to attack this position, he saw Lance Corporal Harman run forward towards the bunker. He got under the trajectory of the enemy machine gun, took a four-second grenade from his belt, let the lever go, could be heard to count "One, two, three" and dropped it through the bunker aperture where it exploded almost instantaneously. He then jumped on top of the bunker, went inside and reappeared with the machine gun. The company commander found that he had killed both the enemy soldiers.

The West Kents had to withstand counter-attacks every night; then one night the Japanese got into one of their forward trenches on the southern slopes of DIS. The next day this incredibly brave man, Corporal Harman, asked his mates to give him covering fire and charged down the slope with fixed bayonet. He shot one or two Japs, bayoneted another and the rest fled. As he was returning back up the hill, the enemy opened fire from Jail Hill and he was mortally wounded. He died in his company commander's arms, his last words being, "It was worth it." For Corporal Harman's outstanding courage he was posthumously awarded the Victoria Cross.

At about this time the Japanese captured GPT Ridge and mounted a 75mm gun, which could shoot up the valley and into the features on Kohima Ridge. Whoever was in possession of GPT Ridge also controlled the water supply, so the Japanese cut it off. Orders were issued to restrict all men in the Garrison to one pint a day, which was mostly collected in water bottles and chagals (canvas water containers) from a stream or a spring; this was a slow and laborious process that could only be done by creeping out at night to avoid snipers.

The weight of the successive waves of Japanese attacks forced the Garrison to contract still further. As the situation deteriorated the Garrison had to give up DIS and Kuki Piquet on the night of 17–18 April. In the meantime the British 2 Division was moving up from Dimapur; as it got nearer to Kohima, it had to fight its way forward and capture enemy road blocks. It finally made contact with 161 Brigade on 15 April.

As General Slim wrote in his book *Defeat into Victory*, 'Sieges have been longer but few have been more intense, and in none have the defenders deserved greater honour.' The Garrison had suffered 600 casualties and there were many sick. The privations they suffered were horrendous; short of water and food, and a supply of ammunition that had to be carefully conserved, they were forced to live among the dead of British, Indian and Japanese that littered the many acres of ground that had been contested for about three weeks. There were positions where no new trenches, including latrines, could be dug. Many of the fly-blown corpses had to lie where they were, the smell becoming worse as their black swellings grew and then decayed.

Although Garrison Hill and its defenders had been relieved, the centre of the town and, more importantly, most of Kohima Ridge was still held in strength by the Japanese. It was an immensely strong and natural defensive position, with a succession of steep jungle-covered hills. Quoting General Slim again: 'Wooded ridges had been improved by the Japanese genius for inter-supporting field works and concealment, until it was as formidable a position as a British army has ever faced'.

The relieving troops were hard-pressed from the moment of their arrival and became engaged in hand-to-hand fighting as they attacked and were counter-attacked, particularly around the DC's Bungalow and the Tennis Court. On 4 May the 2 Division's plan was to put in attacks on Kuki Piquet, FSD and DIS, but it only managed to cling to their positions on FSD. Because of the Japanese tenacity and machine-gun cross fire from Kuki, DIS and Jail Hill, the troops had to be withdrawn from FSD. It became clear to the Corps Commander, Lieutenant General Montagu Stopford, that the Division's progress was too slow and that the pressure against the Japanese must be maintained so our 33rd Indian Infantry Brigade, commanded by Brigadier Loftus-Tottenham, was called forward.

The Battalion left Dimapur for Kohima by Motor Transport at 6.30am on 6 May. It was a drenching wet day, doubtless the prelude to the full monsoon orchestra which gradually develops into a crescendo towards the end of May in Assam. At about Mile 28 there was a sign saying that we were in view of the enemy, and from there on the convoy had to keep well dispersed. As we neared Kohima, from Mile 36 onwards, we received many different orders about debussing, marching and carrying kit, undoing blanket rolls and carrying them ourselves. I received three orders in as many minutes, so I told the Company to do nothing until I found out. I commandeered the Assistant Provost Marshal's jeep and went on ahead to see the CO. But I drew a blank, as he had gone up well ahead; after some quarter of an hour's searching I met the Brigadier and asked him. He was naturally rather upset that there should be so many different orders. However, he gave me the debussing point, which was the most important piece of news, as the last thing I wanted to do was to motor the Battalion into battle. On returning to the Battalion, we drove off immediately, reaching the debussing point at Mile 42, where the road junction was known as Lancaster Gate, and debussed very quickly in the pouring rain. But there was now a greater urgency to our movements. It was here that we had first heard the screech and thunder of battle around Kohima about a mile away.

We had a long and tortuous climb in heavy monsoon rain for a mile or so, moving slowly towards the battle front as we struggled to get a foothold in the sloshing mud, carrying full arms and equipment, with two days' food in our packs, our own blanket rolls and monsoon capes. At last there came a very much wanted rest at about 2.00pm, when Mervyn(A Coy) and I chatted about what the future might hold for us. We had by now gathered that we were going to attack somewhere along the Ridge the next morning.

When we arrived, Tiny Taylor, who had gone on ahead, put the Company into its position while I and the other company commanders went off to attend the CO's reconnaissance and orders. We went forward to a vantage point. The Battalion was to attack two features at 10.30am next morning, May 7. The objectives were 'Pimple' – C Company and 'Jail Hill' – D Company, followed by A Company, with my B Company in reserve.

From this vantage point, some four hundred yards to the north of GPT Ridge, we could see the area of the Japanese positions about a thousand yards away; it was evident that Jail Hill was the largest feature and fairly central to the Japanese defence as it lay near the middle of the banana-shaped curve of Kohima Ridge. Jail Hill was flanked by DIS and FSD on the left, and GPT Ridge down and across the road on the right. At the time of this reconnaissance those features were in enemy hands and all of them had commanding positions overlooking the Dimapur-Kohima-Imphal road. The Colonel's plan was dependent on GPT Ridge and DIS being cleared of the enemy by 9.00am, so that our own H hour to attack would be 10.30.

As we peered through the rain, the low clouds and smoke from the artillery and mortars, we were looking at what appeared to be a dozen different battles going on in front of us. There were the sustained noises of belting machine-gun fire, the cracks and zips of sniper bullets, punctuated by the shrieks and crumps of artillery and mortar fire. At this stage we did not know whose firing was the heavier, or from where. We were in jungle country, our hills and slopes were mostly at about 5,000 feet, stretching up towards 8,000 feet and higher in the far distance. But, looking towards the battle horizon, the fierce exchanges over the last three or four weeks had shaved off much of the foliage, leaving a million shattered tree stumps. It was paradoxical that, as we carried out this reconnaissance in the heavy rain, we saw that some units were receiving air drops of water. We did not know it then, but those units were so pinned down that they could not get the trickle of drinking water that reached that area as the Japanese had cut the pipeline that went through GPT Ridge which they occupied. It continued raining all night and few of us got much sleep.

After standing down the next morning, the CO saw all company commanders at 6.00am at his Command Post, where we all once more acquainted ourselves with the features to be attacked and the surrounding country, although it was difficult to see much through the pouring rain that alternated with the mist.

The Battalion left its present area at 9.30am and filed along the track in the order C, D, A, Battalion HQ, and then my B Company, although I was moving with the CO's Tactical HQ immediately behind C Company. At about 10.00am we learnt that the attack was put off until 11.30am. From the noise of battle going on over to the right we conjectured that 2 Division had not succeeded in clearing GPT ridge. This unhealthy news was later confirmed.

At 11.30, after a twenty-minute bombardment, C Company moved towards Pimple followed closely by D Company, which passed by them on their left. As D Company passed through, the artillery and mortars lifted on to Jail Hill. Just previous to the bombardment on Jail we noticed from our present command post a smokescreen put down by the Japs immediately in front of the crest of Jail Hill. When C Company confirmed that they had captured Pimple without opposition, the rest of the Battalion closed up on them. A Company was dispatched some ten minutes after D Company moved. Battalion HQ moved to the area of Pimple and Tactical HQ went towards the crest of the Pimple feature. Having gained their objective unopposed, C Company were very soon subjected to very heavy firing from the GPT ridge. When we arrived, John Smyth broke the news to us that Major George Rothery, C Company Commander, had been wounded in the head. A minute or so later we were able to see that a bullet had shaved his forehead from his left eyebrow to his hairline. Another fraction of an inch deeper and he would have been killed. George remained commanding his company for another three days, when the CO gave him a direct order to leave the battlefield. He was awarded a well-earned Military Cross.

Very shortly after John Smyth himself was killed while taking on some enemy who were causing casualties to the company. This was a tragedy; he was very young and had proved a gallant leader in the Arakan during the Admin Box days; he was a very talented, intelligent and good-looking man with a warm smile. In the Arakan he used to rally his men with his hunting horn, which he carried tucked into his shirt right up to the time of his death.[1]

I learnt later that day of the gallant effort his batman, Private Collyer, made trying to drag John up the slope away from the enemy after he had been hit; he did manage to retrieve the hunting horn.

By 11.40am our artillery concentrations on Jail Hill had lifted and D Company had begun their climb up the spur just this side of the road. As the haze and smoke of the bombardment lifted they soon came under very heavy cross-fire from DIS and FSD on their left and from their right by machine guns firing straight down the road, probably from positions on GPT. Through my field-glasses I could see D Company moving with determination, but I could also see what a terrible time they were having as men were hit and dropped to the ground; they were getting casualties before they crossed the road. Then they moved up the hill itself, one platoon to the right and one up the left. Over the wireless set the CO gave the OK to A Company to go.

While this battle was going on for Jail Hill, things were happening around us at Tactical HQ. Pimple and the small track and area around us were being shelled and very heavily sniped by machine guns and rifles. We had previously thought ourselves defiladed, but, after our shelling on Jail Hill had lifted, this impression was soon dispelled as enemy bullets whipped into the bashas (bamboo huts) and on to the small tracks on our hill, knocking some of our men down as they scrambled up the bank for further cover. Battalion HQ moved back some 150 yards to behind the next hillock. It was better here, but any movement brought with it an instant response from a Japanese machine gun. The CO decided on this area as the best of many unhealthy spots. Movement along the track which came out on to the main road was suicidal; the Japs appeared to have a perfect line on the bends of the track as it rounded two small spurs. But, as was invariably the case on arriving in a new area, when we were being fired on we never really knew from where the enemy bullets were actually coming. The Japanese were masters at camouflaging their bunkers and slit trenches and building protective covering over them, which gave them considerable immunity from our artillery and mortar fire, and when that ceased they bobbed up again to harass us with small-arms fire, a fact we had long learnt from our operations in Arakan.

An hour or so later, at about 1.30pm, it was becoming clear that D and A Companies were having a very rough time. A Company was pinned down about a quarter of the way up the slope. Casualties were mounting. This I knew, as I could actually see their progress being interrupted as men got knocked over; I had already dispatched about twenty men to help D Company retrieve its casualties. D Company asked for more men and stretchers and some smoke to cover their evacuation. During this period, I had been with the CO in his Tactical HQ in the area of Congress Hill and was therefore at hand to take immediate action on any orders for me. At this time he was probably agonizing as to whether he would send my B Company out to Jail Hill, and I inwardly agonized as to whether I and my Company were going to be thrown into this cauldron. The air seemed to be scorching hot from the heavy firing of their shells and our shells and the mortaring. It appeared to come from all around us, followed by the crumps as they landed; and from in front of us and from all sides there was the staccato noise of small-arms fire, all of which was orchestrating the thunderous battle noises, which were not confined to Jail Hill, but the whole length of this mile-long battle of Kohima Ridge, which was about half a mile in front of us.

This was one of those occasions when fear could hijack normal thought processes. Those in command on a battlefield, from colonels down to lance-corporals, have tremendous responsibilities for the safety and well-being of their men. They make plans and have to undertake many mental and physical actions to put the plans into effect, and consequently their minds are fully occupied. Even so, all men can be afflicted by fear: it is a characteristic of battle. But the private soldier only has responsibility to his mates as part of a team, and his mind will not always be filled with the 'how', but could be filled with 'when' and 'what if'. The mind of the private soldier in the midst of horrendous battle noises can so easily be overtaken by fear. I have seen apprehension in faces, but I have not been aware of abject fear being expressed. No doubt this is largely due to his mental strength propped up by his morale, his personal discipline that goes to make up the collective discipline, and confidence in his leaders. One can only guess at some of the horrors of the future that may all but overwhelm him and me, and the more so if there is a hint of any fear in the face or voice of his leaders. Soldiers will look across to their commanders for a sign of assurance that sustains their morale against the unknown. In spite of our inward fears we draw strength and reassurance from each other.

Colonel Duncombe came to the decision that he would not deploy B Company to Jail Hill as we were all he had left, and some of the Company were already committed to bringing back casualties. At 2.00pm Major Godfrey Shaw, commanding D Company, spoke to the CO on his 48 wireless set and reported that his right-hand platoon had been held up near the bottom of the hill and that he and the other two platoons had reached the top on the left, but he had only fourteen men who were not wounded with him. The whole hill was being swept by crossfire from enemy machine-gun posts on DIS and GPT Ridge. He also said that Major Mervyn Mansel's A Company were getting casualties as they tried to follow up. Colonel Duncombe then decided to utilize the whole of my Company on rescuing the casualties from and around Jail Hill, as he concluded that Jail Hill would remain untenable unless DIS and GPT were neutralized. Therefore, without consulting higher authority, he gave the order to D and A Companies to withdraw. This order was later confirmed by Brigadier Loftus-Tottenham who had come forward to see for himself. At some time tank support had been considered, but now they could not be used because the road blocks were still in Japanese hands.

Getting in the casualties was a ghastly job; most of the routes there and back were under rifle, machine-gun and enemy artillery fire. The Regimental Aid Post which received our casualties and the Advanced Dressing Station near Brigade HQ had moved further forward to help; our own doctor, Jack Sumner, and his men were doing Heruclean work. The B Company men were no less magnificent; some of them made four or five journeys to the slopes of Jail Hill and back through this hell. It was an uncanny sight seeing the hillside and the road just below Jail Hill, where we were having to cross and recross, being cut up by the unseen streams of bullets as they seared into the ground. During all this time there were battles on the hill features on our left and right, which other troops of 2 Division had not captured, but were still engaging the enemy. Adding to the cacophony of the small-arms fire were the relentless and continuing shrieks and crumps of artillery and mortar bombs, theirs and ours, but we had not any idea from which direction it came. Those B Company men were not only moving around on the muddy slopes and tracks, they were also carrying or supporting badly wounded men, some on stretchers.

Now that the whole of the fighting element of my Company of some seventy men were committed to this rescue, sub-units of three, four and five men being directed by their platoon and section commanders to the units of D Company, I was left with nothing to do. That was ghastly. I could not stay and watch, and so, taking my signaller and his 48 wireless set, I went off to the track junction just below Jail Hill. I can't believe that I did any good except it did me a lot of good to be with them, and perhaps my presence might have helped them while the continuous streams of lead came from all directions and miraculously passed us by.

After D and A Companies had passed through me on their withdrawal, I remained behind with 11 Platoon to see that C Company were all right, in case they suffered casualties in their withdrawal. As all these soldiers passed me, I saw among many of the wounded soldiers Tony Hobrow, Annett and Kirby, all officers and Platoon commanders of D Company. Even Battalion HQ had suffered a dozen casualties. I saw many men walking or on stretchers. Among them were some I feared were not going to make it as they were grey-green or ashen-faced through loss of blood. Many had been hit in the face and had not yet been properly patched up. Having withdrawn from all its hard-won objectives, the Battalion was back in its original harbour area by 5.00pm.

The Battalion had had a bad day. They had to give up the objectives they had won, they were exhausted, thirsty and very tired, and then, as they settled down to rest and sleep, a fair-sized battle was developing above our Company position. The overs came our way, including much tracer. With this noise, and lying in the rain, sleeping was hardly on the agenda. In spite of the awfulness of this day, the demeanour of the men was magnificent. Nothing seems to get them down. How could one thank them for making life so much easier for me? I was fortunate.

The day after that battle, which Arthur Swinson calls 'The Black 7th' in his book *Kohima*, the CO went round to all companies in turn today and gave us a short talk on the previous day's battle; he visited us at 3.00pm. He impressed on us that the battle was by no means a failure and that he himself had taken the law into his own hands and ordered the withdrawal. The situation was such that it would have been a mere waste of manpower to remain in the position with our flanks unprotected. Actually, he said, it was a glorious effort on the part of the Battalion; it had captured its objectives in the face of untold difficulties. Major General Grover, commanding 2 Division – we had been under his command for this attack – had told the CO that it was the most gallant and determined effort he had ever seen. Although we never went into the assault, B Company had ploughed gallantly backwards and forwards under intense fire while evacuating casualties, with the result that every man of the Battalion had been accounted for.

We heard on 8 May that 33 Brigade would soon revert back to 7 Indian Division, as General Messervy and his Divisional Headquarters had arrived up from the Arakan.

This was a great boost to our morale. Somehow we, in our Brigade, instinctively knew that, with our eight months' operational experience in Burma, our knowledge of the Japanese and close-quarter fighting was superior to other units in Assam, and this thought we openly expressed among ourselves.

The night of 8 May brought further Japanese patrols infiltrating above us between the Assam Rifles and a company of the Gurkhas. A fairly heavy exchange of shots began at 4.00pm. and continued throughout the night. The Company collected much of the overs, but none of us were hit and I doubted whether we would have noticed if we had been; we were almost too tired to register. I felt that I could sleep on indefinitely. I did have a good night's sleep and a restful day on 9 May when we had more sun than usual. By that evening the Company had completed the erection of barbed wire around our positions. On the slopes of this hill most of the trees were tall and that enabled the sun to filter through the canopy from time to time and gave us an opportunity to wash and dry our dirty, muddy, sweaty clothes.

The CO gave us a warning order before lunch for the Battalion to attack Jail Hill again on 11 May, combined with an assault by the Punjabis (of our 33 Brigade) on DIS ridge. At that time the Royal Berkshires were still fighting the Japs who were entrenched on the top and reverse slope of FSD, and the Royal Norfolks were still engaging the enemy who tenaciously hung on to bunkers on GPT. These positions would also be attacked on the morning of the 11th.

On 10 May the Colonel held an Orders Group at 11.00am. Before giving the orders, he stressed that our attack was part of a Divisional operation which affected future planning and that, naturally, a hitch by any unit taking part might affect other units, if not the whole plan. It was most important, he said, that every man should know this. A confirmation of the verbal orders followed.

After reconnaissance of our objectives, about 1000 map-yards from our objective, I realized that, up and down, it was going to be much more. The following was briefly my plan:

11 Platoon forward right, myself and Tactical HQ with radio and signaller, runner and batman in centre (to include F.O.O. and party some twenty yards in rear), and 10 Platoon up on left, 12 Platoon in the centre some forty yards in rear. The two forward Platoons to move in extended line with two sections up; extended line was possible as Jail Hill had been stripped of all foliage, only tree stumps remained. On nearing the crest 11 Platoon was to go straight over and take on the bunkers on the crest of the hill, and those beyond, as far as it could. 10 Platoon was to move off to the left just before the crest and swoop down from the high ground on to the Jail spur and deal with any enemy bunkers in the jail building area. 12 Platoon would be held in readiness and would be most likely to be used on the right to deal with any further bunkers on the reverse slope while 11 Platoon contained the enemy; 11 Platoon would also, of course, keep the enemy occupied and protect 10 Platoon's flank while they moved over and down to the left.

After giving out orders I went over to the Punjabis and liaised with their right-hand company commander, Major Johnson.[2] After this, I was invited in to the Punjab Officers' Mess for tea. Later, Brigadier Loftus-Tottenham joined us. All were in very good form and wished me the best of luck, as also did I when I left. I got back as far as the casualty Advanced Dressing Station, where I met Tiny, my Second-in-Command, and he broke some dreadful news to me. The Company had been shelled during my absence and 12 Platoon had suffered eleven casualties, which included Ian Frisby, who was very seriously wounded, as they were having their orders for the next day's battle! I visited all the wounded in the A.D.S.; Ian[3] was in a very poor way and was being given plasma. Fortunately only three of the eleven were killed, but the disaster left us very short of commanders in that Platoon. I got back to the Company at 4.30pm.

The Forward Observation Officer from the Royal Artillery and the Indian Engineer party arrived at about 5.30pm. I was determined to snatch some sleep whenever I could, although I knew that I was unlike many soldiers. I could never take odd cat-naps. Fortunately that day was to be an exception. I took some rest between 4.30 and 7.30pm and fell asleep for at least an hour. I was surprised to find that this hour really did make me feel so much fresher. The Company had supper on standing down at 7.30pm, which was as late as possible. Colour Sergeant Fraser produced another brew of tea for the Company at 9.30pm. At 10.00pm we received the order to move at 10.15.

This single-file night approach march was, in my opinion, very difficult and altogether rather nerve-racking, something I shall never forget, maybe one of the most hair-raising things I had done. We were moving in the order B, C, D and A Companies, followed by Battalion Headquarters. My Company being in the lead meant that I had to navigate the column; in fact I had to lead it, as I daren't put anyone in front of me. There could be no talking. It just had to be my decision to choose which side of a bush, tree or basha we would move to keep on our correct bearing. There were no defined tracks, thick undergrowth, down hundreds of feet, round spurs and up hundreds of feet and across re-entrants, gently hacking, pushing, stumbling, and through ruined bashas. It was a navigator's nightmare. Although I had never had one before, I assumed that this was the nightmare!

We halted many times but I dare not allow anyone to sit down as someone would probably doze off and snore and produce other unjungle noises. From time to time a halt was necessary for me in particular to listen, hopefully to hear nothing, and then to move on very slowly. I had a number of thoughts swirling through my head during this four-hour approach march: had the Japanese been alerted by this army of over 300 fully armed men moving towards them? Surely they must have some reconnaissance or warning patrol in front or on the flanks of Jail Hill, or anyhow something near the road which we would eventually have to cross, and so alert their defence? Our progress was surprisingly quiet; then there was my concern: was everyone actually following me?

> We eventually got to what I thought was the forming-up place at about 3.15am on 11 May. I should mention that only the general direction had been reconnoitred in daylight; it would have been impossible to reconnoitre the route itself or the location of the FUP, because of close enemy observation. Having got there, I laid the Company out into the assaulting formation, and then went on to do a very solo, personal reconnaissance to the main road while it was still dark to check on our position. We were absolutely in the correct position. I recognized some tyres on the side of the road which I had seen through my field-glasses yesterday.

I never noticed the weight of my pack during this approach march, but I did notice the great weight off my shoulders on discovering that we had reached the forming-up place exactly where we should be.

During the early hours of that morning our guns and mortars were harassing the enemy on the three features, and this served as another check that we were in the correct position. Waiting here was cold, but every man who wanted could take a mouthful of the rum that each platoon passed round.

At 4.40am it was still dark, and then suddenly the silence was broken: whistle, shriek, screech, and everything came down on the hill in front and above us with a thunderous crash and clatter: machine guns, anti-tank guns, artillery and mortars, a most impressive noise and the earth shook and trembled. The slopes to the left, above and to our right were silhouetted by the explosions in the darkness. We had one or two shorts from something which landed in the Company area, but no one was hurt. The enemy could not have known that this great army of men was assembled some 300 yards away, as we never had any interference from them. The expected enemy artillery defensive fire never came and no Japanese patrols interfered with us or gave us away.

> Exactly on 5.00am we edged forward; as we did so I went over to each platoon and wished them the best of luck, and then the artillery ceased, only machine-gunfire on flanks and some smoke shells bursting on and around the feature, otherwise quiet. By this time there were the first signs of daylight, the inky blackness was giving way to a grey haze. Up the spur and across the main road on to the enemy-held feature itself. The enemy put nothing down to stop us until about three-quarters of the way from the top, and then it started. Our speed and formation up the hill was grand and the chaps in terrific form.

There was no jungle vegetation, only shattered tree stumps, and so I could see almost every man on my right and left; the fact that we had left our packs in the forming-up place gave us a greater freedom of movement and enabled the men to move up about 300 feet of hill at a relatively cracking pace.

As we all but got on top of a Jap bunker on the left, just this side of the crest, the Japanese beat it and ran back and down the hill to the Jail area; 10 Platoon caught these as they came up on to the top and were about to swing round towards the Jail. Their left-hand leading section caught about eight or ten Japs running down and they gave them everything. Private Day just stood up and sprayed them with bullets from his Bren gun and the section surged on, firing on the move. But the Platoon was not doing this without receiving a number of casualties; they were being heavily fired on from bunkers lower down the reverse slope and from the left, from where the enemy's interlocking fire had been covering the Jap bunkers from which they had just been ousted. We were also getting a great deal of interference from the right in the area of 11 Platoon, who were now up against enemy cross-fire from many and unknown directions. We reached the crest of the hill inside of ten minutes.

During that first thirty or forty minutes the Company had

taken one bunker and driven the Japs out of another small one into the arms of 10 Platoon, but movement forward was a very hard and costly business. 11 Platoon had been hard hit. They had lost their platoon commander and sergeant and three other NCOs. Seeing their predicament, I told them to remain where they were, to hold and contain the enemy, and, when possible, to ease forward so as to improve their position merely by a few yards of crawling. I called up 12 Platoon, which was now being commanded by Tiny Taylor, who had taken over from the wounded Ian Frisby. I had also given them another NCO from 11 Platoon after the previous day's shelling tragedy. I put 12 Platoon round the left of 11 Platoon to encircle round to the right, hoping to drive the enemy across our front towards C Company on our right, and so also to bring fire to bear on the enemy's flank and right rear. As far as I could see there were, anyhow, three bunkers directly barring our way, and there were others firing up the hill from about 100 yards' distance. Before committing 12 Platoon I had another shot with 11 Platoon and, under cover of grenades and a Bren gun, I took about six men forward so that we were only eight or ten yards away from about two of their bunkers. This gave us a better position, as it meant we were well forward of the crest of the hill and looked down on the Japs themselves. Around this section I built up the rest of 11 Platoon, now commanded by a Lance Corporal, he being the senior man left in the Platoon.

Tiny's 12 Platoon did not get very far before they had a number of casualties. They tried worming forward, found themselves almost on top of an enemy bunker, threw some grenades and inflicted a number of casualties on the Japanese and then got into their trench, but the majority of those who scrambled into the trench became casualties from a machine gun on their right, and then almost immediately Tiny Taylor was wounded in the legs near the crutch, and in the arms by a grenade, and could not move. Corporal Goodswen, who was one of the NCOS in 12 Platoon wounded in the leg and arm during the previous day's shelling but would not be evacuated at that time, was seriously wounded again. I gave the men the order to withdraw from this bunker, which was merely a death trap, and take up a position overlooking another Jap position some fifteen yards away.

The general situation for B Company at about 8.30am was that 10 Platoon on the left were still down the hill in the Jail area. I couldn't see them but I could see their 2-inch mortar pair and the section Jim Cato had left on the top of the hill that had covered them down and which was also doing flank protection for us. The other two platoons had one NCO between them and about 50 per cent casualties each, so I thought it prudent to hold what ground we had with 11 and 12 Platoons and reorganize them as far as possible into one platoon. The ground we were now on was decidedly in our favour; we had all the high ground and overlooked the Japs. C Company, the other forward company on our right, had met with a similar situation and were held up by interlocking fire, but they were not quite on the crest. By this time daylight was fully established and the sun had been out for most of the time.

And then, before long, other horrors had become evident. We began to realize that our position was made worse by the fact that enemy bunkers still existed on GPT ridge across the road on our right. The enemy took advantage of the clear visibility and were firing down the road and into the rear of our positions, and it became evident that the Japanese positions on DIS on our left were also still very active, although the Punjabs were on that ridge. Cross-fire from these long-range undetected machine guns and snipers were taking a steady toll. Movement on top or any-where on the flanks, and even down to our rear, was becoming increasingly costly. In effect the enemy could bring down fire on us from all quarters.

Evacuation of casualties and getting up ammunition was, to say the least, very sticky. I went back to Company HQ and got on the wireless to the CO and put him in the picture, and then saw Godfrey Shaw, commanding D Company, who was following up in rear of me. As Godfrey and I were speaking, a burst of machine-gun fire coming from our rear, maybe from DIS, hit the ground around us, from where we moved quicker than any wing forward. However, it came about that Godfrey had only one platoon at his disposal, as the others were being used to hold and cover the main road below us. This platoon he gave to me to be under my command. I intended to get in touch with 10 Platoon and relieve them by putting this platoon of D Company's into the Jail area and so add 10 Platoon to the combined 11 and 12 Platoons.

I moved across to have a word with Pen Ingham, who was commanding the left-hand platoon of C Company and who was immediately on the right of my 11 Platoon. We arranged between us to try and put out the post that lay in between and 20 yards in front of B and C Companies. His platoon was now very short of men. He took about six of them and I got hold of about six men of 11 and 12 Platoons.

Before all those troop movements took place I had arranged for smoke to be put down on the flanks of Jail Hill to screen the Japanese from our activities. This had to be done through our Battalion headquarters, as my Forward Observation Gunnery Officer, from our supporting Royal Artillery Regiment, was now no longer in operation, as his runner and operator had been killed and the wireless set knocked out. This was the greatest tragedy, not only to lose precious lives, but to think, as I did after the battle, that these highly trained and gifted men had come all this way with their equipment and were struck down before they had had a chance to use it to support this attack.

This local attack on to this position was an assault in line under covering fire from our Bren light machine guns. Pen and I started the ball rolling by whistling over some grenades, and then we all ran forward. But the terrain was not easy, there being many shellholes, horizontal tree stumps and the odd trench to negotiate. As we were going down the slope we caught the full blast of about three light machine guns and rifle fire and, of course, grenades as we tried to negotiate the obstacles. This, I am afraid, resulted in more men dropping; we were pinned down about ten to fifteen yards away and there appeared to be only six or seven of us there. I halted the assault and we took up positions in the broken ground and just took on the Japs by firing at any that showed themselves. Company Sergeant Major Buchanan, of C Company, was just on my right, not a yard away, hugging the ground as we all were. I had seen a Jap aim his rifle and fire. Half a second later I fired and killed him with my rifle, which I preferred to carry rather than a Tommy gun; then I turned my head to the right and saw that the Sergeant Major's head had rolled over. He had been shot through the head, as I saw the blood pouring out from his temple. What a chap he was, always full of good humour and fun, and I am sure he should not have been up where he was, but, as in B Company, C Company were using any ranks to make up numbers.

After this there followed a sniping duel, and then things happened the like of which I had never seen before. It was the nearest approach to a snowball fight that could be imagined. The air became thick with grenades, both theirs and ours. We were all scurrying about trying to avoid them as they burst. This duel appeared to go on non-stop for an unreckonable time. We did a fair amount of damage to these little blighters. The Japanese up here seemed to be smaller than those in the Arakan. We saw two creep out of the bunker and make a run for it. They both had their head and arms in bandages. Pen Ingham misjudged a grenade and did not crawl away in time, with the result that he caught a number of pieces under the heart; he was soon dragged clear, but he died about half an hour later. Pen Ingham was barely 23, but he was so much older than his years, very articulate and intelligent, a solicitor in the making and a good hockey player, and I knew he had left a fiancée, Nigs, in London. I put Private Easton in charge of those men in this area as this bunker was no longer causing us too much trouble. Easton had a Bren gun and remained in this position coming under mortar and light machine-gun sniping fire for the rest of the day, he himself continually sniping and harassing the enemy. By his section holding this ground it gave us depth. Private

Easton was awarded an immediate Military Medal for his determined personal vigil, with complete disregard for his own safety, which lasted for some six hours of daylight.

I went back and had a look at Tiny in his shellhole and gave him a tot of rum out of my flask; at the time I was trying to boost his morale, but water would have been medically far more appropriate, had I thought of it!

Mervyn Mansel (A Company), John Scott (C Company) and myself managed to get together in rear of my HQ at about 1030 hrs and had a short discussion to see if we could work our way forward somehow. These were very nearly the last words spoken by any of us. The discussion became shorter than we meant, as a machine gun opened up from somewhere in our rear and the bullets hit a tree stump and a piece of metal landed in the middle of us. Nowhere did it appear to be safe. We quickly decided that B and C Companies should hold on and consolidate our present gains, as we were both fairly hard hit and were not even two platoons strong between us. By now 10 Platoon had returned and taken up a position on the left of the Company, as the platoon of D Company had taken over in the Jail area. In consequence it was agreed that two platoons of A Company were to work right round the right flank of C Company and try to dislodge the Japs from the ridge running down the road.

During all this time the stretcher-bearers and Sergeant Major Thatcher had been working absolutely flat out taking care of our casualties, binding up their wounds with their field dressings and sliding down the hill in and around the shellholes where they could. No praise can be too great for these chaps; the stretcher-bearers are always in the thick of any battle. Corporal French, our own medical orderly and in charge of our stretcher bearers, was untiring the whole day; he had a charmed life on this day, but this gallant man was killed a few days later in the Kohima battle. Tiny Taylor was being helped away by a C Company stretcher-bearer. As usual, Tiny was an unforgettable sight. Even on the drill square Tiny's dress only just got by, although on this occasion it was not his fault that he did rather overdo it. Wearing a broad grin and only a cardigan, a watch and his unlaced boots, he said, "Goodbye Sahib" and saluted me as he hobbled away. He had been a marvellous Second-in-Command to me for a year or so and many were the occasions when he had to fill a gap and command a platoon again, as on this day. We were in almost every way quite different characters but it worked very well for both of us.[4]

From some time after 10.00am, and at odd intervals for the rest of the day, there were low sweeping clouds and mist, which of course brought some rain. This was one of the few occasions when we welcomed this thick mist and rain, as it meant we could move round a little more freely without being fired at from behind, and it gave us an opportunity to backload some of our casualties.

When the sun came out again for a brief period we had a few more casualties and I regret that Captain John Scott (OC C Company) was killed outright by bullets that blew his head out and there, in cold-sweated horror, I saw the contents of that clever head spread out on the ground. No grey and white matter could have been portrayed with such awful clarity. He became the second Company Commander of C Company to become a casualty in our few days in Kohima, and they had had their Second-in-Command killed. John Scott had already been wounded twice and had refused to have his wounds attended to, but now his outstanding gallantry on Jail Hill had come to an end, although the memory of his selfless efforts live on. Like Pen Ingham, he was another highly intelligent young lawyer; he was of short, lean stature, but the activity of his limbs were as articulate as his mind; his strong pragmatic views made him a natural leader of great charm. This was another young officer of only 23 years, a grievous loss to his men with whom he had built up a deep rapport.

For the rest of the day we dug like beavers with everything we could find, our entrenching tools, plates, mugs, bayonets; for this was not the type of digging one was trained to do. We did not dare stand up to use a pick and a shovel for fear of immediate enemy reaction. At this stage we were only trying to make a hole or a scrape, and then burrow and tunnel ourselves forward below ground level. I had reorganized the Company as one platoon, and by the evening we were completely dug in and all section posts linked up; our total strength at about midday was thirty-odd, not including Company HQ. During the mist and the smoke that was put down between 12.30pm and 2.00pm we managed to evacuate the wounded men, less a few of the walking wounded, who remained up with us until the late afternoon. When circumstances permitted, we salvaged what arms and ammunition we could from the dead and other casualties who were unable to carry them. It was impossible and would anyway have been foolhardy to have buried the dead, or even attempted to get them away, as the air was still full of metal. I also had water-bottles collected and re-distributed, as I could foresee we were unlikely to receive any further supplies of food or water, and likewise it was out of the question to go down to collect our packs and monsoon capes. With numbers as they were, I was not prepared to risk any more casualties.

I had been conscious that I may have made an error of judge-ment when I had decided to leave our packs where we had formed up. I had wished that the men would arrive at the top of the hill fresh enough to fight after a stiff and difficult climb. And, as it turned out, we did indeed move around a hell of a lot once we got to the top, so I was pleased we were not burdened with any packs. If we had worn them during the assault up the hill, and then taken them off, they had every chance of being blown or shot up somewhere on the ground and probably never found again by their owners; at least, where we had left them they would be easy to find as they had been laid out in assaulting order.

At about 5.30pm two platoons of the 4/1 Gurkhas came up. One platoon was to fill the gap between B Company's right and C Company's left, and the other platoon was going to harry the Japs by patrolling after dark. Major McCann commanded them.

He was the relief commander, as the original company commander, Major Beaman, had been killed within two minutes of his arrival on Jail Hill. Mac and I shared the same HQ area for the night, as he had no wireless (he was actually under my command). I heard that Mervyn Mansel (OC A Company) had been very seriously wounded in the stomach by rifle fire as he crossed the road from his company to go to Battalion Tactical HQ. This was ghastly news, which did not distress me at the time as I was up to my eyes in troubles around us.

At the first sign of dusk a carrying party from the platoon of D Company on the road came up with some ammunition, mostly grenades, as these were running very short and were proving to be our life blood. The party also brought up some very welcome rum. It had been raining more frequently in the late afternoon, so we were soaking wet and were obviously going to be so for the rest of the night. At about 5.00pm Colonel Duncombe got on the wireless set to me to congratulate us on a magnificent show. I passed the message round to all the chaps, which gave them terrific heart. In spite of everything, their morale was still excellent; they just accepted the difficulties and the casualties and carried on with tremendous spirit. I believe that our morale was so high because we who were left were still mostly in one piece and the euphoria of being alive had taken over. Also, our tails were up as we were firmly on our objective and held all the higher ground, although we shared some of Jail Hill with the Japanese.

Our total strength on Jail Hill at stand-to at 6.45pm was two officers (Jim Cato and myself) and twenty-eight other ranks. Of this total I had Company Sergeant Major Thatcher, and of the non-commissioned officers I had only one sergeant, one corporal and one lance-corporal left. This did not include the Colour-Sergeant, two cooks and a storeman, who were left in the administrative area, nor did it include two of the four stretcher-bearers who remained at the Regimental Aid Post for the night. We had started the attack with seventy men.

We had a fifty per cent stand-to all night, but the reality was that we all remained alert. Sleep was impossible, as it poured with rain throughout, and it was one of the noisiest nights imaginable. Jap machine guns and our machine guns were punctuated by grenade and mortar fire. Three of the enemy bunkers were only about ten or fifteen yards away. The grenading was a little unpleasant, as the range was so close they could not help but fall in and around us. We were fortunate in only having three men wounded during the night. The Gurkhas had a few casualties from grenades, and two men I think killed by automatics. The Company were strong in automatics, as we had seven of our nine Bren light machine guns – two had been smashed up – and at least five automatic tommy-guns were distributed around.

That night was very wet and cold, and we all shivered like jellies. The next day, 12 May, we stood to at 5.00am and stood down at 5.30am when each man had a tot of rum. We were thankful for the daylight and later a little spasmodic sun, although it continued to rain intermittently. There was much exchange of shots during the day; the platoon of Gurkhas endeavoured to oust the enemy from one of their strong posts with negative results. There was still intense automatic sniping from the enemy on DIS ridge. Mac and I had been considering how the remaining enemy bunkers could be knocked out, and at this hour it was difficult to assess how many enemy bunkers remained on Jail Hill. We thought we knew of four across the front. I sent the following wireless message at 6.00am to Battalion HQ:

"Sit.rep. Enemy sniping from D.I.S. flank. Two enemy bunkers still occupied (on my front) and have automatics. Sniping and grenades have come from these. Apart from this, situation O.K.
"To deal with bunker up here, McCann and I think a tank feasible if it can get up the slope and under cover of smoke. Company strength: 2 and 28. Can smoke be arranged for rations and water to be sent up?
5.55am hrs".

231

As a result of this message I was called in to Battalion Tactical HQ to discuss the possibility of using tanks, and had to dodge much sniping going down the hill and across the road. I learnt that the Brigade objective for the day was to mop up and eliminate the enemy posts on DIS and Jail Hill. This was going to be done by tanks in conjunction with the Gurkhas, who were reserve battalion. The tanks could not operate on the previous day owing to road blocks, but these were cleared by the Sappers in the dark in the early hours of this morning. Tanks were to go through the Jail Hill and DIS cutting and blast the enemy bunkers on the reverse slopes of both features. Other troops of tanks were going to blast up the tough bunker, which might almost be termed a small fortress position on the south side of Jail Hill. Down the hill, 20 yards below us, apparently there was also a fourth bunker near the road closer to C Company; the tanks would also tackle the sniper's post on GPT ridge.

I returned to the Company at about 9.30am and sent Jim Cato down to liaise with the tank troop commander to point out the targets. The bunkers on DIS were to be cleared first by the tanks and mopped up by a company of Gurkhas at about 3.00pm. The bunkers on our hill were to be pounded at 3.30pm, and Chris Nixon's company (of 4/1 Gurkhas) and one platoon of Mac's were to deal with the top bunkers. Hamilton's platoon of D Company (under my command) from the Jail area were to mop up the post north-east of us in that Jail area.

During the day another D Company platoon at HQ brought up some sandwiches and dixies of tea and more rum at midday. I should add that the rum was strictly under the Company Sergeant Major's control and was only issued after standing down at last light, and then again in the morning at first light, which would invariably have been a very chilly night. This rum was not always necessary, but at this monsoon time of year we were usually very wet; it was not for nothing that George Grimston, the Battalion Second-in-Command, referred to the rum ration as a 'drop of morale'!

It was an extraordinary sensation being very nearly on the

receiving end of our own tank shells when the Grant tanks shelled these bunkers during that afternoon. In between each shell fired the tank crews poured Browning automatic 35mm machine-gun bullets into the bunker positions, which of course lay between us and the tanks. We all lay flat on our stomachs in our trenches to avoid the mud and timber debris thrown up, and possibly bits of shells, as the positions pounded by the tanks were literally only fifteen yards or so away from us, but we had no casualties during this 15–20 minute onslaught. When the tanks ceased firing we considered they had been completely successful with the far bunker. As the Japs streamed away out of its rear exit they were shot up by the Manchesters' machine-gun platoon and the tanks' automatics. The bunker near the road was shot to pieces and Japs were seen to be blown clean up into the air. Hamilton's Platoon dashed through the Jail buildings and old bunkers as soon as all firing ceased and encountered no opposition but long-range sniping from DIS or Treasury Hill (still occupied by Japs).

Taking advantage of the remaining Japs' dilemma, the Gurkhas tried to tackle the big bunker next door to us. While they were doing this, our Company HQ had a grandstand view of the Gurkha company tackling the bunker on DIS, the next ridge on our left. So good were our sniping opportunities that Sergeant Major Thatcher and I took on this role as the Japanese fled the persistent tank firing and the Gurkhas' assault; the enemy were far too occupied to notice us firing from a range of about 400 yards away as we looked right down on them. While we shot, the Subedar-Major of Mac's company spotted for us. This was the first time that our position was free from sniping from the DIS ridge, and now here we were reversing the charges, as it were. I am afraid the Gurkhas did not manage to clear the large bunker on Jail Hill, which still appeared to have four automatics.

At about 5.45pm a very welcome draft of ten men joined the Company. They were mostly old B Company sick and wounded men returning to us, and two new sergeants. They arrived in the middle of a large shoot-up by Gurkhas and the Japs; this served as a good initiation to our reinforcements, as they were forced to keep on their stomachs and crawl into positions. They arrived a few minutes ahead of a memorable dixie of tea and another dixie of stew at about 6.00pm. Although we had had some rain, our conditions and anxieties had contributed to dry mouths and a feeling of de-energised dehydration; so, as always, that strong mug of tea laced with as much sugar as could be spared went some way to recharge our mental and physical systems.

Although there was a considerable amount of enemy cross-fire today, the sniping was not as heavy as yesterday, and so we managed to slip a few men at a time down to fill up water-bottles and collect packs. Altogether we only had one killed and two wounded today. In the early evening the Japanese began firing three or four 70 mm guns (the flashes of three could be seen by us), from a position just beyond and overlooking GPT ridge, the guns were almost certainly on Aradura Spur. They fired at a rapid rate for fifteen minutes, the shells appeared to be aimed at us as they just whizzed over our heads; and were falling on the road and DIS just beyond us. This was an interesting experience as the crack and whistle of the shells screeching a few inches above us could be heard before the crump of their landing behind us, and then would follow a triple thunder-like crack which was the noise of the shells being fired from about three miles away.

I sent out a four-man fighting patrol under L/Cpl. Edmunds to worry and do some damage to the nearest leg of the Jap bunker. They went out at 7.45pm and returned at 9.30pm. They threw many grenades into the post and fired the odd burst of tommy-gun. There was no answering fire from the post, although the Jap had been blazing away earlier in the evening. By about 2.00am all firing on the feature seemed to have died away.

I sent out another patrol as daylight broke; the Gurkhas did the same from their platoon on our right. Patrols reported that the bunkers were empty. At 6.00am I got a telephone message (cable was reeled out to us yesterday at midday) telling me to report to

Battalion HQ. This, again, was to discuss how to deal with the remaining large bunker on Jail Hill opposite the Gurkhas.

The Colonel and others were pleased to see me at HQ and gave me and my batman a marvellous breakfast, almost real food, but included a soya link, which I never liked, but it soon became evident that this was quite the best sausage I had ever eaten, as, looking back towards Jail Hill about 800 yards away, we saw something we had all been praying for. There were our men and Gurkhas walking all over the Hill! It was confirmed by telephone that our patrols and those of the Gurkhas had found the bunkers empty.

On my arrival back at the Company I found the men searching the bunkers. The main bunker position in front of us and the Gurkhas had a large central position and four legs coming out diagonally from the centre; it could have held about forty to fifty Japanese.

The central bunker had steel shutters on the inside, which could have been effectively closed up against both grenades and small arms fire, and the bunker was so deep that no bomb or shell would have caused much if any damage. This could explain the Japanese ability to weather the onslaught of our shelling and mortaring, to reappear when our shelling ceased, then to engage us from the defensive fox-holes that were connected to the strong point. The fortress position of this central bunker had been constructed with considerable skill and had been so well camouflaged that it was only when we got into it could its shape and size be assessed. At the time it seemed that nothing could survive the mighty bombardment Jail Hill had received, but now we understood how it was that this courageous enemy could survive, and at the same time it was a testimony to his efficient fieldworks.

When Jail Hill had been finally cleared of the Japanese, we found twenty bunker positions; all had been occupied when the attack began. Although we never discussed it at that time, in retrospect we marvelled at the incredible tenacity of the Japanese as they invariably continued firing from their positions after they had been, or so we thought, completely destroyed by gunfire.

There was a quantity of kit in and around the main enemy position: rifles, ammunition, very rusty machine guns, a battered Bren gun, stacks of Jap grenades, and our 36 grenades. Several of our men got hold of Japanese flags. The ten dead Japs we found inside were searched and five Jap diaries were handed to me. An interesting thought is the way that some Jap units were issued with quantities of their national flags; I suppose it did something for their morale. No man could be more patriotic and dedicated to his cause than the British soldier, but I cannot see him including our Union flag in his kit and hanging it out!

Colonel Graham Duncombe, George Grimston, our Second-in-Command, and Dick Kensington, the Adjutant, came up together with Major Sir Christopher Nixon, a 4/1 Gurkha company commander, and had a look round the area. An amusing, but very fortunate, incident occurred during their visit: a Jap sniper from somewhere, probably GPT Ridge, fired a couple of shots at them, followed by two long bursts; their escort party, commanded by Sergeant Hunter, returned some fire in that direction. The CO's party automatically jumped into the nearest trench. It so happened that the CO and Adjutant jumped into what turned out to be an old Jap latrine; the mire was made deeper by the past rain. With the aid of a rifle, George Grimston and Chris Nixon pulled the Colonel and Dick out of the oozing mire. It was evident that they had been up to their waists in pure bog. I think the CO laughed louder than the troops and waved a cheery goodbye, their stinking clothes taking with them its share of our flies.

That morning we buried all our dead; most were taken down and buried in a Battalion site below the road and about 300 yards north-west along it from the 47th milestone, in sight of Jail Hill. Some with fragmented bodies had to be buried on the hill. This was a time when the significance of the identity discs proved their value. All arms, ammunition and equipment, etc, were salvaged and sent back to the road and were later collected by Bren gun carriers and taken to the salvage dump-head. Barbed wire came up at about 0930 hrs and we had wired the whole area in with trip and a single-apron fence by about 1430 hrs, the Company frontage being about 200 yards.

There was very little firing on the Battalion front that day, 13 May, although snipers were still spasmodically active from the south, maybe GPT Ridge, but DIS ridge and FSD had by this time been cleared of all Japs. So life on Jail Hill became pretty relaxed. There was a considerable battle going on in the Treasury Hill area about a mile to the north of us between 2nd Division's troops and tanks against the Japs still dug in there.

It so happened that at about 1.00pm I picked up my field-glasses to have a look at their battle, and then I noticed figures dodging away from the hill and crossing the road diagonally across our front about 900 yards away; first they came in ones and twos, and then larger parties. They were obviously Japs running away from their positions. This was too good to miss. I warned all those of the Company on that face of the perimeter and we began to snipe. Then more came down the hill, about thirty of them. In the meantime I acted as the Forward Observation Officer to our Battalion 3-inch mortars, and our gunner FOO got the artillery's 3.7-inch guns on to them. Sergeant Major Thatcher was spotting and indicated the targets to the men. There were probably about fifteen of us altogether and included three Bren machine guns. This was terrific fun, as we were carrying out real controlled aimed fire at the Japanese as they crossed the road and tried to take cover behind bushes, tin and bamboo huts. This firing by the men sounded grand. We were getting a great kick out of this. The shells and bombs fell very accurately indeed and moved with the enemy as they tried to get to shelter in a re-entrant. Some fifty of the enemy must have crossed our front; there was no realistic way we could assess their casualties but between us and the guns and mortars we must have hit them fairly hard.

The words 'terrific fun' and 'getting a kick out of this' would probably not have been used with hindsight, but at that moment there was a thrill of battle enjoyed by my soldiers as they had a freedom to kill without retribution, and hence the words found their way into my diary.

The enemy did a little spasmodic shelling on some of our wiring parties in the early afternoon, and shelled and mortared the road below us and DIS ridge. Jail Hill had been blasted so much from the air and artillery of both sides and our tanks that there was not a leaf or a blade of grass left on it. It had, of course, been thick jungle; some of the tree stumps still remained standing. Jail Hill was void of any cover except shellholes and battered bunkers; it was littered with kit, smelt of death and rotting flesh.

The desolation was augmented by millions of flies as they tried to do justice to the feast that 'civilised' man had delivered to them, moving from corpses to latrines, then to our food and pricking and sucking the naked parts of our bodies, such as hands and faces, which might then absorb some disease.

> They have been so thick on this now battered, barren and debris-scattered hillside, that complete corpses have been almost buried by them. I, for one, have eaten several of the largest filthy-looking bluebottles, having settled on a bully-beef sandwich between the hand and the mouth.
>
> Telephone message from the Battalion in the afternoon to say that we are to be relieved tomorrow, 14 May at 10.00am. No regrets, cheers all round. We had a quiet night and a little rain, but who cared? We were being relieved.
>
> The next day I sent out patrols fairly well forward to search the area primarily for stay-behind Jap parties, their dead bodies and any kit they may have left behind. The patrols came back with about four more diaries, papers, sketches, etc. They had come across some more weapons, some British, a store of clothing and hundreds of tins of milk, and some wrist watches. I sent out a party to gather in as much as possible. I collected a Jap rifle and

bayonet off the hill, which I intended to keep not only as a souvenir, but to have cut down and use as a sporting rifle. The Punjabis of another division relieved us; the relief was completed by 1045 hrs and I came away with the last section.

Whilst we were thinning out, one Jap plane (Zero) came over and dropped a bomb in the area of Divisional HQ. Ten minutes later about a dozen 97s and Zeros came over and bombed and strafed the rear divisional area. They were successfully driven off by anti-aircraft fire, and were met by Spitfires on their way back. A half an hour of aerial dog fights broke up an otherwise boring day.

The Battalion had returned to its original area which it left on the 10th. It was good to be back here. Those who had to remain out of the front-line battle area, and there did have to be some administrative staff who looked after the stores, the food and the cooking and so forth, were overjoyed to see us, rather like a returning home after months of absence, but in reality only four days. The cooks prepared a tremendous meal for us, and thank heaven for our blankets for this night; the following day Colour-Sergeant Fraser was able to give us all a change of clothing.

Our green battledress had been sweated through and through again and again by our exertions, to the extent that the white salt of our sweat had soaked through everything, and then in turn the battledress was washed by the monsoon rains whilst we wore them and much of it became caked in mud, where we had sat or lain in it, and then occasionally out would come a burst of hot sun that baked the oozing mixture. It was a marvellous luxury to exchange the ten-day-old dirty clothes, a further fillip to the morale, and we all drew added strength to see each other with that sharper edge restored.

It was only after the successful battles for the Kohima Ridge that one learnt a little about the thinking of our Brigadier. When he had received his orders and made his reconnaissance for the impending objectives and battles that his 33 Brigade would become involved in, Brigadier Loftus was quite clear about the momentous task facing his Brigade. After the battle he said, "We were faced with clearing five or six strongly defended positions. . . . This filled me with some dismay. Though I knew I could rely 100 per cent on the spirit of the troops, I did not relish the prospect of returning to my Division in a highly mauled condition." In time, some of us also learned about a medical assessment of the Brigade, which had recently borne the considerable burdens of the battles in Arakan, and had been promised "a good rest in the Assam valley". The troops had been medically classified as "suffering from malnutrition as a result of the Arakan privations". The medical opinion was that September, which was about four months ahead, was the earliest that we should be committed to battle again. In spite of that medical opinion, malnutrition or no malnutrition, the Brigade succeeded in capturing all its objectives!

We might have thought that the Brigade's successful battles so far were possibly the last in Kohima, but this was not to be.

Naga Village

The Battalion casualties during the week of the Jail Hill battles were very nearly 40%, with a disproportionately high rate among the officers, sergeants and corporals; they were such that Colonel Duncombe decided to hold a conference for company commanders on 15 May to discuss the Battalion's reorganization. Since that week all companies had received reinforcements of about ten men. B Company, including its administrative element, was fifty-three strong, and the other companies were marginally larger; all companies agreed to reorganize to about sixty and to operate on a two-platoon basis. We received the bad news that Mervyn Mansel had died of the wounds to his stomach; gangrene had set in. His dying from his stomach wound might have been inevitable. Even so, it was a great shock to all of us. The sadness to his parents, brothers and sister must have been all the more painful, as Mervyn had known, and they would have known, that he was due for repatriation to England very shortly, as he had already completed five years and four months in the Far East, longer than any officer in the Battalion. Everybody, not least the girls, fell for him. He greeted everyone with a natural, warm charm. He was a tall, good-looking sensitive man and I had known him for more than four years, longer than any other officer in the Battalion. We had done so many things together, jollied along by his infectious and characteristic laugh. He had been Adjutant of the Battalion during much of our time on the North West Frontier and was meticulously efficient. As a company commander, he was a leader that everyone would instinctively follow and respect.[5]

After the conference I was told that B and C Companies were to amalgamate under my command and then move further up our ridge to relieve the 4/1 Gurkha company, about thirty-five minutes' walk beyond our present position and about 200 yards below the Assam Rifles at the top of the ridge.

It sounded the simplest of moves, as indeed it was, but it entailed moving all the administrative bits and pieces. We had all the blankets and mosquito nets, as well as our change of clothing, reserve ammunition, which included 2-inch mortar bombs, grenades, tommy guns, sub-machine gun ammunition and two boxes of .303 rifle ammunition. The ammunition alone required six mules. Additionally there were the cooking pots, cooking oil, two days' rations, picks, shovels and water. That was a total load of about twenty-six mules, but we only had twelve at our disposal. Colour-Sergeant Fraser, as always, worked it all out and saw all the kit up from the bottom, our own mules working on a shuttle service. He also had to sort out all the bundles of kit that belonged to our casualties so that it did not get sent up with everything else. We had our midday meal at noon and left the old area an hour or so later.

Our new positions had been well dug by the Gurkhas. Large logs and earth had been built on top of the dug-outs. We found that we were to occupy a series of ring contours that were connected by narrow saddles. The position was fairly well wired, but it needed to be strengthened in places. I liaised with the Assam Rifles about patrols. Starting the next day, they would send down a patrol to us at first light and then we up to them on alternate days. This was jungle country, but the trees were for the most part much taller and the jungle undergrowth was sparser and not so close and tight as in Arakan, occasionally giving up to about 20 yards visibility; the saddles that connected the platoons' positions had been cleared to give reasonable fields of fire.

> The rest of the Battalion and Battalion HQ were about 500 feet lower and 600 yards away to the north of us.
>
> By stand-to (7.00pm) we were fully organized, including a telephone to Battalion HQ and an extension to 10 and 11 Platoons, which had been combined to make one strong defensive platoon of about forty men and were commanded by my only officer, Jim Cato. Dear old 12 Platoon had had to be subsumed into 10 and 11 Platoons. The C Company combined platoon position was commanded by Brian Grainger.
>
> In the evening I spoke to all the Company and congratulated them on the magnificent successes they had had over this last week.

What no one in my Company knew at the time of the Battalion's two attacks on Jail Hill was that, prior to our attacks, two brigades of 2nd Division had been held up in their attacks on adjoining features by accurate machine-gun fire from Jail Hill. The Japanese defended their positions with fanatical stubbornness. Their tenacity and courage were well known. It was one thing to reach one's objective but it was quite another to drive them out of their positions. It was not in their creed to surrender, although they had so often suffered artillery and air bombardment during which they would seek protection in their deep bunkers. When the bombardment ended they would pop up again and staunchly defend the position that was covered by their interlocking, supporting machine-gun positions sited in depth and from the flanks. From there onwards the battle was invariably won through the spirit, determination and courage of our infantrymen, when it was the small 5–6 men section size units that influenced the battle as they closed with the enemy.

At last more barbed wire and pickets became available on 17 May. It had arrived on a small convoy of mules, which had staggered and slithered their way up as they tried to move through the muddy, porridgy slopes, that had been freshly creamed by the night's torrential rain. We finished off the wiring of all positions and made new knife rests, which are mobile imitations of the wiring pattern that would allow us easy exit and entry into the position. These defended localities were now a very tough proposition for anyone trying to intrude. The rain continued from time to time during the day.

The following day the rain became even more troublesome. The monsoon was really finding its feet as we were losing ours. Some of the dug-outs leaked and all our kit was more or less permanently wet. There was a perpetual slow drip down at the far end of my foxhole. Private Sear made an effective arrangement of sandbags, groundsheet and an empty bully beef tin that harnessed the cascading water into a chagul. Although there was plenty of water running all around me, this arrangement gave me an instant personal supply of water for my washing, shaving and a cup of tea the next morning.

When not in the battle area one knew that there were rats around, nosing their way into our rubbish pits. During the early hours of one morning in this position I saw a rat silhouetted against the night sky through the foxhole exit. It was idly walking over the monsoon cape across my legs and then jumped on to a ledge. It was the only time I saw a rat actually sharing my foxhole.

At 8.00pm on 18 May very heavy firing began in the Treasury Hill and Jail Hill area. After a time this seemed to become more intense and spread over to the left and then appeared to be behind us. After three-quarters of an hour the battle moved from the left, as if the Japs were beaten off, and went round again from the Treasury and Jail area to GPT ridge and finally finished above us in the area of the Assam Rifles and Burma Regiment. And then, an hour later, there was absolute hell let loose just above us. I had just stood the Company to when Dick got on the field telephone and told us to do so. The general battle going on gave me an impression that it was a large-scale counter-attack by the Japs on the Division's front.

The battle above us spread farther and appeared to be all around us. There were bullets, red tracer and Very lights whipping across our position, and I honestly thought that we were being attacked. A burst of automatic hit my command post dugout. It took me about half an hour to discover whether it was us being attacked. Only one of our own posts (not my amalgamated platoons) had opened up, and all they had contributed to the noise were six grenades and four rifle shots. I asked them if they had seen anything, but no. They had just seen some rather close rifle flashes and had fired at them. It soon became apparent that, officially, we were not included in this battle.

This conflagration across the whole front went on until midnight and gradually petered out in the early hours of 19 May, then seemed to subside back to the Treasury Hill area.

> While we were standing-to this morning after a very wet night, the patrol from the Assams came down to us. The officer commanding the patrol came and saw me with apologies to say that there were in reality no enemy on their front. But they had picked up the pattern of the firing which had become infectious, and then it ricochetted around their posts. Well!
>
> But the origin of the firing, I learned later that day, was indeed a large-scale attack on Treasury Hill, and that there were other Jap patrols out, trying to draw our fire by firing wildly at our Brigade positions, including Brigade HQ and the gunners. One officer (cipher) and one sergeant were killed in our Brigade HQ.

By daylight all firing had ceased and things were once again normal. The only damage to the Company were some water chaguls, equipment and plates holed. During the day we repaired the tracks between our own positions to make them rather more mule-able for rations and a constant resupply of drinking water.

An extract from our Battalion Intelligence Summary published on 19 May 1944, gave us an indication of what was going on around us:

> Prisoner-of-war surrendered Jail Hill. States he deserted because he had passed limit of endurance and believed Japs could not win. His battalion now (in) Aradura area. (Their) company strengths very low, none exceeding sixty, also officer casualties very heavy. (And their) battalion guns at present without ammunition.
>
> Own Troops: 4/7 Rajput on Jail Hill. 1/1 Punjabi returned Dimapur Yesterday's air strike was by twenty-four Hurri-bombers on east end Naga village. Reported very accurate and successful.

In the letter I wrote to Ma and Pa on 20 May thanking them for a parcel that arrived on about 1 May and had taken about six months, I added that recently we had a big battle with the Japanese: "But everywhere in men and material we are superior. They can't win in the long (I hope short) run. We are killing them off so easily, but then they don't readily give ground. They literally die at their posts, each one having to be winkled out. . . . We are getting excellent food: eggs and flour and plenty of tinned milk with which our cooks can work wonders." I congratulated my parents on their 26th wedding anniversary on 2 May (1918) and hoped they would forgive me for not sending my usual telegram on the day.

Although the centre of Kohima Ridge had been cleared of the Japanese, they clung determinedly to their positions in apparent strength on the extreme flanks of the Ridge, in the Naga Village area to the north and to the south on Aradura Spur about three miles away. After bitter fighting, a brigade of 2 Division had been fought to a standstill in Naga Village, and so our 33

Brigade were to take this on, and the fight to capture Aradura Spur continued to challenge 2 Division.

Perhaps the morale of the Japanese soldier had peaked; certainly the above Intelligence Summary suggested that the enemy were in a poor state. But it was very evident that, to us, the enemy's 31 Division still defended with determination and the apparent ammunition situation was such that, to our soldiers on the ground, it was still able to put up determined opposition to the two divisions of our XXXIII Corps.

All company commanders had to report to the CO's Command Post at 9.30am on 21 May and from there we went on a reconnaissance with him and Brigadier Loftus-Tottenham, together with the commanders of the 4/1 Gurkhas and the 4/15 Punjabs to the area of the Naga Village. We went by jeep convoy as far as the DC's bungalow and Treasury Hill area, and then walked through the remainder of what was left of the bazaar. This and the town were mostly a heap of rubble with corrugated iron sheets strewn around.

It was at this reconnaissance that I first met the new commanding officer of the 4/1 Gurkhas, Lieutenant Colonel Derek Horsford. He had taken over after Colonel Hedderwick had been killed by a sniper while carrying out a reconnaissance with Brigadier Goschen (4 Brigade), who was also killed by another bullet, within minutes of each other, in early May. Colonel Horsford was only 27 and must have been one of the youngest COs in the Army at that time.[6]

We reached 4 Brigade HQ in mid-morning just short of Naga Village after half an hour's climb. Our Queen's Battalion was to take over the south-eastern perimeter with the Punjabis on our left, and the Gurkhas took over all of the Treasury Hill area linking up with us on our right. The Jap positions were about 150 yards from us on a spur.

After being shown round the area, the Company Commander of the Worcestershire Regiment (his company had only just moved into this post) very kindly gave me tea in their Battalion

RAP, where we exchanged recent experiences. The Worcesters were taking over the positions we had just left.

Arriving back at the Battalion in the early afternoon I heard that the Brigadier had given permission to the CO to send Major George Grimston, the Second-in-Command, Dick Kensington, the Adjutant, and 'Pokey', Captain Polkinhorne, our Signal Officer, on leave. They deserved a break. I do not think that they had been away from operations since our first arriving in Arakan in September 1943.

The CO held another conference concerning our move to Naga Village on 22 May. After the conference he took me aside and said that he was going to order me to go sick, as he knew that malaria was in my system, but in the meantime he was recommending me to go to the Staff College. However, I said I wasn't too keen about going to the Staff College, as I had already been away from England nearly five years and it was my understanding that I would have to remain out in the Far East a year or so after a staff course. If I accepted, I would be away from my Ma and Pa and England for nearly seven years. I believe that my weakness through being riddled with malaria for months had made me completely disinterested in a staff course. Colonel Duncombe's order did rather shake me and I argued rather feebly against reporting sick, but it was really the only sensible way to look at it, as I knew, as did he, that I could only get worse.

The Battalion began to move out at 6.00am, companies following each other at half-hourly intervals.

B Company left at 7.30am, taking reserve ammunition, its cooking pots, tools, water and rations with it; the blankets, mosquito nets and spare clothing would follow on after we had moved off.

After walking for about ten minutes with the Company a message came to me from the CO requesting me to ride up with him in his jeep, so I returned to him at his Tactical HQ. The CO and I arrived at Naga Village at about 10.00am, just as my Company were arriving on foot. The take-over was completed by 11.00am. The whole position smelt of decaying matter and was generally filthy. The defensive wiring was virtually non-existent and the slit trenches were thin and shallow. I did not blame those from whom we had just taken over, as they had only been there a few hours themselves and doubtless the area had been shelled, re-occupied and re-shelled many times over. Anyhow, this new B Company position was very exposed, except for about four leafless trees, and another quite beautiful pink and white cherry blossom tree that had somehow survived the battles around Naga Village. This sweet little tree stood alone and was about twelve feet high. There being no other living vegetation near it, one's eyes were naturally drawn to this gentle colour. I suspect that few of us had seen such a tree as this since leaving home. It conjured up a memory of the villages in Surrey or Berkshire or indeed anywhere in England in the month of May.

Very soon we discovered that the war had not deserted this slice of Naga Village. The afternoon was spent in getting the place organized, first digging, then wiring, and then the enemy found us and was obviously watching us work as he sniped and shelled during much of this period. One shell landed within five yards of my dug-out. There were some casualties in A and C Companies, and some among the Indian engineers, who were in position just behind us. One thing of interest I managed to pick up from among the debris on a track was a British medical compendium, all in pieces and very muddy but complete, called *The Handbook of Physiology and Biochemistry*.[7]

From 22 May all the 2-inch and 3-inch mortars of 33 Brigade had been pooled and were in position in the Naga Village. From 6.00pm that night the 18 × 3-inch mortars and the 36 × 2-inch mortars, that would have been the maximum number of 2-inch mortars if they were all in working order from the three battalions, (I know that two of ours had become casualties) blasted off a two-round concentration at ten minutes to every clock hour, and then again at the hour. The idea behind the Brigadier's plan was to school the Japs into taking cover at these times and then, instead of a concentration of mortar bombs coming down at the clock hour, infantry would suddenly pour onto the positions. These concentrations were to go down for forty-eight hours at least, and would start this evening.

It rained a great deal during the night and early in the morning, 24 May. The Company continued with digging and wiring during the morning, but, as we had made good progress in getting ourselves below ground level, I called a halt to the digging for an hour before our midday meal so as to transfer our efforts into a grand-scale clean up of everything around us. The hour's hard work made a whale of a difference: less flies, not so much smell and no tins to trip over. Looking from this position across to the south, where we had been on Jail Hill, one could see what used to be the reverse side of the Kohima central ridges. It appeared that there was really only one portion of the town that had hardly been touched by the past battles and that was the barrack area where the Assam Rifles lived before April. These red-roofed barracks were almost intact. As with many things, the Japanese had an eye for anything that might be of use to them after their 'victory'. Examples included the motor transport they did not destroy in Arakan, the rice and other food they picked up, and the bakery in Kohima. Perhaps they thought the barracks would just suit them.

At first light on 25th the artillery 25-pounder guns put down smoke all round the Naga Village. This was done to enable tanks to get up the track to the top of the hill. Three tanks came up, preceded by a bulldozer that widened the track. All this activity on the hill, which was on B Company's flank, produced some enemy harassing fire. Soon after the smoke had cleared, one of the tanks on top of the hill suffered two direct hits. Another shell landed among the six-pounder anti-tank gun ammunition, which caught fire and made the Battalion HQ area a little unhealthy. 11 Platoon suffered some ineffective sniping while they were wiring. Our chaps retaliated with the Bren, but I do not think it was at anything they could see.

Jack Sumner, our Medical Officer, came over and saw me

after breakfast and said that he would make out my field medical card so that I could be evacuated soon after lunch. Aggravated by monsoon weather, my malaria had got worse. I managed to drink plenty of odd brews of tea during the day, but I was quite unable to eat any food, much to the surprise of those who knew my normal appetite.

During the morning I went round all the Company posts, maybe over twenty of them, and saw all the men at work and said goodbye to each of them. They had done marvellously; all positions had been enlarged and many were now connected up. They were amazingly hard workers, so good and thoroughly reliable; even the most recently joined were caught up in the spirit, and fully realized the value of some few hours' hard work for the sake of more comfort and safety later on.

Saying goodbye could never have been easy when one had been in the same company for nearly four years. How does one say goodbye and thank the men adequately in their ones and twos as they stood in their bunker-type foxholes? It would have been easier to have had the sixty or so men all together on parade and made one short valediction. But that could not be done. In the event, as I went round, I felt pleased that I could speak personally to each of them. I had dreaded that moment of departure, as one got attached to the men under command. They had contributed so much, indeed everything, in helping to build up such a battle group as this B Company that I had been privileged to command on and off for over three years. The bond between a commander and his men becomes the greater when there have been some shared moments of danger, hunger, an exhausted tiredness and a thirst which sometimes borders on dehydration when the water output nearly exceeds the water intake. Our worst experience was seeing some very close friends brutally carved up, suddenly never to be able to speak to them again.

Some of those casualties were very young, perhaps barely 20, and had no chance to experience life. There were many who were in their 20s and 30s, recently married with babies and young children. The impact of those losses did not hit one at the time, but it did when the heat was off and one had time to reflect. It said so much for their loyalty, dedication and discipline that they endured and overcame the mental and physical extreme conditions of fighting a tenacious enemy. I could not recall a moment when anyone hesitated to do some probably frightening task, and having to carry out a similar task a few days later for the second and possibly third time. The individual's pride in himself and his unit is such that it engenders a spirit that ensures he never lets his mates down. These soldiers had built up small teams of interdependent mates where none of them would dare let the side down: they cared so much for the safety and welfare of each other in the team; they had an inbuilt discipline that was fanned by a collective discipline and nourished by high morale. Time and again one heard of and saw soldiers put themselves at risk to look after or save another. They looked upon their Battalion, the Company and its sub-units, as their surrogate family.[8]

I have to say that my task was made easier by the British soldier's robust and ready sense of humour and sense of the ridiculous, which invariably popped up spontaneously when conditions were tricky and would take the sting out of a problem.

The time eventually came when I had to leave; the jeep was ready at the Quartermaster's area. I bid my final adieux to Colonel Graham, George Grimston[9] and others in Battalion Headquarters in mid-afternoon; Privates Sear and Dunkley (Jim's batman) staggered down to the jeep with my kit, most of it having been retrieved from the administrative area and included my bedding role which had had a fairly cushy war, as it only got into the action when we were destined to be in a protracted defence.

The jeep took me to Mile 36 (Zubza), where I was picked up by a Gurkha military policeman's truck to the next hospital at Mile 28. From there I travelled in an ambulance convoy of the American Field Service. In my ambulance was another man of B Company (malarial case). During the latter stage of the journey I began to feel quite ill and sick. We finally arrived at Number 66 Casualty Clearance Station in Dimapur at 9.00pm.

The malaria got its chance to break out the following day in the warmth of a super bed with plenty of blankets. My red blood cells were apparently being savaged by a mosquito parasite. I was fortunately suffering from the benign variety, which recurs over a period of years. I had originally been bitten in 1940 on the North West Frontier of India, in the days before the invention of prophylactic pills. My temperature and much liquid was taken at very frequent intervals over the next few days.

On the evening of 26 May I heard the news on the hospital wireless set that the Battalion had been heavily mortared and shelled and that the whole of our 33 Brigade had been counter-attacked by the Japanese, but that all positions held. There was a 7 Indian Division order that no one would fire at night. Only grenades and bayonets would be used, except in case of big attacks. I was to learn from our Regimental History that the word went round the other units in Naga Village, "This is a real attack; the Queen's are firing." This was a great tribute to the Battalion's fire discipline.

According to diaries and some history books, the 4/15 Punjabs put in a battalion attack on the strongly held Church Knoll, which overlooks the rest of Naga Village. This quite excellent Indian Regiment sustained many casualties in their attack on 28 May, but on this occasion they could not overwhelm the Japanese. The Brigadier was anxious that 33 Brigade's magnificent fighting reputation should be maintained and that the whole of Naga Village should be cleared before handing over to another brigade on 1 June. In consequence on 30 May B Company, now commanded by Lieutenant Greig after my departure, infiltrated on to the flank of Church Knoll to within 80 yards of an enemy bunker. Then D Company passed through and put in a holding attack on this still strongly defended position, with orders not to get too heavily involved; in time they had to withdrew. The next day the bunker position was again shelled by our tanks, followed by an attack by A

Company, but they were shelled and mortared off by the Japanese before the company could dig in.

All intelligence reports had stated that the Japanese had lost a very large number of men in the Kohima battles. They were apparently sick, demoralized and half-starved, and yet, in spite of having been shelled by artillery and tanks, mortared by the infantry battalions, withstood the jets from flame throwers, and sometimes bombed by our airforce, they never gave up. Their outstanding courage was boosted by an apparent bottomless pit of ammunition. I did, however, learn much later that their ammunition and food supply system was very sorely tested by the length of their lines of communication across Burma, a situation so often experienced by armies who plunder someone else's territory.

It became the turn of the 4/1 Gurkhas to have a crack at the Japanese on Church Knoll. Colonel Horsford had seen the frontal attacks fail, so he put a new plan to the Brigadier, who agreed it. After extensive patrols to locate the enemy's positions and strengths, the Gurkhas infiltrated behind them, and, after a series of battles, took the positions behind Church Knoll, from where the Gurkhas could bring down fire on the enemy's rear. The complete success of this operation enabled my old B Company to capture the position at about 10.30am and under cover of heavy mist and rain, they were able to consolidate and dig in.

The Battalion was relieved by the South Lancashire Regiment, after which 1 Queen's returned to Dimapur for a well-earned rest. This was the last battle by 33 Indian Infantry Brigade in Kohima, which had now captured all its objectives on the very day it was due to hand over to another brigade. From a Regimental point of view, it was perhaps a happy augury that it should be on the day of one of our great battle honours, 'The Glorious First of June' of 1794, one which we share with the Royal Navy and the Worcestershire Regiment and, in peacetime, celebrate each year.

My conscience felt a little better when I learnt that the

Battalion had moved down to Dimapur for some rest and entertainment and had followed me there exactly seven days after I had left them at Naga Village, but by 1 June 1944 I and some 100 other sick and wounded were on a river steamer going down the Brahmaputra River. On 6 June a trainload of us sick and wounded somehow heard the news of the D-Day Landings. The boost to morale that this news gave us brought cheers from all ranks as the news was absorbed, and made us forget our discomforts. We felt that at last, after nearly five years, the war was turning the corner in our favour, with the victories against the Japanese, and now the Allies landing in France. All this was premature thinking, but the euphoria carried us through those five days as we chugged and steamed our way across India and then found ourselves unloaded at number 136 British General Hospital in Dehra Dun, near the foothills of the Himalayas.

After a month or so at this hospital dysentery tried to get into the act and overtake my malaria, but for a time they travelled together until the dysentery proved that the ball was in its court. Many months of poor sanitation had allowed the microscopic amoebae to get into my large intestine where they were doing battle and making a feast of me. Then, as I was recovering from these, I began to feel really ill. I could not play a game of cards or write without throbbing pains everywhere – headache, bones, joints and muscles, everything ached, and the nausea was such that I could not look at food. I had apparently succumbed to jaundice, which, I learnt, was not a disease but a general condition of debility. My weight at that time was about 8 stone, which meant that I had lost about three and a half stone. As I convalesced, I was moved from Dehra Dun Hospital to the British Military Hospital at Landour further up the foothills, near Mussouri, which must have been 2,000–3,000 feet higher. When cloudy, as it mostly was at that time in July, it had a temperate climate and was cool at night. As I recovered I played Bridge every night with the CO of the hospital, his wife and usually a colonel recovering from something. This was a small hospital with about 20 officers and some other ranks, but in my time only about six of us played Bridge.

While in that hospital I received letters written by Pa and Ma from their house in St. Ives, Cornwall. They had both written on the same very memorable day of 6 June, D-Day. Pa referred to that part of my letter which said, "We had them on the run", his comment being that it was a target an infantryman dreams of and hardly ever gets. He had been given a week's holiday for being a good boy, working in the Royal Observer Corps. His holiday apparently did Ma much good, as she worked very hard at home and in the troops canteen. He made no reference to D-Day, but Ma covered it well: "I am writing you on The Day. Everyone is wild with excitement. . . . I haven't moved from the wireless. . . . We knew things were about to happen Sunday last, as the armada passed our very windows. It took over two and a half hours to pass. What a sight. One thrilled with pride to think we had such ships. . . . Poor devils are fighting along the coast we know so well. . . . Do you remember our last lunch at Cabourg on (our) way to Dinard? You slept all the way in the car." What marvellous memories. Ma had made a very emotional statement, because that lunch was the very last time, just on five years ago, a few days before war was declared, that we actually had lunch together. She just had to write and bring me into her thinking, praying as she did so; as I read that, I was thinking would we ever have another lunch together again? Cabourg is about 20 miles from Caen and 30 miles or so from Falaise, all in the area of big battles to come as the Allies thrust their way across France towards Germany during 1944–1945.

Chapter 12

Reflections

I doubt that there was anyone of us below the rank of Lieutenant Colonel who was present at Kohima who appreciated at the time the real strategic importance of those victories against the Japanese. We knew we had to eject the invader and save India, but the scale of the defeat and destruction of the Japanese 31st Division at Kohima and on its jungle-clad mountains has, in the words of some senior British commanders and other writers, confirmed that the sacrifice of our troops was rewarded, as the outcome of those battles proved to be the turning point in the war against the Japanese in Burma.

It was some time after the battles before one began to realize that we privileged survivors had taken part in an important phase of the war.

To illustrate that importance, some of the difficulties involved and the reactions of others to the performance of our soldiers, I shall quote from other sources:

The Fourteenth Army Commander, General Sir William Slim, wrote in his book *Defeat into Victory*: "The gains thus made in a few days since 10 May changed the whole picture around Kohima. . . . We had the town, or rather where the town had been, for the whole area in mud and destruction resembled the Somme in 1916."

Brigadier Sir John Smyth VC MC whose son, John, was killed in the battle, referred in his book *The Valiant* to a conversation he had with our Brigadier Loftus-Tottenham about our Battalion. He wrote that the Brigadier "emphasizes that the Queen's captured the first Japanese prisoners in any theatre of war and that they were part of the Brigade which forced on the Japs their first and disastrous retreat (in Arakan). They were completely unflappable and whether in attack or defence 100 per cent reliable. I remember, as I was moving up to Pimple on 7 May, meeting a man badly wounded in the head and neck who was staggering back to the Advance Dressing Station. I had met him previously and knew he was a recent transfer from . . . regiment. He said to me, 'I have one request to make to you, sir. When I recover, will you see I am posted back to the Queen's?' "

Among the British casualties in that period were one brigadier killed and two brigadiers wounded. Two lieutenant colonels commanding battalions were also killed. The total casualties suffered by our Battalion during its twenty-six days in Kohima were:

Killed	4 Officers	65 Other ranks
Wounded	6 Officers	118 Other ranks

The proportion was particularly high among the commanders, officers and down to the most junior lance corporals. Those of our officer casualties at Kohima included two company commanders killed and two wounded, and two seconds-in-command of companies wounded; my B Company were fortunate to have only two officers wounded. The 2nd Division cemetery is sited on Garrison Hill and is maintained by the Commonwealth War Graves Commission; it includes the graves of 1,387 men, of whom about 300 are those of the Indian Army or Gurkha battalions. There are a number who fell in the mountainous jungle who have no known grave. Their memory is recorded on their regimental memorials.

It will be recollected that 33 Infantry Brigade initially fought under the command of 2 Division during our battles for Jail Hill.

On the higher ground above the cemetery is the 2 British Division's war memorial at Kohima, on which the inscription reads:

"When you go home
Tell them of us and say
For your tomorrow
We gave our today."

Many have thought that this epitaph was composed by a regimental padre. In fact the original version was composed by the Greek poet Simonides to commemorate the gallant action of 300 Spartan soldiers, under the command of Leonidas, who successfully held a mountain pass at Thermopylae against a large invading Persian army under their King Xerxes in 480BC.

The over-all estimate of the Japanese 31 Division's casualties in the fifty days of their non-stop attack, defence and retreat from around Kohima, was between 4,000 and 6,000 killed, with a much larger but unknown number of wounded.

The book *Tales by Japanese Soldiers*, published in 2000, was jointly written and edited by Dr Kazuo Tamayama and John Nunnelly, who was wounded in Burma, tells of the experiences of 62 Japanese soldiers during the Burma campaign, 1942–1945. One of the stories told by a Japanese private soldier at Kohima tells of the terror they suffered from our shelling: "as shrapnel burst upon us with tremendous force so that officers and men were cut to pieces . . . as they ran for cover. We watched as enemy reinforcements arrived by truck with more and more arms and ammunition. . . . It was only about three o'clock in the afternoon when they took their tea break, as we could see through our telescopes, that we had respite from the shells." This was a perceptive statement, maybe unconsciously, about the British afternoon tea, taken perhaps an hour early on this occasion, but the Japanese were probably not aware that that cup of tea would have given British soldiers more fire in their belly.

Having had the privilege of a lifetime to be responsible for the lives of British soldiers in times of mortal danger, I do wish briefly to trace some of the movements of the men of my old B Company as they fought their way down the length of Burma until the surrender of the Japanese while I was back in England. With the aid of the Battalion Diary and the Regimental and Divisional histories, I can do this, but with only meagre justice to their achievements.

After the Japanese retreat from Kohima in June 1944 there was a slight pause on that front as 2 Division and 7 Indian Division and the Japanese forces regrouped. As far as our Battalion was concerned, many members went on leave and a few older soldiers were repatriated back to England.

The next overall objectives were to open the road to Imphal, join up with IV Corps and defeat the enemy on the Imphal Plain, which was about 3,000 feet below Kohima Ridge. The Battalion, down to barely 300 men by mid-June 1944, set off again with the rest of 33 Indian Infantry Brigade to do a right hook round the enemy, on an all-pack basis along tortuous jungle tracks that were sometimes knee deep in monsoon mud, struggling up 8,000-feet mountains along knife-edged ridges, whose glutinous and sometimes slippery narrow tracks overlooked deep gorges that caused a few mules and their loads to slither down. In time the soldiers learned which were the potential danger points that the mules might not be able to negotiate and became adept at fielding those mules that went adrift. During the march they received air drops when crossing the valleys. This march through the jungle hills took the enemy by surprise as the Brigade surfaced in their rear at Ukhrul.

One of the great changes during this rest period was that the CO, Lieutenant Colonel Duncombe, left the Battalion and George Grimston took over. Colonel Duncombe had led the Battalion gallantly and ensured it was a happy team. It was not only his leadership that percolated down to the men, it was also his sense of humour and fun that put a smile into their hearts and faces. He was one of those Colonels who led from the front, quietly demanding high standards that rewarded all of us. He also saw to it that his Battalion would not be messed about by higher authority. He was awarded a richly deserved Distinguished Service Order.

After a period of rest and reorganization between September 1944 and March 1945 the Battalion crossed the River Chindwin; followed by battles in the area of the oilfields of Chauk and Yenangyaung. In July 1945 the men were in the swamps of the Sittang River, patrolling, attacking and being counter-attacked. Movement in that waterlogged country, with its high humidity, was exhausting. The troops could barely move more than one mile an hour in daylight.

On 29 July 1945 the Battalion took part in its last battle against the Japanese in the swampy area sixty miles north of Pegu. My old B Company was once again down to sixty men and was commanded by Major Joe Mullins, who had been with me during the previous year. The Company carried out this attack in the gloom of fading light and into the darkness, all at very close quarters. Their success cost the Company two officers and fourteen other ranks killed and nine wounded; their gallantry was rewarded by Joe receiving the Military Cross and two of his men the Military Medal. It will be noticed that the ratio to killed and wounded was on this occasion a reversal of the usual. In later years Joe told me that, when he took off his steel helmet after the battle, he saw that there were two holes through it and realized that it was possibly heavier than usual. Then he saw that a bullet was lodged in it and that it had just broken the skin and drawn a little blood on the top of his head!

The historian of 7 Indian Division, Brigadier M.R. Roberts DSO, in his account of this Battalion's final battle, writes:

"Between the wars the Queen's in India had built up a reputation for soldierly bearing and smartness. Crowds used to watch their guard-mounting parades in Delhi, individual soldiers on leave in hill stations were usually turned out as if they might meet the Sergeant-Major round the next corner. In fact the Queen's were rather proud of the Queen's. . . . This discipline and that soldierly bearing was still there in spite of the mud, sweat and overpowering tiredness, and they carried the position at the point of the bayonet, at a cost of twenty-five casualties, a noteworthy performance on the part of very tired men against a well-dug-in and determined enemy."

On 6 August, barely a week after B Company's attack, the American air force dropped an atomic bomb on Hiroshima. A few days later a second atomic bomb was dropped on Nagasaki. On 14 August Japan surrendered.

From Pegu in Burma a party of two officers and thirty-seven other ranks of the Battalion were flown to Bangkok on 6 September for special duties. A week later the news came back to say that the aircraft carrying Lieutenant Pattie, Sergeant-Major Goodchild and nineteen men had crashed and that there were no survivors. That was the saddest news that hit the Battalion – within a month of the end of a savage war – devastation for their families back in Britain, who had only recently celebrated VJ Day. A relief party was sent to Siam immediately.

At the end of the war in Burma the 7th Indian Division was told to ensure the liberation and pacification of Siam. The Battalion was moved by sea and air from Rangoon to Bangkok in early October 1945. The change from jungle conditions to a city, seemingly untouched by war, with cinemas, restaurants and shops that had plenty of things to buy, brought considerable cheer to the men, whose first task was to scrape off the Burma mud and regain their traditional smartness.

The enthusiasm with which they entered into the spirit of their new world is shown by a letter from the Commander-in-Chief, South-East Asia Command, Lord Louis Mountbatten, to the Colonel of the Regiment, General Sir George Giffard: "I was recently invited by the King of Siam to pay an official visit to Bangkok. I decided to have a big Inter-service Parade in order to put up British prestige within Siam. . . . I enclose a photograph showing the march past of the Queen's guard of honour in columns of sixes followed by the Queen's detachment in columns of threes. The photograph gives little idea of the tremendous impression which the bearing, turn-out, drill and marching of the Queen's guard of honour made on all the spectators. They received a special ovation from the crowd and everyone commented on them. Their marching was head and shoulders above the rest of the parade. . . . General Evans further informs me that the behaviour of your men on leave in the town has been exemplary and had greatly raised the prestige of the British Army in Siam. I hope you as their Colonel will accept this small but sincere tribute from me."

Most soldiers would recognize that anything that this Queen's Battalion, and B Company in particular, accomplished, was not just their prerogative but would have been witnessed in other units throughout the British Army, but as I had the privilege of serving with them, I wish to add my appreciation to those words of Brigadier Michael Roberts and Lord Louis Mountbatten, which express so clearly the valour and loyal dedication of the British soldier in war and peace. It was a magnificently high note on which to end the Second World War.

The story of these men, as witnessed and told by others, could be hidden in the archives of museums and regimental diaries, but I consider their achievements should be known and publicized – lest we forget.

References

Prologue

1 Lieutenant Colonel de Wiart had already fought in South Africa and Somalia before the Second World War. He had been wounded eleven times, including the loss of eye and his left hand. In the Second World War he saw active service in Norway and was taken prisoner on his way to Yugoslavia. He became Lieutenant General Sir Adrian Carton de Wiart VC, CMG, DSO

2 In the context of the white feather, I must mention the book *The Four Feathers* by A.E.W. Mason. This romantic story of cowardice and bravery is centred on the campaign in the Sudan in 1885, when the British were fighting the Dervishes to relieve Khartoum. The gift of a white feather illustrated the stigma of a coward in the mind of the donor.

3 In addition to its cricket ground, White Waltham had an airfield. Enthusiastic weekend pilots were training to fly and have fun. Here, and at other airfields around Britain, many of these pilots became caught up in the RAF's defence of the country during WW2.

Chapter 1

1 A few weeks before the war Cecily Barnett, whom I first met when she was eleven and I was twelve, was my partner at a dance at the Officers' Club Aldershot. Here we joined up

with two young unmarried couples of the Regiment. Apart from my family, she was the last girl I saw before going abroad. During the war she worked with some Intelligence organization. My sister Marny worked with the Red Cross and became a VAD. After the war Cecily and I went to the Berkeley and the Dorchester for many dinner-dances, often followed by night clubs. Over the years we have kept in touch.

2 Colonel Buller was a very large man who had won the Army boxing heavyweight championships in 1914 and then again in 1919.

Chapter 3

1 The Three Colours were the King's Colour, the Regimental Colour and the Third Colour. I believe that this Regiment is the only one in the British Army that has a third colour. In the early days of the army each company carried a colour as a rallying point. In 1686 King James II authorized payment for ten colours of the Regiment. In 1836 King William IV had allowed the Regiment to retain this Colour so long as it was never carried on parade.

2 A few years later he took over command of the 2nd Battalion of the Queen's when they were part of the Chindit force deep in Burma. He was wounded in a very early action. When I was about to take over command of the 1st Battalion (Queen's Surreys) some twenty years later, and he was Colonel of the Regiment as a Major General, one of the first things he did was to invite me to lunch with Colonel J.B. Coates. They gave me a good send off.

3 He was to become my very excellent Colour Sergeant in Burma some 2–3 years later, and one of my Quartermasters as a major in Aden and Hong Kong in the 1960s.

4 Private Boyne was killed in 1943 in Arakan, Burma.

5 John Dring was a most articulate speaker, who clearly had many contacts on the 'other side'. He was an expert on all Mahsud affairs. I learnt sometime after the partition of India

and Pakistan in 1947 that he was transferred to Africa and knighted.

6   This Battalion of Gurkhas was commanded by Lieutenant Colonel Loftus-Tottenham, whose son by mutual arrangement was soon posted to our Battalion on the Frontier before being gazetted to his Gurkha Regiment. Loftus-Tottenham became our Brigadier in Burma in 1943–1944 and was then promoted to command a division.

7   HMS *Excellent* was the Naval Gunnery School on Whale Island, Portsmouth. The Regimental links with the Navy go back to the battle of The Glorious First of June 1794, when over 300 officers and men of the Regiment served on board five naval ships of Admiral Earl Howe's Fleet, including the Flagship *The Queen Charlotte*: HMS *Excellent* is that ship's successor.

8   On my return to England before the end of the war in Europe, I met and enjoyed the company of these marines, whose training included assault boat landings and climbing the rocky Cornish escarpments. Four of the officers' families were billeted in my parents' flats, which formed a wing to the house they lived in.

9   Tony was about a year senior to me. I found myself under his enlightened and entertaining instruction in my early days in the Battalion. From the 1960s we were members of the same shoot in Wiltshire and Somerset; we played Regimental cricket against the Royal Navy on Whale Island on many occasions.

10   From the time of Peter the Great (17c) through the years of Catherine the Great and into the 19th century, the Russians made many incursions into Central Asia and into Afghanistan with the aim of invading India, as indeed had the British invaded Afghanistan to deter a Russian invasion. This to-ing and fro-ing across frontiers referred to by Rudyard Kipling in his book *Kim*, which portrayed intelligence-gatherings across that frontier: "Now I shall go far and far into the North, playing the Great Game." In the

1990s Peter Hopkirk wrote a brilliant book which traced the Russian and British activities into Afghanistan, he borrowed Kipling's words for the title of his book *The Great Game*.

Chapter 4

1   I had the opportunity to appreciate this remarkable soldier as I sat next to him at lunch when he visited 164 Officer Cadet Training Unit in Staffordshire in 1946: he was Chief of the Imperial General Staff at the time.

2   I was to meet up with Tony and some fifteen of our ex-Sandhurst friends at a very memorable and rather alcoholic lunch at the Dorchester Hotel in Park Lane in that euphoric period towards the end of the war in Europe in 1945.

Chapter 6

1   An account of this action was given in the *Indian Army Training Manual* as an example of training and discipline.

2   I found myself in the same headquarters on the staff of British Troops Austria. He was Commander of the Royal Signals and I was Military Assistant to the General Commanding our troops in Austria in 1951. Pat Hobson was awarded the Distinguished Service Order for his gallantry and counter-attacks in the Admin Box battles.

3   When at the School of Infantry, Warminster, about 20 years later, I met Colonel Mattingley's son, who was attending a course. He was probably about 26 years old and would have been about six when his father was killed. I gave him a copy of my Diary "An Infantry Company in Arakan and Kohima". He joined the King's Own Scottish Borderers and became a Brigadier.

Chapter 7

1   While commanding a division in the Western desert, his headquarters were overrun by the Germans and he and some of his staff were captured. The story was told that before the

officers and men were segregated he managed to tear off his badges of rank but left his medal ribbons on his chest. When a German officer came along and saw him sitting with the men, he said, "You're a bit old to be a private soldier"; the General was alleged to have replied that he knew this was so, but it was the drink that was always the problem. In the course of being backloaded he and some other troops managed to escape.

Chapter 9

1 In the following year two more VCs were awarded: one was a Sikh in the 4/15th Punjab in our Brigade, and the other was a Gurkha.
2 He took over command of the 81st West African Division at the end of 1944. Loftus had a second son killed later on in the Burma campaign. After the war I saw a great deal of Loftus and his wife, and their third son on occasions.

Chapter 11

1 John Smyth was a very keen horseman. In our training days a year or two before he was killed, John and I came first and second in a Point-to-Point – Gymkhana sports day organized by the Division. After the war John's father, Brigadier Sir John Smyth VC, had a copy made of his hunting horn, which he gave to Private Collyer. The original was given to the Officers' Mess of the Battalion.
2 Major Johnson was killed in the Punjab assault on 11 May.
3 Ian Frisby was very seriously wounded by this shelling. A man of weaker disposition would have died. I was in hospital with him some months after his evacuation; he told me that he remembered an orderly saying rather loudly, "Cor he's a gonner".
4 Tiny and I met up a few weeks later in hospital in India. It took about two years before he was finally and successfully operated on. He and his wife came over from their home

in the Channel Islands and stayed with us in Wiltshire in the 1970s. He was not altogether surprised to see me commanding a flock of sheep among 101 foxholes, but he was surprised to see that, when sheep moved from one pasture to another, they invariably followed each other in single file. "Do sheep always move like that even when they are not in the jungle?" he asked with his memorable grin!

5   I met his father when I was a cadet at Sandhurst. After the war I got to know his mother (his father had died by then), two brothers and his sister, and was in and out of their house at Sunningdale. His elder brother John had been a Territorial officer in 5th Queen's and was captured in France in 1940. John became quite a hero in his prisoner of war camp: his trade was an architect and he was a superb artist: He made the passports and travel documents for those that escaped; he proved too valuable for their success and so remained a prisoner for the duration of the war in Europe. His calligraphy was such that he defeated the German inspections of his documents. One of his tricks was to introduce a 'minor printing error', say the letter 'h', that was repeated throughout his thousands of documents. He became best man at my wedding to Rua. He was a natural link as he also knew my future wife's family. In the 1950s I became a Godfather to one of his daughters.

6   For 40 years after the war many officers of 33 Infantry Brigade, including Major General (as he became) Derek Horsford, met up at reunions. In 1981 he came to live within three or four miles of my house. It was not until I read some histories that I realized what a dedicated professional soldier he had been; he had an astute perception of reading a battle. He was awarded two DSOs in Burma.

7   Having had the tattered book bound in India, after the war I sent it with a short history to the Royal Army Medical Corps Museum at Aldershot.

8   In December 1968 I received an unexpected one-and-a-half-page typed A4 letter from an ex-private soldier who had

been with me in B Company in the Arakan and at Kohima. I proudly reproduce parts of his long letter: "When you get this letter, you will wonder who on earth it is from, I am sure you wouldn't remember me. However, I am one of the lucky ones who arrived back home after exploits in Burma and Siam with our old Regiment, the 1st Bn. Queen's. I am, sir, one of ex-B Company, Sgt Charlie Thatcher's Platoon in Arakan days in front of Hill 162, flying from there to Dimapur and up to Jail Hill, Kohima (which I know you remember so well) then on to Church Knoll. I vividly remember you. You woke me up one night in the Arakan for snoring, your leadership and spirit at all times, especially the early hours of the morning when we took Jail Hill, in fact I can see you now shaking hands with all of us after Church Knoll, it was I think when you left us for repatriation." He said he had much enjoined reading Arthur Swinson's book *Kohima*, from which he learnt that I had written a book, but could not find any copy. Could I help? Sadly, I had no spares.

His letter goes on, "Going back to Burma days, even now many of those times were wonderful, I never ever had before or since such good friends. . . . Like many others, I had serious bouts of malaria and dysentery and was in and out of Hospital. . . . I would, sir, love to hear from you. I know when you left us you were a sick man, but as always you wouldn't give in.

Yours Sincerely 6020041 ex Pte F. Watson." That was good for my morale; and we are now on each other's Christmas card list.

9   Before I left the Battalion, George insisted that I contact his wife, Stella, who lived in Guildford. I rang her up and she invited me to tea where I met George Grimston's sister, Frances Thesiger, and his three nieces in March 1945. At a cricket match three years later at Reigate, I met Donald Thesiger, the father of these three girls. He rather liked my 1930/31 4.5 litre Bentley and invited me to stay with them

in Scotland; "and be sure and bring the Bentley", but he had overlooked the petrol rationing which allowed me about 100 miles a month. More importantly, I fell in love with the middle girl, Rua, and married her a few years later. I doubt we would have met had it not been for World War II.

Bibliography

John Colvin, *Not Ordinary Men, The Battle of Kohima re-assessed.*

Major R.C.J. Foster, *The Regimental History of The Queen's Royal Regiment, Vol VIII, 1924-1948.*

Sir Martin Gilbert, *First World War.*

Christopher Lee, *This Sceptered Isle.*

Major M.A. Lowry, *An Infantry Company in Arakan and Kohima.*

Sir Fraser Noble, *Something in India.*

John Nunneley and Kazuo Tamayama, *Tales by Japanese Soldiers.*

Lieutenant Colonel Frank Owen, *The Campaign in Burma.*

Brigadier M.R. Roberts, *Golden Arrow, the story of the 7th Indian Division in the Second World War*

Field Marshal the Viscount Slim, *Defeat into Victory*

Brigadier Sir John Smyth VC, *The Valiant*

History of the 8th North Staffordshire Regiment

Arthur Swinson, *Kohima*

W Beach Thomas, *With the British on the Somme*

War Diaries of the 1st Battalion The Queen's Royal Regiment, 1940-1945

Index

274